Faulkner and Slavery
FAULKNER AND YOKNAPATAWPHA

2018

# Faulkner and Slavery

FAULKNER AND YOKNAPATAWPHA, 2018

EDITED BY
JAY WATSON
AND
JAMES G. THOMAS, JR.

UNIVERSITY PRESS OF MISSISSIPPI
JACKSON

The University Press of Mississippi is the scholarly publishing agency of the Mississippi Institutions of Higher Learning: Alcorn State University, Delta State University, Jackson State University, Mississippi State University, Mississippi University for Women, Mississippi Valley State University, University of Mississippi, and University of Southern Mississippi.

www.upress.state.ms.us

The University Press of Mississippi is a member
of the Association of University Presses.

Copyright © 2021 by University Press of Mississippi
All rights reserved
Manufactured in the United States of America

First printing 2021
∞

Library of Congress Cataloging-in-Publication Data

Names: Faulkner and Yoknapatawpha Conference (45th: 2018: University of
Mississippi) | Watson, Jay, editor. | Thomas, James G., Jr., editor.
Title: Faulkner and slavery / Faulkner and Yoknapatawpha, 2018; edited by
Jay Watson and James G. Thomas, Jr..
Description: Jackson: University Press of Mississippi, 2021. | Includes
bibliographical references and index.
Identifiers: LCCN 2020058519 (print) | LCCN 2020058520 (ebook) | ISBN
978-1-4968-3440-9 (hardback) | ISBN 978-1-4968-3441-6 (epub) | ISBN
978-1-4968-3442-3 (epub) | ISBN 978-1-4968-3443-0 (pdf) | ISBN 978-1-
4968-3444-7 (pdf)
Subjects: LCSH: Faulkner, William, 1897–1962—Criticism and
Interpretation—Congresses. | Slavery in literature—Congresses.
Classification: LCC PS3511.A86 Z78321157 2021 (print) | LCC PS3511.A86
(ebook) | DDC 813/.52—dc23
LC record available at https://lccn.loc.gov/2020058519
LC ebook record available at https://lccn.loc.gov/2020058520

British Library Cataloging-in-Publication Data available

One of the hopes of this project is to help shed light on how the pernicious ideology of white supremacy weaponizes language. At times, some of the contributors felt it necessary to quote words that would be inappropriate in a spoken context in order to analyze how language functions in that instance. This is in no way an endorsement of the use of such slurs in a non-academic context.

# Contents

Introduction   VII
   JAY WATSON

Note on the Conference   XXIX

Slave Capitalism in Faulkner   3
   JOHN T. MATTHEWS

Loosh   23
   MICHAEL GORRA

Beyond the Door of the Big House: Slavery and
Poor Whites in Faulkner and the Slave Narratives   32
   ANDREW B. LEITER

Ritual Architectures: Doorless and
Makeshift Boundaries in Faulkner's Slave Quarters   44
   AMY A. FOLEY

Race, Family, and Architecture at Faulkner's Rowan Oak   57
   EDWARD A. CHAPPELL

Faulkner, Slavery, and the University of Mississippi   82
   W. RALPH EUBANKS

More than Running: Redefining Movement in *Go Down, Moses*   91
   ERIN PENNER

Playing Monopoly with William Faulkner   105
   TIM ARMSTRONG

The Expropriated Voice: Sonority, Intertextuality, Flesh   126
   JULIE BETH NAPOLIN

Jason Compson, Belated Slave Master    146
    JULIA STERN

A Literary Genealogy of "Slavery's Capitalism"
in Chesnutt and Faulkner    155
    STEPHANIE ROUNTREE

Melodrama, Turbulence, Titillation: Silhouetting Slavery
in the Works of William Faulkner and Kara Walker    173
    RANDALL WILHELM

Emancipating Faulkner: Reading *Go Down, Moses* and
Jesmyn Ward's *Sing, Unburied, Sing*    194
    SHERITA L. JOHNSON

Contributors    211

Index    215

# Introduction

## Jay Watson

In April 1930, William Faulkner entered into a purchase agreement with the Bryant family of Coffeeville, Mississippi, for the antebellum Oxford home known to locals as the Bailey place, the home that has become iconic under the new name Faulkner soon gave it, Rowan Oak.[1] Later that year he placed a story with the *Saturday Evening Post*, "Red Leaves," that was at once his first sustained fictional portrait of Southeastern Indians and his inaugural effort in an intense twenty-year span of novels and stories that imagined the lives and experiences of enslaved African Americans in the US South.[2] Suddenly, there it all was, across a scant eight pages, and in the most popular among the American "slicks" to boot: a tribe of slaveholding north Mississippi Indians, already lured disastrously into the modern economic world-system by the white man; the anonymous "Guinea man" whose flight from his Native captors represents Faulkner's earliest engagement with the fugitive slave narrative, a New World genre he would return to often in his work; the slave community of the plantation quarters; and even the New England ship captain, pious, drunk, and obscene, who conducts the Guinea man across the Middle Passage, firmly implicating New England shipping and merchant interests alongside southern agriculture in the rise of the peculiar institution in the United States. Here in a nutshell were the enabling conditions—the specter of land theft and Indian Removal (under which Red *leaves* northern Mississippi), plantation slavery and the international slave trade, the tentacular grip of the money economy—that made not only Yoknapatawpha County but the modern nation possible.

The timing of these events—the purchase of Rowan Oak, the publication of "Red Leaves," the closer, deeper look at Native and African American lives and antebellum histories—may not have been so purely arbitrary. Faulkner had given passing notice to chattel slavery in some of the flashbacks and reminiscences of *Flags in the Dust*, where, however, the function of the enslaved was mainly to serve as witnesses to the glamorous Civil War exploits of Colonel John Sartoris, or, as in the case of the formerly enslaved Simon Strother, to comment disapprovingly, in classic plantation-school fashion, on the superiority of antebellum ways to those of the modern moment of 1919–20; certainly the more incisive portraits of the Sartoris enslaved in the stories of *The Unvanquished*—Ringo, Loosh, Philadelphia, Louvinia—were still years away. Faulkner had acknowledged the Native ground of his fictional territory in *Flags* as well, baptizing his county Yocona, a word derived from a Chickasaw root meaning "earth" or "land." But in drawing up the new deed and establishing title to his new residence in 1930, Faulkner might have had occasion to view the mark of E-Ah-Nah-Yea that initially conferred the property to one of the area's first white settlers in 1836—an archival reminder of Native dispossession.[3] Certainly he must have contemplated the name of Robert Sheegog, an owner of slave plantations in four Mississippi counties who acquired the property in 1844 and not long afterward completed work on the two-story, Greek Revival town house Faulkner would eventually call his own; the name recurs, slightly altered to Shegog, in section 4 of *The Sound and the Fury*, where Faulkner suggestively assigns it to an African American preacher. Though designed by a white architect, the Sheegog residence was undoubtedly constructed with enslaved labor, perhaps primarily so. By 1930, then, the author inhabited just the sort of house that, at the other end of the decade, one of his characters would describe as the work of slave "sweat."[4]

Faulkner's own maternal and paternal ancestors included antebellum slaveholders, and the biographical evidence is strong that his great-grandfather, William Clark Falkner, had at least one child with an enslaved woman in the 1860s.[5] In a literal sense, moving into Rowan Oak, christening and presiding over the estate like a proper planter, may have brought these histories and legacies closer to home, and closer to Faulkner's fiction as well. If they awakened a new and more serious interest in the meaning of slavery, other forces at work in US society and culture may have kindled that interest further. The onset of the Great Depression prompted much reflection on the Civil War, in a search for insight into how a people weathered a great national crisis. The seventy-fifth anniversary of the war would arrive later in the decade, of course, as would a massive archive of slave narratives, recorded by WPA workers across the country—450 in Mississippi alone.[6] Seven decades after Emancipation, then, the problem of slavery was much on the minds of Americans in the 1930s, and much on the minds of the nation's writers, if historical fictions ranging from Arna Bontemps's *Black Thunder* to Margaret Mitchell's *Gone with the Wind* (both 1936) are any indication.

Faulkner was no exception, taking up the subject of slavery directly in *Absalom, Absalom!* (also 1936), *The Unvanquished* (1938), *Go Down, Moses* (1942), and *Requiem for a Nun* (1951), all of which feature prominent action set on Mississippi slave plantations and in the antebellum Jefferson community that serviced them. But slavery's shadow also falls more subtly across numerous other fictions from this period. Three generations of the Burden family of *Light in August* are thoroughly and fatally embroiled in the debates over slavery, abolition, Emancipation, and Reconstruction; and Gail Hightower learns about his Civil War grandfather in large part from a formerly enslaved woman. The ruin of the Old Frenchman Place, an enormous slave plantation in the southeastern part of Yoknapatawpha County, figures crucially in *Sanctuary* (1931) and *The Hamlet* (1940). In *Intruder in the Dust*, African American Lucas Beauchamp, first encountered in the stories of *Go Down, Moses*, continues to sport the beaver hat and gold watch chain once owned by his slaveholding grandfather, L. Q. C. McCaslin, the white man who both owned and sired Beauchamp's father. Born free in 1874, Lucas into his sixties still grapples daily with legal, racial, and economic legacies handed down directly from slavery times on McCaslin land. Even *The Wild Palms* (1939), set entirely in the period from 1927 to 1937, drives each of its entwined narratives toward conclusion at Parchman penitentiary, the notorious prison farm that was one of the many places where US slavery went to hide in plain carceral sight after the ratification of the Thirteenth Amendment. In this context, the seemingly incongruous scene in which the Tall Convict glimpses a grand plantation house burning above the Mississippi floodwaters of 1927 offers less reassurance than we might hope that slavery's afterlives were slowly being extinguished in the twentieth-century South.[7] Instead, it might signal that the torch of plantation enslavement has passed to mass incarceration—a subtext of the title story of *Go Down, Moses* as well.[8] With the exception of the 1935 aviation tale *Pylon*, this roster includes every novel Faulkner published between *As I Lay Dying* (1930) and *A Fable* (1954). To it we could add several short stories published during the period—"A Justice," "Mountain Victory," "My Grandmother Millard," "There Was a Queen," "Wash"—as well as the unpublished "Evangeline."

As it turns out, ownership of Rowan Oak also tied Faulkner directly, though in ways he might not have been aware of, to the history of slavery at the University of Mississippi, whose Oxford campus lay just a half-mile walk through Bailey Woods from the novelist's residence. Though the house, grounds, and surrounding woods became part of the university only with their acquisition by the institution in 1972, their connection to the university was actually much older than that. Not long after building his Oxford town home, Robert Sheegog leased a number of his slaves to the university to assist with the construction of the antebellum campus between 1846 and the institution's opening in 1848. Some of these workers may have been from the same cohort on whom Sheegog drew to build his house; according to US census information for Lafayette County, Mississippi, there were eight enslaved persons residing on the Sheegog place in 1860.[9] Faulkner biographer Joseph Blotner evokes the scene there in the early 1840s, when a kiln on the property baked bricks for the original foundation.[10] It's possible that this kiln remained in use afterward to produce bricks for campus structures like the Lyceum (1848), the Chapel (1853), or the Observatory (1859), all of which remain standing today. It's also possible that the clay for this brickwork was drawn from deposits along a creek behind Sheegog's residence, in woods Faulkner would later own. If so, the "branch" where he played with his daughter Jill, and the paths through the woods he would later ride on mounts like Tempy and Stonewall, would have entangled him all the more inexorably in local histories and networks of slavery.

If such speculations seem downright Faulknerian in their conjectural nature, they have also helped prompt important historical and archaeological research at Rowan Oak itself in recent years. In the wake of Craig Steven Wilder's groundbreaking scholarship in *Ebony and Ivy*, a number of American colleges and universities are taking stock, and taking historical and moral ownership, of the role of the enslaved in the economic histories and built environments of their institutions, and of the role of higher education in laying the intellectual foundations—philosophical, political, scientific—that gave legitimacy to colonial and antebellum slavery.[11] At the University of Mississippi, such efforts gained momentum with the formation in 2013 of an interdisciplinary working group of faculty, staff, and students to study the history of slavery in the university. The group, now several dozen strong, calls itself the University of Mississippi Slavery Research Group (UMSRG). UMSRG has delved deeply into the archives, archaeology, and architecture of the campus to uncover the foundational role of enslaved labor, slave wealth (wealth in the form of human chattel), and proslavery ideology and interests in the history of the university, from the discussion and debate leading to its charter in 1844, through its closure in 1861 and the enlistment of many of its students in the Confederate Army, to its reopening after Emancipation, all the way to the university's integration by James Meredith in 1962, and beyond.[12] The group has sponsored guest lectures; created campus tours; disseminated its findings through conference activity, scholarly publication, and online resources; contributed to history and contextualization efforts on the campus; and collaborated with community members to discover, share, and preserve more inclusive stories about local history. By widening its net in these ways, UMSRG aims to integrate the story of slavery at the University of Mississippi more fully into the history of slavery in north Mississippi and in American higher learning more broadly. The William Faulkner residence has emerged as a critical space where these histories converge.

At the 2018 conference on "Faulkner and Slavery," ample space was set aside on the program for UMSRG to share its research with Faulkner scholars. Registrants were introduced to the history and mission of the group on the opening day of the conference. UM anthropologist Jodi Skipper discussed her work with the Behind the Big House project in Holly Springs, Mississippi, a richly curated tour of former slave dwellings that runs alongside the annual spring pilgrimage to the town's celebrated antebellum homes: a kind of pilgrimage-from-below that provocatively contextualizes the history and splendor of the plantation houses. Later in the week, Skipper led a guided tour to Holly Springs so a lucky group of conference attendees could experience Behind the Big House for themselves. From members of the UM's Arch Dalrymple III Department of History, the conference audience learned about the rate and extent of slaveholdership among the university's antebellum students—vividly documenting just how privileged this group of young men was, even among the Mississippi elites of the period; about an enslaved man who was able to exercise a degree of influence upon his work assignments and working hours on the campus, finding room to maneuver between and among faculty and administrators; and about the role of student debate societies as incubators of states'-rights ideology during the university's antebellum years. A student in the Southern Studies program discussed the challenges and rewards of interpreting slavery at local historic sites like Rowan Oak and Burns Belfry, the African Methodist Episcopal church that served as a communal anchor for postbellum Oxford's Freedmen Town—Faulkner's model for the similarly named and located part of Jefferson traversed by Joe Christmas in chapter 5 of *Light in August*. Finally, a trio of visiting archaeologists and architectural historians returned us to Rowan Oak, sharing the results of a Phase I archaeological survey done on site in 2017—the first stage in a search for material clues to the nature and texture of slave life on the premises—and providing a detailed architectural profile of the residence as well as the brick structure Faulkner used as a storeroom and smokehouse, originally a two-room slave dwelling and now arguably the most historically and architecturally significant building at the residence. Though much of this UMSRG-sponsored scholarship has been published or is forthcoming elsewhere, it is represented in this volume by two essays: Edward Chappell's fascinating account of how owning and occupying an antebellum home built by a planter and slaveholder shaped Faulkner's self-image and self-fashioning over the better than three decades he lived at Rowan Oak, and Ralph Eubanks's rereading of *Absalom, Absalom!* in the context of the University of Mississippi's antebellum and slavery histories.

Yet Faulkner's critical engagement with chattel slavery was hardly limited to tales of enslaved persons, slaveholders, or antebellum times, at the university, at his homeplace, or elsewhere. He clearly understood that slavery's logics continued to inform the twentieth-century world about which he more often wrote, in systematic and traumatic ways. In *The Sound and the Fury*, for instance, Benjy Compson's provocatively racialized circumstances—his enforced immobility, his lost birth name, the perceived sexual threat he poses to white womanhood, his need for continuous supervision—serve to remind us that the roots of his family's status and influence lie in African American slavery, and that by 1928 that particular legacy of violence and incarceration is coming home to roost. By the same token, the backyard cabin from which Dilsey Gibson emerges in her Easter finery in section 4 of *The Sound and the Fury*, and in which she manages to create a modicum of domestic warmth and stability that even the Compson children can feel and value, is in all likelihood a former slave dwelling attached to the original mile-square Compson homestead. Such details reinflect, and severely ironize, Jason Compson's offhand, self-aggrandizing comment that his family *once* owned slaves.[13] The histrionic structures of feeling surrounding Joe Christmas's flight from the law at the climax of *Light in August* owe more than a little to white affect in the era of the fugitive slave, before Percy Grimm steps in as a latter-day patter-roller and the home of a defrocked minister fails in its intended role as way-station on Jefferson's Depression-era version of the Underground Railroad. Rider's bereaved roamings across the Yoknapatawpha landscape elicit similar anxieties in another representative of police power, the addled deputy sheriff of "Pantaloon in Black." Faulkner takes pains to reveal that the jail that holds Nancy Mannigoe in *Requiem for a Nun* once housed runaway slaves, a historical connection that invites reflection on the origins in antebellum slavery of the mammy role that Nancy, as caregiver to Temple Drake Stevens's children, so disastrously misperforms—or, seen another way, that she exposes as never tenable, mere myth, in the first place.[14]

Nor are even the Snopeses altogether exempt from implication in the slave-made modernity they thrive in. Faulkner once assigned Flem Snopes's arrival in Frenchman's Bend to the 1880s, though *The Town* and *The Mansion* would date his marriage to Eula Varner in 1908.

Either way, however, his career would appear to make the rise of the Snopeses a thoroughly post-slavery affair. Yet we might do well to historicize more fully the strategies at the heart of the Snopeses' peculiar economic genius. As John T. Matthews has recently pointed out, their real gift—Flem's gift especially—lies in their ability to literally capitalize on the wave of financialization coursing through the twentieth-century US economy, the particular form of capital—Matthews calls it "making money off nothing"—that allows Flem and his kinsman to mobilize and commodify immaterial assets like insider information, skillfully salted rumor, ephemeral visual images, personal reputation, family name: the hovering threats and possibilities (like that of a burned barn) whose conversion into tangible, material gain gives Flem his start as a human fire insurance policy in Frenchman's Bend.[15] In this respect, it's surely no coincidence that the masterstroke that propels Flem from the Bend to Jefferson is the sale of the Frenchman Place, the worthless property—a slave plantation without slaves or indeed any labor force at all—into which Flem manages to inject the insinuation of value, financializing the local legend of buried antebellum treasure with a carefully placed postbellum silver dollar or two.

But there's even more to it than that. As scholars are increasingly recognizing, the modernization of the credit economy and the roots of twentieth-century financial capitalism can be traced to the development and increasingly widespread use of economic instruments like insurance, mortgages, notes of hand, stock exchanges, and paper currency over the seventeenth and eighteenth centuries, the peak years of the international trade in African slaves. Among the most common and flexible forms of collateral or capital during this period were enslaved human beings. It wasn't just their stolen labor that drove the Enlightenment-era global economy; it was also their commodification, the ease with which they could be bought, sold, traded, mortgaged, insured, speculated in, and (as in the hideous case of the 1781 *Zong* massacre) all too literally liquidated for economic gain.[16] This is an important part of what contemporary economic historians mean when they refer to "slavery's capitalism": not only a mode of production centered in slave labor but a mode of circulation centered in slave value, as a stimulus to financial innovation, investment, and exchange.[17]

As Walter Johnson, Edward Baptist, Sven Beckert, Joshua Rothman, and other contemporary historians have argued, slavery's capitalism received another powerful boost in the nineteenth century in and from the opening of the lower Mississippi River Valley to cotton cultivation.[18] As Faulkner's fictional chronicle reveals, white settlement in the region was predicated on Chickasaw Indian Removal. It was also accompanied by a frenzy of speculation—in land, in slaves—on which fortunes were made and lost at a pace and a level of volatility hitherto unprecedented in US economic history. At the same time, amidst the turmoil was a creative ferment in which, as Baptist in particular has shown, emerged new credit arrangements and other paper instruments that helped power up the modern banking industry and the financial turn of US capitalism in subsequent decades, including, eventually, Faulkner's formative years. Much of the liquidity that enabled and demanded this transformation was supplied by mortgaging slaves, thereby creating enormous uncertainty and instability in the lives and families of the enslaved themselves. So pause for a moment to reconsider Flem's ascent from the Frenchman Place—whose antebellum grounds, as his sharecropping father knew well, were salted not with specie but with slave sweat—to the presidency of Jefferson's Merchants and Farmers Bank and the ownership of his predecessor's mansion. Though it seems unlikely that his antebellum ancestors would have owned slaves, the path he traces, not so unlike that of old Bayard Sartoris before him (and culminating at the same bank), is the path of slavery's capitalism, slavery's modernity.

To assess the place of slavery in Faulkner's creative life and personal history, then, we must cast a wide net, remaining mindful of post-Emancipation histories and alert to subtle textual enregistrations of slavery's effects alongside the writer's more explicit accounts of the enslaved and their enslavers. Individually and in the aggregate, the thirteen essays gathered here do just that, taking up slavery's subjects, spaces, lives, afterlives—and, yes, its capitalism—as they bear, and bear down, on the writer and his people. Starting with the premise, shared by many of the new economic historians, that "Atlantic capitalism came to rely on a global system of enslaved labor" at a formative level, John T. Matthews traces these entwined systems of commodity exchange, financial flows, and human trafficking as they wind through Faulkner's work. Extending some of the insights into financialization developed in his essay for the 2019 *Faulkner and Money* collection, Matthews's "Slave Capitalism in Faulkner" comes to rest on *Absalom, Absalom!* as the novelist's most thorough and incisive account of how "the traffic in human chattel" gave modern industrial capitalism its "most propulsive new fuel." Beyond the immediate value of their labor and their fungibility on the auction block, slaves were "financialized as insurable lives," "as sexually reproducible merchandise; as contracted wage earners; as speculative investments; and as collateral for mortgages, loans, or the purchase of other goods bought on credit, including more slaves." What is more, this maelstrom of economic innovation surrounding slavery was especially turbulent during the so-called flush times of Mississippi, when Indian Removal opened up vast swaths of land for cotton production and/or financial speculation. This is precisely the moment, of course, when Thomas Sutpen descends upon Yoknapatawpha County with his grand design and swashbuckling financial legerdemain. Behind the Spanish gold, the rumors of steamboat gambling and armed robbery, the loans of seed cotton, and the acquisition of a respectable wife, however, lurks the shadow of the slave trade, slave-fueled credit, the financialization of the human body. This sets the horizon against which we should read mysterious transactions like the bill of lading over which Sutpen and Goodhue Coldfield end their unspecified business partnership, a relationship that none of the novel's twentieth-century narrators seems eager to delve into, even though the shady dealing is a key episode in Sutpen's rise to dominance among the county's slaveholding planters. Sutpen's eventual downfall, argues Matthews, "allegorizes how the South was destroyed by the slave capitalism that had borne it," though, tellingly, the narrators opt instead to chalk up Sutpen's ruin to sexual effrontery, bigamy, incest, miscegenation—anything, it would seem, but the economic piracy and African bondage that made the cotton kingdom possible. The novelist does better than his narrators, however, by developing stylistic and other aesthetic strategies that translate "the capitalist derangements of personhood and time" into literary forms capable of "resist[ing] capitalism's demands" even as they evoke and impugn chattel slavery's constitutive violence.

Michael Gorra explores the actions, words, and historical context of an understudied figure who is among Faulkner's most intriguing enslaved characters: the Sartoris slave Lucius, whom the family refers to as Loosh. In his essay, simply titled "Loosh," Gorra sets out to examine "the conditions of slavery on the Sartoris plantation," with an eye open not only for what Faulkner "shows us about the lives of the enslaved" but also for "what he just as crucially doesn't." He then zeroes in on the key transition point in *The Unvanquished* when Loosh decides to assist the Union soldiers in their raid on the Sartoris plantation and liberate himself in the process, whereupon, Gorra observes, he also "leaves the page" for a substantial stretch of the novel, only to resurface on the plantation in the Civil War's aftermath. Gorra offers some historically grounded reflections on what might have happened to this self-emancipated man as Yoknapatawpha moves from wartime to peacetime and from a slave society to a post-slavery regime that is very much a work in progress. The much diminished, pointedly marginalized Loosh we encounter tending the Sartoris horses in "An Odor of Verbena" represents a broken promise, a forfeited potential for forceful agency, self-assertion, and property ownership, perhaps meant to evoke, at the level of characterization, the nation's broken promises to the newly freed during the Reconstruction era and afterward. "What would have driven him back there?" Gorra wonders, thus illustrating how Faulkner's narrative aesthetic of omission and reticence compels readers to engage actively with the legacies of slavery, to "think our way inside a postwar experience that never quite gets on the page."

Probing the Faulkner oeuvre, including *The Unvanquished*, for further "insight into the enslaved condition," Andrew B. Leiter comes to the perhaps surprising conclusion that the writer's temperamental and thematic "prioritization of whiteness" leaves its mark on his portrayal of antebellum society in the South, where "the poor-white presence" plays a disproportionate role in the shaping of Faulkner's conceptualization of slave experience. "Beyond the Door of the Big House: Slavery and Poor Whites in Faulkner and the Slave Narratives" argues that the relatively gentle treatment of enslaved characters by southern planters in Faulkner's writings only underscores the fiction's way of "displac[ing] the brutalities" of the peculiar institution onto "poor-white suffering." The experiences and careers of Wash Jones, Ab Snopes, the Appalachian clan of "Mountain Victory," and the Sutpens of Tidewater Virginia illustrate this pattern of white abjection and bitter enmity between slaves and poor whites, a reciprocal antagonism not actually borne out by the historical record. As a corrective, Leiter turns to the work of contemporary historians like Jeff Forret and Keri Leigh Merritt and to antebellum slave narratives by Frederick Douglass, Harriet Jacobs, and Charles Ball. These sources attest to the existence of cordial and even mutually sympathetic relations between the enslaved and the white poor. For Leiter, the bristling antagonism Faulkner portrays performs a "twofold displacement" that "reconfigures the traumatic violence of slavery in two crucial ways": first by "remov[ing] the planter class from association with . . . physical violence" against slaves, then by substituting the poor-white body for the enslaved body "as the site of traumatic antebellum violence." For Faulkner, Leiter concludes, it was the white poor rather than commodified Africans who were excluded from the plantation "family" of paternalist ideology.

Slavery was not just a legal or economic regime; it was a fundamentally spatial one as well. Four essays explore the spatial and architectural arrangements that governed the lives of the enslaved and in turn consolidated and challenged the power of slaveholders in Faulkner's Mississippi, with profound implications for the author's life and writings. Amy Foley ranges widely across the Faulkner oeuvre to illustrate the author's sensitivity to fundamental differences between a European poetics and politics of space and an African one as the two systems weave their dialectical way through Yoknapatawpha history. "Ritual

Architectures: Doorless and Makeshift Boundaries in Faulkner's Slave Quarters" detects an African architectural legacy at work in the "permeable" forms of both white and Black housing that dot the antebellum Yoknapatawpha landscape, from the doorless cabins of the slave quarter in "Red Leaves" to the unexpected architectural porousness of plantation houses like the McCaslin big house, with its ersatz animal-skin doors and windows, and Sutpen's Hundred prior to its master's marriage, the "Spartan shell" whose austere solitude, devoid of windowpane or doorknob or furniture, signifies the personal agency and individualistic ethos of a white man unencumbered by the feminized trappings of Euro-American imperial "civilization." These open or semi-open dwellings ventilate the binary Western spatial scheme of inside and outside to create room to maneuver for enslaved figures like Tomey's Turl and latter-day fugitives like Joe Christmas, "allowing different pathways and ranges of movement for their inhabitants" that forged perspectives on place and space "alternative to Euro-American capitalist-driven definitions of property and borders." Foley proposes the concept of spatial "exemption" rather than spatial *freedom* to capture the creative but circumscribed forms of slave agency and social existence that open up in and around such fluid, unpredictable fields of movement. The "spatial confusion between owners and slaves" so characteristic of Faulkner's mature work thus underscores "the complex power dynamics" of the antebellum plantation regime.

Edward A. Chappell takes this interest in slavery's spaces from the Faulkner page to the Faulkner homeplace in "Race, Family, and Architecture at Faulkner's Rowan Oak." Close attention to the domestic world Faulkner lived in, Chappell observes, "reveals things about him and his conception of race and slavery that you will not find in his writing." Placing the structures that Faulkner built or maintained at Rowan Oak in the architectural and historical context of North Mississippi, Chappell reminds us that the antebellum slave quarters and dwellings of the region were conceived as "model worker housing" and "intended as a defense of slavery and an expression of owners' expendable wealth." The slave dwelling that remains at Rowan Oak was no exception, and when Faulkner took possession of the residence in 1930, he placed himself and his family in relation to that architectural, ideological, and racial legacy. We need to see the improvements he made to the property in 1933 and 1952 in that light. For one thing, Faulkner opted not to house his resident Black employees in the "slave-tainted space" of the antebellum quarter built by original owner Robert Sheegog, which the writer used primarily as a smokehouse and for storage space, but instead by 1933 had constructed a new two-room residence he referred to as servants' quarters. His decision "to build the servants' house farther from the main house" than the original slave dwelling "and to buffer it visually by garden plantings" allowed Faulkner to present Rowan Oak as "a modern 1930s home," free of "the specter of black workers occupying a scruffy slave quarter . . . and moving conspicuously back and forth between the house and quarter." At the same time, this modernizing effort observed many of the principles of the Colonial Revival movement popular among affluent middle-class Americans in the 1920s and 1930s, "with its affection for the preindustrial past and respect for the buildings and furnishings of a more tasteful old regime." A collaborative project between Faulkner and his wife, Estelle, focusing on "a workable home" and graceful living, the 1933 expansion also, significantly, "graded [its] spaces by race," with distinct "physical transition[s] between predominately black and white sections of the house." These "racial zones" were continually breached in the observance of day-to-day affairs, including Faulkner's writing, which he often did in the kitchen during the winter months. By contrast, the 1952 construction, supervised by Faulkner alone in the absence of wife and daughter, concentrated on functional improvements and used stock rather than restoration-grade materials. Chappell finds both "race and taste" "less evident" in these additions, which included the office where Faulkner iconically plotted out the main events of *A Fable* on the walls. Here "privacy and marital separation" seemed to be the order of the day, even as Faulkner was turning away from direct representations of the enslaved in his own writings.

For Ralph Eubanks, Rowan Oak is a key thread tying together Faulkner's writings and the institution of higher learning located in his hometown. "Faulkner, Slavery, and the University of Mississippi" turns to the historical record—the UM archives—and the fictional one—*Absalom, Absalom!*—to explore these ties in more detail. When Faulkner purchased the home in 1930, he entwined his own story with that of slavery—via the slaveholder who originally built the residence; via the university, since the home is now owned and maintained by UM and curated by University Museums; and via slavery *at* UM, since, as documentary evidence from the 1840s and 1850s reveals, Robert Sheegog was among the local slaveholders who loaned enslaved people to the institution as "servant hires." Many of these "hires" were involved in the construction of the antebellum campus, which opened in 1848. Eubanks observes that the history of slavery in Mississippi, including slavery on campus, was debated at the university during the very years that Faulkner was thinking his way into *Absalom*; he might well have known of, even read, faculty member Charles Sydnor's 1933 book *Slavery in Mississippi*, for instance, on the way to setting key scenes and relationships at the university in his great novel of slavery. Eubanks finds in Charles Bon "a University of Mississippi student whose ancestors were once slaves," a living symbol of slavery's role in the university's founding, noting moreover that Faulkner places Bon and Henry Sutpen at the university at a time when Robert Sheegog and his neighbor Jacob Thompson received payments from the institution for the use of their slaves. During this period, students were assessed each term for "servant hire" and assigned abolitionist literature to read and critique. Such practices helped normalize the institution of slavery "among the sons of the landed aristocracy" who attended the university. By laying fictional history so carefully and provocatively alongside actual history, *Absalom* anticipates the findings of contemporary historians like Craig Steven Wilder, reminding us that "American colleges and universities were not passive beneficiaries of the institution of slavery." The ghosts of the peculiar institution that linger at UM need to be recognized among the many revenants that haunt the pages and the characters of *Absalom*.

Erin Penner turns from specific architectural spaces to spatialized mobility in "More than Running: Redefining Movement in *Go Down, Moses*," finding in the itineraries of African American figures like the enslaved Tomey's Turl of "Was" and his successor Rider of "Pantaloon in Black" a set of carefully constructed alternative mappings of the Yoknapatawpha landscape that offer "very real benefits to minor and disfranchised characters" whose "stories rarely emerge in full force through words" but whose "routes complete . . . stories they are not given room to tell." Misunderstood, indeed mis-mapped, by white narrators who shoehorn their stories into inhospitable genres like the hunting tale and the fugitive slave narrative ("Was") or the myth of Black bestiality and inhumanity (the deputy of "Pantaloon"), Turl and Rider nevertheless author competing accounts of their lives and world through their movements. Noting that both characters unexpectedly make "return" rather than escape "the goal of their running," Penner argues that Turl's peregrinations and homecoming both inscribe his links to the McCaslin family upon the local landscape and exploit those connections in service of a love story; for all his legal and natal alienation from the McCaslin landholdings, then, Turl still finds a way to "reclaim the very land that Ike McCaslin will relinquish." Eighty years later, by defying the white deputies' assumption that he would flee the law and the lynching posse to Tennessee, Rider insists "that his story is mapped within Yoknapatawpha County; he will not allow . . . injustice [to] occur off the map." The map he draws with his movements points to the woods as a space of "temporary reprieve," not escape, from the "habits of plantation life" that "continue to define his world" and the circuits of white power that pulse through the dwellings and workplaces and along the roads of that world. Ending his run at his own porch, where he quietly awaits arrest by the sheriff, Rider ultimately emphasizes "family connection" over labor or flight, "echo[ing] Tomey's Turl's routes to Tennie." Spatially constructing identities and commitments "grounded in family and community ties," these characters, in slavery and in freedom, "articulate their narrative arc through [a] Faulknerian landscape that has been established by the dominant narratives," including those of their white creator, "but not defined by them."

Tim Armstrong follows the afterlives of slavery into a pair of structuring conceits in the Faulknerian imagination. "Playing Monopoly with William Faulkner" first dives deep into the conceptual territory of the predial, a common-law term under which slaves and serfs were held to be attached to the land they worked. Prediality acknowledged multiple stakeholders in a given piece of land: not just the "dominant" claim of the owner but the "subservient" claims of others whose intimate relationship to soil gave them certain rights to it as well. Perhaps learning a thing or two from Charles Chesnutt's conjure tales, whose protagonist, the former slave Julius McAdoo, is said to exhibit a "predial" attitude toward plantation land owned by a northern transplant and investor, Faulkner infused his fictions of Lucas Beauchamp in *Go Down, Moses* and *Intruder in the Dust* with a similar attitude, traceable to the slave plantation, under whose terms everyone in Yoknapatawpha recognizes Lucas's rights to his ten acres of McCaslin land, in what amounts to an ethical more than a strictly legal claim. Noting the "postage-stamp" shape of Lucas's farm and linking it both to Faulkner's account of Yoknapatawpha itself as his postage stamp of native soil, and to the Monopoly game board, patented in 1904 as a way of illustrating the economic theories of Henry George, Armstrong goes on to posit, in the topology of the square, a spatial "emblem" for the linked ownership of land and slave that supplies the historical as well as the geographical contours for Faulkner's Mississippi domain. To this topology Armstrong opposes an alternate one, working itself out in ellipses and ovals, clockwise and counterclockwise circuits, within which Faulkner experiments with redistributionist notions that might, in some modest way, alleviate the injuries and inequities handed down from slavery—as when Lucas's kinsman Ned McCaslin turns a racetrack into a source of personal enrichment and score-settling in *The Reivers*. Armstrong thus looks to "the apocryphal shapes of Faulkner's texts" to uncover a "cultural poetics of in-forming" trajectories at work there, a poetics both informed by slavery and pursuing recourse to it.

Julie Beth Napolin comes at slavery's lives and afterlives in Faulkner through the Yoknapatawpha soundscape. "The Expropriated Voice:

Sonority, Intertextuality, Flesh" taps into a long tradition in Black studies that focuses on the transmission of "social feeling" and political possibility through voices and other sounds. At the center of much of this scholarship, and Napolin's own essay, lies the scream, as the zero degree of articulation for and by flesh denied personhood. Napolin aims to reconstruct something of a genealogy of the scream as it pierces and echoes through the "circumambient" air of Yoknapatawpha and the slave histories it continues to vector into the twentieth century. The result is an extraordinary acoustic network whose sonic roots and routes lie in the chattelization of African flesh and the "expropriation" of voices denied the "sanctified dimension of personal property": the scream of the lynched Joe Christmas in *Light in August*, displaced aurally into the unbearable wail of a police siren; the moans of Benjy Compson in *The Sound and the Fury*; the uncategorizable "Negro" sounds (like singing and yet not like singing) of Nancy Mannigoe in "That Evening Sun"; the wild wailing chorus of Raby's daughters and granddaughters in "Evangeline"; and the array of voices Faulkner releases in *Absalom, Absalom!*; from the screams of white Henry Sutpen at his father's ritual brawls with his slaves to the imperious commands of Clytie Sutpen, a formerly enslaved woman of color with "perhaps the most authoritative voice" in the novel; to the vibrating "sonority" of Rosa Coldfield as it courses across the italicized pages of chapter 5; and on to the howlings of Jim Bond, grandson of an enslaved courtesan, that end the narrative proper before the cartography-work of the endpapers plunges the text into silence. These soundings, and the complementary acts of listening that allow them to live, take the human voice "beyond property," writes Napolin, and as such beyond the "metaphysics of liberal personhood" and the "poetics of possession" that provided philosophical scaffolding for the slave trade and the modernity it made possible. Intriguingly, the sonic lineage that Napolin excavates is ultimately a matrilineal one as we push farther back into Yoknapatawpha history, from Christmas, Bond, and Benjy in the twentieth century, to Clytie and Rosa at the Civil War's end, and finally to Clytie's mother, the unnamed slave woman whose voice we never hear in *Absalom*, its silenced urgencies and intensities nonetheless serving as "the origin of the novel's claim" to a counterdiscourse that might speak to Saidiya Hartman's poignant question, "What was the afterlife of slavery and when might it be eradicated?"

Julia Stern follows slavery's afterlives to a perhaps surprising destination in "Jason Compson, Belated Slave Master." Acknowledging that *The Sound and the Fury* "would seem to unfold at a long distance from the lived reality of African American slavery," Stern nonetheless draws on Orlando Patterson's influential sociological work in *Slavery and Social*

*Death* to limn Jason Compson IV's "anachronistic incarnation of a plantation master." In his brutal relationship with his niece Quentin we can see elements of Patterson's natal alienation and social death: "ripped away" from her mother and forever ignorant of her father, she is also denied a surname throughout Jason's monologue. Instead, arrogating the role of father-surrogate, Jason imposes much the same sort of fictive kinship upon her that, according to Patterson, slaveholders imposed on their bondpeople. Jason's attitudes toward Dilsey Gibson and her family sound the Pattersonian motif of human parasitism, wherein masters complain of "being eaten out of house and home" by their servants, while also illustrating the rhetorical phenomenon Patterson calls ideological reversal, in which "the idea of who produces and who consumes" in the slaveholding household "gets flipped on its head" by masters who "claim elaborate credit for production" while "slaves are identified as . . . rapacious consumers." When she absconds with Jason's embezzled hoard of cash, however, Quentin proves herself a match for her would-be master, improvising a latter-day version of slave *taking* to counter the systematic *stealing* Jason has been doing from her and her mother for fifteen years. Nor is Quentin alone in throwing off the "old ways" Jason would like to preserve on his "plantation." Stern finds in Dilsey's grandson Luster—son of a Pullman porter and a girl who once placated the Compson children with a jar full of fireflies—a figure whose interests reach beyond the economics of slavery to "aesthetic" and "performative" passions with the potential to carry him beyond Jason's imperious reach.

Moreover, focusing on slavery's afterlives invites us to consider Faulkner's imaginative engagements with slavery in comparative context. In addition to Leiter's essay, the volume's final three chapters take up that challenge, with impressive dividends. Stephanie Rountree finds slavery to be inextricable from "the logic of US liberal democracy" both before and after Emancipation. In "A Literary Genealogy of 'Slavery's Capitalism' in Chesnutt and Faulkner," Rountree introduces the concept of "anteliberalism" to designate a national literary history probing "the triangulation of capitalism, citizenship, and corporeality in post-Emancipation US governance" as it continues to answer to "enslaving logics." Rountree traces this critique of liberalism from *Light in August*—where slavery's biopolitical legacies can be seen not only in the corporeal discipline and racialized (non)citizenship of Joe Christmas but also in the depleted, hookworm-infested bodies of Doane's Mill, Alabama, upon the departure of the rapacious industrial lumbering operation once situated there—back to Charles Chesnutt's 1900 story "Lonesome Ben," whose character-narrator Julius McAdoo witnesses to the ongoing consumption of enslaved bodies into the post-Reconstruction decades and beyond. Chesnutt's Ben is a runaway slave who subsists by eating clay from a local stream bank, only to discover that the yellowish soil leaves him pale-skinned and unrecognizable to his loved ones and even his master. Lonely and dejected, he pines away at the clay bank until his death, whereupon his decomposing body returns to the soil now eaten, a generation later, by poor whites who replicate his lethargy and sallow complexion—symptoms that happen to mimic precisely those of hookworm. In Rountree's genealogy, Chesnutt's characters thus anticipate both the hookworm-afflicted denizens of Doane's Mill and the young Joe Christmas, whose toothpaste-eating in the dietitian's closet falls afoul of the biopolitics of respectability advocated by Booker T. Washington and leads immediately to his racial denigration. For Rountree, these stories allegorize how the liberal nation-state actually tightened rather than relaxed its grip on the body-servants of US capitalism in the wake of Emancipation. Like other writers in the antiliberal tradition, Chesnutt and Faulkner offer sobering reminders that slavery's constitutional abolition has not brought an end to slavery's capitalism.

Randall Wilhelm notes the curious fact that the period between 1790 and 1850, the heyday of chattel slavery in the United States, was also the era of a "silhouette rage" in American popular and visual culture: an art form that rendered all its subjects equally pitch-black just as philosophers, anthropologists, and pseudo-scientists were consolidating racial Blackness into a somatic badge of inferiority. The ironies and implications opening out of this historical juxtaposition invite a reconsideration of the function of silhouettes, visual and verbal, in Faulkner's art and set the stage for fruitful comparison and contrast with the contemporary artist most renowned for working in the silhouette medium, Kara Walker. "Melodrama, Turbulence, Titillation: Silhouetting Slavery in the Works of William Faulkner and Kara Walker" mines the creative possibilities of an aesthetic "space where visual details *cannot* be seen within a shape that *can* be seen," as the two artists capitalize on that potential to different but partially overlapping ends. Faulkner, Wilhelm argues, "manipulates silhouette effects to evoke the mysteries of many racialized and sexualized characters," especially at sites of contact between and among them, in a typology of silhouette structures ranging from the "visual-visual" constructions of *The Marionettes*, the Symbolist verse-drama that was Faulkner's most sophisticated creation as a visual artist, to the "verbal-visual" cues, lighting effects, assemblages, and entire passages that show up with surprising frequency in his fiction. Walker doubles down on the silhouette's fundamental indeterminacy by ramping up the affectivity of large, complex installations like her most celebrated and vilified work, *The End of Uncle Tom and the Grand Allegorical Tableau of Eva in Heaven*, in which paper cutouts serve as "entry points for murder and mayhem, power and cruelty, sexual depravity and pleasure, melodrama and turbulence, titillation and ambiguity." Targeting "the clichés, stereotypes, and irreality of plantation life that have become so ingrained in the popular American imagination," Walker nevertheless refuses to provide clear resolution in her contemporary slave narratives, or to offer "more accurate representations of African American history and culture" to revise or redeem her wild grotesques. Thus educated by Walker in the possibilities of the genre, Wilhelm can return to an underappreciated Faulkner novel like *The Unvanquished* with a sharper eye for its "shadow games," the Walker-like aesthetic that focuses on "silhouette-like meetings and mergings" of "said and unsaid, sign and signifier, language and experience," in an "affective turbulence that can grow with deeper analysis and reflection."

Finally, as contemporary "new abolitionist" thinkers and activists have stressed, one of the most insidious of slavery's afterlives in US society today is the rise of mass incarceration as a means of systematically depriving African Americans of their liberty and once again turning their bondage into a source of profit. Sherita L. Johnson explores this legacy as it informs the work of Faulkner and one of his most celebrated Mississippi successors. "Emancipating Faulkner: Reading *Go Down, Moses* and Jesmyn Ward's *Sing, Unburied, Sing*" finds common ground between the two writers in the way "figures of the enslaved" become "reimagined as black male convicts" in their fictions, but Johnson ultimately concludes that Ward's story offers a "lyrical key" that can not only open Faulkner's novel to new critical insight but also temper its pessimistic visions of twentieth-century Black lives still under slavery's long shadow. As Johnson argues, incarcerated figures like Rider of "Pantaloon in Black" and Butch Beauchamp of "Go Down, Moses" are drawn with sympathy, historical understanding, and "moral conviction" yet "cannot escape narrative entrapments" that channel them toward tragedy rather than liberation or healing: "they remain enslaved by circumstance," hemmed in by "generational curses" the narratives cannot ultimately transcend. By contrast, Ward's novel, which features a trio of characters incarcerated over multiple generations at Mississippi's infamous Parchman Farm, not only achieves "fuller expression" for the enslaved through dialogue, reminiscence, and song but also follows its convicts to and through the point of their release from imprisonment, a physical and psychic event that *Go Down, Moses* seems unable to stage or even imagine in 1942. Indeed, for one of Ward's prisoners, the spectral Richie, this release is metaphysical: murdered decades ago by a trusty guard, Richie is finally able to "end his long unburial and return home" by sharing his story, across the ontological gap between death and life, with young Jojo, himself the son and the grandson of Parchman survivors. Thus, in what amounts to an "exorcism" of slavery's curse, Ward "breaks the frame of black male enslavement" in her novel, charting new "routes out of Yoknapatawpha" and its sense of historical entrapment by "emancipat[ing] not only enslaved African Americans and their descendants but also Faulkner from th[e] slave past."

That Johnson's Faulkner had to wait over half a century after his death to be emancipated by Ward's 2017 novel attests to the continuing hold of that slave past on his world and hers, and to the difficulty of the wake-work[19] needed to eke out zones of maneuver and possibility among the many forms of confinement—spatial, economic, psychological, ontological—that slavery and its auxiliary forms have imposed on those worlds, modern worlds they had a constitutive role in creating. As Faulkner recognized, slavery remains a curse afflicting Black, brown, and white in the Americas, albeit in incommensurable and deeply inequitable ways.[20] Though he seemed to despair of ever lifting that curse, he explored it, indeed inhabited it, with a tenacity matched by few American writers, and even fewer white ones. His finest novels—*Light in August, Absalom, Absalom!, Go Down, Moses*— unmask African slavery as the historical crucible and agon of the nation and indeed the hemisphere, though, as his Chickasaw and Choctaw characters might add, not the only one. In these works and the others discussed here, Faulkner has left us a rich and troubled imaginative record of American slavery, yet another of its tangled afterlives.

NOTES

1. Joseph Blotner, *Faulkner: A Biography*, vol. 1 (New York: Random House, 1974), 653.

2. William Faulkner, "Red Leaves," *Saturday Evening Post*, October 25, 1930, 6–7, 54–64. The story was then included, slightly revised, in Faulkner's *These 13* collection (New York: Cape and Smith, 1931), 127–66, and in the *Collected Stories* volume (New York: Random House, 1950), 313–41.

3. Blotner, *Faulkner: A Biography*, vol. 1, 651.

4. William Faulkner, "Barn Burning," in *Collected Stories of William Faulkner* (1950; repr., New York: Vintage, 1977), 12.

5. Joel Williamson, *William Faulkner and Southern History* (New York: Oxford University Press, 1993), 64–67.

6. Neil R. McMillen, "WPA Slave Narratives," *Mississippi History Now*, accessed October 4, 2019, www.mshistorynow.mdah.state.ms.us/articles/64/wpa-slave-narratives.

7. William Faulkner, *The Wild Palms [If I Forget Thee, Jerusalem]* (1939; repr., New York: Vintage International, 1995), 59.

8. On the mass incarceration of African Americans as a form of twentieth- and twenty-first-century neoslavery, see Michelle Alexander, *The New Jim Crow: Mass Incarceration*

*in the Age of Colorblindness* (New York: New Press, 2010); Angela Y. Davis, *The Angela Y. Davis Reader*, ed. Joy James (Malden, MA: Blackwell, 1998), 61–109; Houston A. Baker Jr., *Turning South Again: Re-Thinking Modernism/Re-Reading Booker T.* (Durham, NC: Duke University Press, 2001), 79–98; Dylan Rodriguez, *Forced Passages: Imprisoned Radical Intellectuals and the US Prison Regime* (Minneapolis: University of Minnesota Press, 2006), 225–39; Alexander Weheliye, *Habeas Viscus: Racializing Assemblages, Biopolitics, and Black Feminist Theories of the Human* (Durham, NC: Duke University Press, 2014), 86–88; and Patrick Alexander, *From Slave Ship to Supermax: Mass Incarceration, Prisoner Abuse, and the New Neo-Slave Novel* (Philadelphia: Temple University Press, 2017). See also Ava DuVernay's splendid documentary *13th* (Kandoo Films, 2016).

9. I'm grateful to Mississippi historian Jack Elliott for providing this census information, cross-checked against a November 1, 1860, inventory of Robert Sheegog's personal property at his Oxford "home place," sent to the University of Mississippi Slavery Research Group in an email of August 6, 2017. Elliott found the inventory in the estate file for Sheegog at the Lafayette County Chancery Clerk's office.

10. Blotner, *Faulkner: A Biography*, vol. 1, 651–52.

11. Craig Steven Wilder, *Ebony and Ivy: Race, Slavery, and the Troubled History of America's Universities* (New York: Bloomsbury, 2013).

12. University of Mississippi Slavery Research Group, www.slaveryresearchgroup.olemiss.edu.

13. William Faulkner, *The Sound and the Fury*, rev. ed. (1929; repr., New York: Vintage International, 1990), 239.

14. On the mythology surrounding the mammy figure, see, among many others, Kimberly Wallace-Sanders, *Mammy: A Century of Race, Gender, and Southern Memory* (Ann Arbor: University of Michigan Press, 2008); and on Faulkner's deconstruction of the mammy role in his 1951 novel, see Deborah Barker, "Demystifying the Modern Mammy in *Requiem for a Nun*," in *Faulkner and Film: Faulkner and Yoknapatawpha, 2010*, ed. Peter Lurie and Ann J. Abadie (Jackson: University Press of Mississippi, 2014), 71–97.

15. John T. Matthews, "Financialization and Neoliberalism: A Snopes Genealogy," in *Faulkner and Money: Faulkner and Yoknapatawpha, 2017*, ed. Jay Watson and James G. Thomas, Jr. (Jackson: University Press of Mississippi, 2019), 59–77.

16. For a brilliant account of the *Zong* massacre in historical, economic, and literary context, see Ian Baucom, *Specters of the Atlantic: Finance Capital, Slavery, and the Philosophy of History* (Durham, NC: Duke University Press, 2005).

17. See the essays collected in Sven Beckert and Seth Rockman, eds., *Slavery's Capitalism: A New History of American Economic Development* (Philadelphia: University of Pennsylvania Press, 2016), and the following essays in Sven Beckert and Christine Desan, eds., *American Capitalism: New Histories* (New York: Columbia University Press, 2018): Seth Rockman, "Negro Cloth: Mastering the Market for Slave Clothing in Antebellum America" (170–94); Christopher Tomlins, "Revulsions of Capital: Slavery and Political Economy in the Epoch of the Turner Rebellion, Virginia, 1829–1832" (195–217); Michael Ralph, "Value of Life: Insurance, Slavery, and Expertise" (257–81); and Kris Manjapra, "Plantation Dispossessions: The Global Travel of Agricultural Racial Capitalism" (361–87).

18. Edward E. Baptist, *The Half Has Never Been Told: Slavery and the Making of American Capitalism* (New York: Basic Books, 2014); Sven Beckert, *Empire of Cotton: A Global History* (New York: Knopf, 2014); Walter Johnson, *River of Dark Dreams: Slavery and Empire in the Cotton Kingdom* (Cambridge, MA: Belknap Press of Harvard University Press, 2013); and Joshua Rothman, *Flush Times and Fever Dreams: A Story of Capitalism and Slavery in the Age of Jackson* (Athens: University of Georgia Press, 2012).

19. With my phraseology here, I'm invoking the concepts of the ontological "wake" of Atlantic slavery and the Middle Passage, of the "hold" in which Black life and being remain confined in the African diaspora, and of the "wake-work" necessary to avoid succumbing to such restrictions on human flourishing, developed by Christina Sharpe in her important study *In the Wake: On Blackness and Being* (Durham, NC: Duke University Press, 2016). For related arguments see Dionne Brand, *A Map to the Door of No Return* (2001; repr., Toronto: Vintage Canada, 2012); and Saidya Hartman, *Lose Your Mother: A Journey along the Atlantic Slave Route* (New York: Farrar, Straus and Giroux, 2007).

20. The Faulkner at Virginia audio archive contains this exchange between Faulkner and an unidentified interlocutor, perhaps a student or professor, at the University of Virginia in 1957:

> Unidentified participant: Mr. Faulkner, throughout your work there seems to be a theme that there's a curse upon the South. I was wondering if you could explain what this curse is and if there's any chance of the South of escaping it.
>
> Faulkner: The—the curse is slavery, which is a—a—an intolerable condition. No man shall be enslaved, and the South has got to work—work that curse out, and it will, if it's let alone. It—it can't be compelled to do it. It—it must do it of its own will and—and desire, which I believe it will do, if it's let alone.

See the transcript of "Blotner and Gwynn's Classes, tape 2," April 13, 1957, Faulkner at Virginia: An Audio Archive (2010), ed. Stephen Railton, accessed December 12, 2019, https://faulkner.lib.virginia.edu/display/wfaudio06_2.html#wfaudio06_2.10.

# Note on the Conference

The Faulkner and Yoknapatawpha Conference, sponsored by the University of Mississippi in Oxford, took place Sunday, July 22, through Thursday, July 26, 2018. Thirteen presentations on the theme "Faulkner and Slavery" are collected as essays in this volume. Brief mention is made here of other conference activities.

The program began on Sunday afternoon with a reception at the University Museum. Following the reception, Edward E. Baptist delivered a keynote lecture in Nutt Auditorium on the subject of "Where the Line Draws Blood: Faulkner, Ward, and the Policing of Race." Following Baptist's keynote, a panel included a discussion on the subject of "Understanding Slavery and Its Legacies at Robert Sheegog's Estate" between Jillian Galle, Tony Boudreaux, Maureen Meyers, Jeffrey T. Jackson, Edward Chappell, and Carl Lounsbury.

Following a buffet supper at Rowan Oak that evening, Oxford mayor Robyn Tannehill and University of Mississippi chancellor Jeffrey Vitter welcomed participants, and Jenna Grace Sciuto, secretary-treasurer of the William Faulkner Society, introduced winners of the 2018 John W. Hunt Scholarships. These fellowships, awarded to graduate students pursuing research on William Faulkner, are funded by the Faulkner Society and the *Faulkner Journal* in memory of John W. Hunt, Faulkner scholar and emeritus professor of literature at Lehigh University. Katie McKee, McMullan Associate Professor of Southern Studies and associate professor of English at the University of Mississippi, presented the 2018 Eudora Welty Awards in Creative Writing. A panel on "Community Engagement and Interpreting Slavery in North Mississippi," which included presentations by Jodi Skipper and Suzanne Davidson, W. Ralph Eubanks, Charles K. Ross and Jeffrey T. Jackson, and George McDaniel, concluded the evening.

Monday's program began with Terrell L. Tebbetts leading the first "Teaching Faulkner" session, "Slavery's Very Words: What Were We Thinking!," followed by a panel on "Legacies of Slavery in *The Sound and the Fury*," with Shawn Salvant, Julia Stern, and Kenneth Estrada. A panel on "Spaces of Slavery" followed and included papers by Amy

Foley and Leigh Anne Litwiller Berte. The day's program also included a Brown Bag Lunch presentation by Seth Berner on "An Introduction to Collecting the World of Faulkner"; a keynote lecture, "Slave Capitalism in Faulkner," by John T. Matthews; and presentations on the topic of "Current Research on Slavery at the University of Mississippi," presented by Chet Bush, Andrew Marion, and Anne Twitty.

Tuesday's program included the second "Teaching Faulkner" session, "Faulkner, Slavery, and the AP/IB Classroom," led by Brian McDonald, followed by a panel on "Sexual Properties" that included papers by James B. Carothers, Jenna Grace Sciuto, Julie Beth Napolin, and Rebecca Starr Nisetich, with a response from Erich Nunn. The panel "Houses of Slavery," which included W. Ralph Eubanks, Anne MacMaster, and Michael Gleason, closed the morning sessions. Lunch included a progress report by Jennie Joiner, Erin Penner, and Stephen Railton on the *Digital Yoknapatawpha* project at the University of Virginia. That afternoon Tim Armstrong delivered the keynote lecture "Playing Monopoly with Mr. Faulkner," followed by a panel on "Slavery and Its Futures: Liberation, Survival, Trauma" with Michael Gorra, Robert Jackson, and Amber Zinni. A cocktail party at the Oxford Depot completed the day.

Wednesday's program began with Anders Walker and Linda Chavers delivering papers on the topic of "Grand Designs: Present, Future, and the Prism of *Absalom, Absalom!*" Concurrent panels followed on "Faulkner and African American Representations of Slavery," with Andrew Leiter, Tim A. Ryan, and Randall Wilhelm; and on "Slavery and Its Afterlives in *Go Down, Moses*: Traces and Testaments," with Laura Wilson, Lael Gold, and Garry J. Bertholf and Zoran Kuzmanovich. Concurrent panels on "Faulkner, Chesnutt, Ward, Beyoncé," with papers by Stephanie Rountree, Kim Manganelli, and Sherita L. Johnson, and on "Planters Plantations, Plaçage," with papers by Sarah E. Gardner, Murphy Wood, and Jennie Lightweis-Goff, ended the morning. Richard Cellini spoke on "The Ethics of Memory: The Search for 272 Georgetown Slaves" at the J. D. Williams Library, and Stephen Best's lecture "Wrongful Life" and a panel on "'Distensions' and Extensions: Beyond the Popular Icons of Slavery," which included presentations by Peter Lurie, Charles Peek, Theresa Towner, and Sarah Gleeson-White, followed in Nutt Auditorium. A late-afternoon walk through Bailey Woods ended at Rowan Oak, where the annual picnic on the grounds concluded the day's events.

Guided tours of north Mississippi, including Oxford and Lafayette County, the Mississippi Delta, and New Albany and Ripley, took place on Thursday, along with a "Slavery in Holly Springs, Mississippi" tour by Jodi Skipper. The conference ended with a closing party and book signing at Square Books. The University Press of Mississippi exhibited Faulkner books published by members of the American Association of University Presses.

The Faulkner and Yoknapatawpha Conference at the University of Mississippi is sponsored by the Department of English and the Center for the Study of Southern Culture and coordinated by the Division of Outreach and Continuing Studies. The conference planners are grateful to all the individuals and organizations that support the Faulkner and Yoknapatawpha Conference annually. In addition to those mentioned above, we wish to thank the College of Liberal Arts, the Office of the Provost, Square Books, the City of Oxford, and the Oxford Convention and Visitors Bureau.

Faulkner and Slavery
FAULKNER AND YOKNAPATAWPHA

2018

# Slave Capitalism in Faulkner

## John T. Matthews

It is fitting that we should be gathered here this week to think about Faulkner's representation of slavery following last year's conference devoted to Faulkner and money. One of the central consequences of the burgeoning scholarship on capitalism over the last decade has been the conclusive case it has made for how fundamentally Atlantic capitalism came to rely on a global system of enslaved labor. Slave capitalism enabled European investors to extract enormous profits from colonial agricultural enterprises; to establish dominance over the production, manufacturing, and trade in premier commodities like cotton; to build prominent financial industries such as banking and insurance; and to amass vast institutional and personal wealth. In recent years, prompted by economic crises in the West such as the near meltdown of investment banking in 2007–8 and exponentially increasing income disparity, works like Thomas Piketty's *Capital in the Twenty-First Century* (2014) have signaled a new determination to understand the economic mechanisms of hyper-financialized capitalism amid a scene of extreme social damage.[1] Financialization, which we normally think of as a more contemporary development, was key to modern industrial capitalism from its emergence out of earlier forms in the eighteenth century, and its operatives developed an assortment of devices to multiply the profitability of that capitalism's most propulsive new fuel: the traffic in human chattel. Historians of global capital have also been mindful that unearthing the extent of American capitalism's dependence on racialized slavery matters vitally to understanding continuing racial conflict. As Sven Beckert and Seth Rockman write:

> Slavery often bubbles to the surface of the national political and cultural discourse in response to tragedy, such as the 2015 massacre at Charleston's Emanuel A.M.E. Church; the subsequent removal of the Confederate battle flag from the grounds of several southern statehouses provided

opportunity for a public discussion of the Confederacy's investment in slavery. Sustained attention to police violence against black bodies, political mobilization against mass incarceration, and student protest against racial exclusion on college campuses have created new space to consider slavery and its legacies in American society.[2]

Recent monographs and collections by Beckert, Greg Grandin, Walter Johnson, Ian Baucom, Edward Baptist, Stephen Best, Tim Armstrong, Craig Wilder, and others have elaborated the crucial role of the US South in the global slave economies that became the chief driver of capitalism's ascent.[3] What has been most revelatory to me in the new scholarship on the reciprocity of slavery and capitalism is the prominence of finance in slavery's capitalism. As Bonnie Martin remarks about the US South, "Slave owners worked their slaves financially as well as physically from colonial days until emancipation."[4] Her point reflects wider new investigation into the variety of ways human chattel was capitalized by owners beyond being goods sold for profit and labor bought to convert into further profit. Slaves were, in addition, financialized as insurable lives whose loss turned their nonexistence into money; as sexually reproducible merchandise; as contracted wage earners; as speculative investments; and as collateral for mortgages, loans, or the purchase of other goods bought on credit, including more slaves.[5] Such financialization augmented slavery's role in the development of modern capitalism, since it was not just the massive advantage of uncompensated labor that propelled the dominance of Atlantic world plantation economies but also the emergence in the eighteenth century of instruments and institutions of advanced capitalism such as personal credit, nautical insurance, and finance banking.[6]

Faulkner's chronicle of the South's plantation regime does expose its foundational dependence on heavily financialized forms of slave capitalism, although that evidence invariably appears obscured in discourses of denial authored by its practitioners and complicit beneficiaries. As has been examined from numerous standpoints, Faulkner's historical fiction concentrates more on the repression of devastating knowledge than on the rehearsal of what is known. In this essay I want first to consider some particulars of financialized slaveholding as they retain legibility under attempted expungement by not-narration. The first thing Thomas Sutpen says he needs to defend himself against the insults of planters like Pettibone is "money."[7] We can track Sutpen's career along a timeline of Atlantic slave capitalism, from his birth in 1807, the year Great Britain and the United States outlawed the international slave trade, through the conception of his life-design on a Virginia Tidewater plantation, his foray into the hemisphere's first dominant colonial economy based on sugar production; his arrival in frontier Mississippi in 1833, the year Great Britain abolished slavery altogether and thereby spurred a boom in America's cotton economy; and on to his becoming the "biggest single landowner and cotton-planter in the county" (56) by the height of the Deep South's Cotton Kingdom in the 1850s. Sutpen's subsequent ruin allegorizes how the South was destroyed by the slave capitalism that had borne it, the "shifting sands of opportunism and moral brigandage" undermining the very foundation of the South's "economic edifice" that they constituted (209). Sven Beckert summarizes: "Slavery, colonialism, and forced labor, among other forms of violence, were not aberrations in the history of capitalism, but were at its very core" (*Empire of Cotton*, 441). Yet the story of slavery is not one that any privileged character in Faulkner wants to tell, abide though it does as the story of all other stories, the story all those other stories mean not to tell, the pebble rippling through the history of the modern Atlantic world. More broadly, the refusal by its beneficiaries to admit the slave capitalist foundation of southern society symptomizes a national blindness to the whole country's economic dependence on slavery—a practical ignorance that the new histories of American capitalism characterize variously as forgetting, inattentiveness, erasure, not telling, or, as Edward Baptist has put it acutely, "a mutually-agreed-to-structure of lies that . . . made the nation" (*The Half Has Never Been Told*, 36).[8]

Compounding the abuses of forced labor, the financializing of enslaved humans rendered them property whose value could be abstracted as paper assets. So perverse a capitalist fantasy levied extreme violence on bound people, who were treated as amalgams of the physical and fiscal—as both laboring Black bodies and white financial interests. Chattel slaves were monetized before birth and after death, doubled as collateral, and could instantaneously be liquefied as capital. The temporalities of capitalism recalibrate slave "life-cycles" as profit cycles, as Daina Berry puts it, and redefine human lifespans according to sliding financial value ("'Broad is de Road dat Leads ter Death,'" 146). Faulkner suggests how slave capitalism fantasized Blackness as the investment of white financial interest in slave bodies and how new market temporalities altered cognitive rhythms. After considering in more detail the way Faulkner's fiction reflects on the capitalist derangements of personhood and time in his representation of slavery, I turn in my conclusion to the way his aesthetic responds to slave capitalism's infliction of such violence. Faulkner's fiction formalizes the distortions of slave capitalism, but he redeploys such distortion in narrative and stylistic forms that resist capitalism's demands. Faulkner's modernist reconfiguration of the novel owes something to his position as a close witness to modernity's perhaps earliest and most radically transformative force, slave capitalism.[9]

## *"getting richer and richer"*

Sutpen creates himself, constructs his design, from the material of the plantation world he inhabits. From the instant he suffers the initial insult of his exclusion from full personhood, through the devising of his design, to his ascent to elite cotton planter, Sutpen makes himself as slave capitalism makes him. Louis Althusser's formula would run: the capitalist subject comes into being through the enactment of ideology, that ideology materialized in the embodying of it. In historical terms, Sutpen redresses his insult on an established Tidewater plantation by realizing opportunities presented by the Mississippi frontier more than a decade later. In that interval, cotton had expanded to what was then called the Southwest, with notable differences in scene. As Beckert writes, "The old paternalism of East Coast planters, shielded partially by the mercantilist logic of mutually beneficial and protected exchange between motherland and colony of the greater British imperial economy, had given way to a freer, more competitive, and fluid social order mediated by merchant capital" (*Empire of Cotton*, 117). The scale of development of the new cotton frontier depended on foreign investment and other forms of financial capital. Against such a background our hundred-square-mile Sutpen seems a bit less outsized, less Faustian, Luciferian, Beelzebubian. Beckert notes that frontier cotton's "patterns now followed the competitive logic of markets rather than the whimsy of personal aspiration and regional circumstance—capital moved to wherever cotton could be produced in the greatest quantities and the cheapest cost." Sutpen's prosaic need for money reflects standard methods of cotton capitalization. His first move has been subsidized by European money increased in value by its stop through the Caribbean plantation colonies; his next is to target Goodhue Coldfield, who allegorizes the "merchant capital" newcomers required.

Rosa gets starchy about Sutpen's disreputable origins, pointing out that he's "no younger son sent out from some old quiet country like Virginia or Carolina with the surplus negroes to take up new land, because anyone could look at those negroes of his and tell that they may have come (and probably did) from a much older country than Virginia or Carolina but it wasn't a quiet one" (Faulkner, *Absalom, Absalom!* 11). Her use of the word "surplus" to describe a slave force no longer of use on coastal plantations inadvertently evokes the whole history of the internal slave trade. Once Great Britain had abolished slavery altogether by 1833, New

World cultivators completed a pivot away from sugar and toward cotton that had begun with the conclusion of the Haitian Revolution in 1804. The Mississippi and Alabama territories craved slaves, while the East Coast plantation regime, much of its land exhausted, converted its work force into merchandise. Rosa's word betrays her understanding of the surplus value congealed in slaves as commodities—"negroes" who in Mississippi in 1833 were more likely to have been bought in New Orleans than brought by a Tidewater scion. Sutpen's troubles in Jefferson have something to do with his disregard for this established, if noxious, domestic trade. By 1807 the United States had banned the importation of slaves, in part to protect against the infiltration of insurrectionist sentiments from abroad after the Haitian Revolution. Not only does Sutpen's "crew of imported slaves," as Mr. Compson refers to them, pose a potentially fatal danger to the locals, who view them as "a good deal more deadly than any beast" (28), they also represent a threat to the livelihood of those involved in the internal slave trade. I've always wondered why the novel's narrators make such a point of identifying the unruly demonstrators at Sutpen's wedding as coming from outside Jefferson. They're described as a "mob," "traders and drovers and teamsters" who, after the ceremony, "returned, vanished back into the region from which they had emerged for this one occasion like rats" (44).[10] Traders, drovers, and teamsters are occupations of the internal slave trade. Here's what Frederick Douglass had to say about them in his "The Meaning of July Fourth for the Negro" speech of 1852:

> Behold the practical operation of this internal slave-trade, the American slave-trade, sustained by American politics and American religion. Here you will see men and women reared like swine for the market. You know what is a swine-drover? I will show you a man-drover. They inhabit all our Southern States. They perambulate the country, and crowd the highways of the nation, with droves of human stock. You will see one of these human flesh jobbers, armed with pistol, whip, and bowie-knife, driving a company of a hundred men, women, and children, from the Potomac to the slave market at New Orleans. These wretched people are to be sold singly, or in lots, to suit purchasers. They are food for the cotton-field and the deadly sugar-mill. Mark the sad procession, as it moves wearily along, and the inhuman wretch who drives them. Hear his savage yells and his blood-curdling oaths, as he hurries on his affrighted captives![11]

Such "man-drovers" occupy the liminal space between Jefferson's genteel pretensions and their dependence on the flesh markets wished out of sight. The traders' anger at Sutpen targets his having sidestepped the domestic trade by bringing foreign slaves into Jefferson.[12] Those imports are once referred to as Sutpen's own "brand" of Negro (209). The wedding confrontation comes close to laying bare the feral struggle for gain on the frontier that depended on brutal, competitive traffic in humans. The 1830s were a time of explosive profit in the cotton economy in Alabama and Mississippi: cotton became America's most important export, and prices of land and labor skyrocketed. Joshua Rothman observes that "only recently have scholars begun appreciating how extensively slaves and slavery inflated the bubble of the flush times, and how cotton capitalism rested on the capacity of the enslaved as both laborers and assets" ("The Contours of Cotton Capitalism," 124).[13] That Tidewater slaves would one day be destined for sale during that "inflated ... bubble of ... flush times" in Mississippi is perhaps already reflected on the distorted faces of Pettibone's Blacks in 1820 as Sutpen recalls them in the 1830s: "The nigger was just another balloon face slick and distended with that mellow loud and terrible laughing so that he did not dare to burst it" (*Absalom, Absalom!* 189).[14]

One reason Sutpen urgently needs a second infusion of cash, or at least available credit, may have to do with a subsequent development in the feverish 1830s. Sutpen arrives in Mississippi in 1833; it takes him two years to erect the shell of his mansion; then, without explanation, he stops. The edifice stands partially complete for three more years, until 1838, when Sutpen marries Ellen Coldfield. During the hiatus Sutpen leaves Jefferson a second time, devising some scheme to make use of Goodhue Coldfield's credit, and returning with the "loot" to furnish his house. The dating here suggests that what may contribute to putting Sutpen's plans on hold is the Panic of 1837, in which overproduction and easy credit for expansion were undercut by a drop in demand for raw cotton.[15] Prices had soared in the years between 1832 and 1837, presumably confirming Sutpen's decision to have come to this next place where men go to get rich (as he puts his original decision to head to the West Indies). The Southwest, including New Orleans, was stuffed with foreign investment, but local paper credit far exceeded gold reserves. Just before the time the traders, drovers, and teamsters confront Sutpen at his wedding in 1838, the domestic slave trade had cratered: in 1836, Rothman writes, "'all the public highways to Mississippi became lined ... with slaves,' which severely glutted the market and led to lagging sales" ("The Contours of Cotton Capitalism," 131). Amid a scene of debts called, panicked liquidation of assets, and defaults, Sutpen makes a desperate and illegal gamble.

It's not surprising that Jeffersonians assume Sutpen has robbed a riverboat when he shows up with wagonloads of plunder. Walter Johnson has described the significance of riverboat economics and subculture in the rapid development of the Mississippi River Valley. Steamboats were the third-leading sector of investment behind slaves and land by the 1830s, with transportation of cotton to world markets and the reciprocal procuring of goods, including slaves, crucial to the growth of the frontier economy. Johnson describes the especially rough-and-tumble underworld created by low entry barriers for investors, huge profits, ruthless business practices, and the ersatz glam of riverboat luxury. Such vessels literalized the speculative nature of the frontier, with their flat-bottomed, high-risk designs, their faux opulence, and the tendencies of their high-pressure boiler engines to blow up. Such open spectacularization of slave capitalism contributed to an effect Johnson characterizes as "the steamboat sublime" (*River of Dark Dreams*, 73), the sort of effect that, following Slavoj Žižek, we can understand as enabling slavers to convert the barbarity of speculative slave capitalism into a form of pleasure.[16] In discussing Sutpen's original options, Rosa in fact confirms that riverboat larceny would have been the obvious shortcut for a "young man without any past that he apparently cared to discuss, in Mississippi in 1833, with a river full of steamboats loaded with drunken fools covered with diamonds and bent on throwing away their cotton and slaves before the boat reached New Orleans" (*Absalom, Absalom!* 11). But Rosa is intent on denying that Sutpen's motive in Jefferson could have been as simple as "clearing virgin land and establishing a plantation in a new country just for money." So she insists that "nobody knows how" Sutpen does anything he does (10). What she denies about the Sutpen of 1833, however, is exactly what he's accused of doing five years later, when he's confronted by Jefferson's "vigilance committee" as he returns to town having, as one citizen puts it, "stole the whole durn steamboat" this time (34).

Whatever Sutpen and Coldfield have dreamt up to make a quick hit, there's evidence they are relying on the customary financial tools of international slave capitalism to do it. As Quentin learns from his father, "It was something about a bill of lading, some way he persuaded Mr Coldfield to use his credit" (208). A bill of lading is a document that certifies the receipt of goods for shipment. Bills of lading were key instruments in the development of international finance capitalism, including the commerce in slaves, because they allowed the transfer of capital over large distances. They were also crucial to Mississippi River commerce, since insurers were reluctant to cover goods traveling by such high-risk transit; instead, purchasers typically accepted responsibility for loss themselves by signing bills of lading. Such agreements would put recipients at high financial risk, the sort the town assumes would have destroyed Coldfield's name and finances if Sutpen's trickery had failed. Still, that Coldfield initially agrees to Sutpen's proposal suggests his own ambitions. Individuals like Coldfield actually were migrating to the territories in hopes of moving up themselves from merchant to planter. The storekeeper arrives on a tide of upwardly aspirant settlers. Coldfield knows where he's going and what's there.[17]

What Coldfield may not have figured on is the repugnance of direct profiteering from financialized slave trading. Like northerners and other Atlantic investors, Coldfield practices complicity with a system he hopes to keep at arm's length. His efforts to appease his conscience and perform a "moral fumigation" (38)—for himself as much as for Sutpen—begin with his withdrawal from their business deal and the forfeiture of profits when he sees it will, against all odds, succeed. But Coldfield's economic complicity is structural, not just personal. To secure a wedding for Ellen and Sutpen, he determines to "employ" his church "exactly as he might or would have used any other object, concrete or abstract, to which he had given a certain amount of his time"; he has "invested a certain amount of sacrifice and doubtless self-denial and certainly actual labor and money for the sake of what might be called a demand balance of spiritual solvency, exactly as he would have used a cotton gin in which he considered himself to have incurred either interest or responsibility, for the ginning of any cotton which he or any member of his family, by blood or by marriage, had raised." The simile loops back on Coldfield here, implicating moral fumigation in the very economic system that has generated the need for it. Such figurative self-cancellation measures the conundrum of those who disapproved of slavery in the Atlantic world but who found it impossible not to continue to enrich themselves by it.[18]

Coldfield equivocates between profit and conscience, but his handling of the manumission of the only slaves he ever owns—tellingly, as collateral for a failed debt—underscores how inescapable complicity could seem: Coldfield makes the two financialized chattel earn not their market price but the equivalent of what's owed him, as if to avoid selling them himself while refusing to take a loss. In effect, he's outsourced the commodification of the slaves.[19] Coldfield's circumstances allegorize the predicament of northern banks and foreign financial institutions that ended up as inadvertent owners of plantations and slaves when loans to southern planters failed. The slave constitutes credit returned to capital in a most liquid if also most morally objectionable form. Eventually, banks like the Rothschilds' pulled out of direct credit markets for southern cotton planters altogether, in part because of moral scruple, in part because of even more lucrative new prospects in commercial finance banking.[20]

Telling the story in 1910, Quentin and Shreve improvise a farcical rejoinder to the absurdity of financializing humans as they imagine the counterplot of Eulalia Bon and her lawyer. Eulalia represents the returns of the racial subject under capitalist calculation. The New Orleans lawyer compiles a plantation ledger in caricature, one that mocks the monetary valuation of everything under slave capitalism:

> *Today he finished robbing a drunken Indian of a hundred miles of virgin land, val. 25,000. At 2:31 today came up out of swamp with final plank for house. val in conj. with land 40,000. 7:52 p.m. today married. Bigamy threat val. minus nil. unless quick buyer. . . . Son. Intrinsic val. possible though not probable. . . . Emotional val. plus 100% times nil. plus val. crop.* (241)
> 
> *1859. Two children. Say 1860, 20 years. Increase 200% times intrinsic val. yearly plus liquid assets plus credit earned. Approx'te val. 1860, 100,000. Query: bigamy threat, Yes or No. Possible No. Incest threat: Credible Yes.* (248)

This is inspired parody. It's as if the two Harvard undergrads have been reading *The Half Has Never Been Told*, or at least *Go Down, Moses*. It's somewhat less likely that they have actually been studying slave capitalism, although they would have learned a lot in a course in American history offered by Albert Bushnell Hart, a specialist in southern history and the author of a book titled *Slavery and Abolition*, as Natalie Ring suggested in a recent paper at the "Faulkner and History" conference.[21] Tables turned, Sutpen's property, including the two white children he acknowledges as his own, is commoditized, Eulalia and Charles Bon put precisely in a position to capitalize on their purported Blackness. That recursive doubling back creates an effect of the uncanny: the lawyer repeatedly describes the cultivation of Eulalia's interests and her nurturing of Bon's resentment as if they were plantation fields themselves. Shreve refers to the lawyer as having a "mad female millionaire to farm," in fact having "already been plowing and planting and harvesting [Bon] and the mother both" (241).[22] Bon's situation as a claimant to indemnification may even reflect the prospect of post-Emancipation reparations, an idea that actually gained some public support in the years following Reconstruction.[23]

## *"compounded each of both yet either neither"*

When the over-narrator of *Absalom, Absalom!* describes Quentin and Shreve's identification with their fictional subjects Henry Sutpen and Charles Bon as being not merely the two of them become four, "but compounded still further, since now both of them were Henry Sutpen and both of them were Bon, compounded each of both yet either neither" (280), Faulkner's syntax compacts the fluidity and inextricability of identity as it is formulated via the history of slave capitalism. That "compound" denotes *mixture*—or, given Bon's purported mixed "blood," the more apt synonym *amalgamation*—draws Quentin and Shreve into the mix: Quentin, who has witnessed stable racial identity liquefy and alchemize in the modern North; Shreve, who may all too cheerfully be appropriating southern racist rhetoric to his own crypto-nativism.[24] "Compound" also sounds the financial note in blood mixture, reminding us that Blackness in the plantation New World was at base an economic invention, an expedient to rationalize the claim of financial interest in another person.

The scene of Quentin and Shreve's confabulation itself suggests the financial interests that structured the plantation world they both are indebted to, and on whose very premises they meet. Spying the outwardly servile Deacon, Shreve teases Quentin about his shameful southern past: "Just look at what your grandpa did to that poor old nigger."[25] And Quentin puts Sutpen's ambition as bluntly as possible: "'Yes,' Quentin said, 'The design.—Getting richer and richer'" (209). Quentin is at Harvard in the first place thanks to the wealth accrued from plantation capitalism; his forebears include lawyers, slaveholders, landholders. The last liquidation of Compson realty involves selling off Benjy's pasture, Quentin's freshman year at Harvard in effect the monetized compound profit extracted from generations of Luster's people—Luster, who spends a good deal of his time looking for lost money. Quentin and Shreve's reconstruction of the story of the South in a Harvard dormitory is acutely ironic, although it took the new studies of slavery and capitalism to appreciate it fully.

Five miles from my office at Boston University stands the big house of what was once a six-hundred-acre slaveholding plantation. In 1732 Isaac Royall acquired property called Ten Hills Farm in Medford, Massachusetts, and saw to its rebuilding over the next five years as an impressive country estate, crowned with a Georgian-style mansion. A New Englander, Royall derived his wealth from a sugar plantation in Antigua, where he lived for forty years, amassing a fortune in trade with Boston. When he eventually returned to Massachusetts, he brought with him twenty-seven slaves for his family's personal use. His mansion, as well as one of its outbuildings constructed as slave quarters, still stand today. Royall's predecessor had been a rum merchant, slave trader, and lieutenant governor of Massachusetts named John Usher, who had, in his turn, bought the land from the family of no less an eminence than John Winthrop, the first governor of the Massachusetts Bay Colony. Winthrop's son and nephew had developed plantation enterprises of their own in the West Indies, and the Winthrops began trading native

American slaves for African ones between Boston and Barbados.[26] It turns out that part of Isaac Royall's fortune was bequeathed by his son to found a first professorship in law at Harvard College, and that bequest eventually led to the establishment of its School of Law, where there is still an Isaac Royall chair. Although this uncomfortable legacy has been addressed directly by Harvard in recent years, as well as by other institutions with similar histories, it is the case that northern complicity in the New World's colonial slaveholding plantation economy and society has often been treated as an open secret.

Craig Wilder has excavated the dependence on the slave economy of preeminent institutions of higher learning from the early republic onward. Schools like Brown, Georgetown, and Harvard not only benefited from bequests made by families who had amassed their wealth from business in the Atlantic world of slave capitalism. The first American universities also functioned to educate the elite class of investors and directors who profited most from that economy.[27] Quentin and Shreve's identification with Henry and Bon then is also compounded, in the sense of "worsened," because they do not realize that the interest they take in telling about the South overpasses advantages deriving from a system in which, as rising members of hemispheric elites, they were deeply invested long before they were born, their interests already "compounded still further" before they ever matriculated.[28]

## "a time altered to fit the dream"

Slave capitalism measured time in unnatural new ways to accommodate the diverse forms of slave financialization. Faulkner absorbs such violent reconfigurations of temporality into a modernist aesthetic that reckons with slave capitalism as a prime mover of modernity. One temporality of this sort is the *instantaneity* with which human assets are willed to change form. The imposition of the commodity-form itself redesignates person as good immediately upon entry on the market. Whatever the ongoing and unresolved struggle between personhood and objecthood in the slave as commodity, a saleable human has changed status for the purposes of commercial transaction. Baucom points out as well how the labor value of slaves at a stroke became monetary value as insurable goods. Once slaves were insured against accident in transit, they were already prospectively dead with respect to their financial value. Labor to insurable good in an instant, nothing between: this is the temporality of the commodity. The actual death of a slave involved a similar instantaneous conversion of value in the field or market to monetary indemnification. Faulkner's fiction displays the violent changes in human apperception that such financial mutilations of time caused: think of the occasions in which individuals experience psychic blows that suddenly replace one self with another. Imagining what it must have meant for Bon to realize he was likely Henry's brother and so Sutpen's son, Quentin and Shreve describe him as "almost touching the answer" that soon "would reveal to him at once, like a flash of light, the meaning of his whole life, past" (250): Black not white, the presumption of bondage not freedom. That "flash," that "glare" corresponds with Sutpen's own instantaneous realization of his inferiority to Blacks on the plantation: "It was like that, he said, like an explosion—a bright glare that vanished and left nothing" (192). This kind of instantaneous revalorization persists in the secondary effects of Sutpen's design as well: the no-time it takes him to propose to Rosa (*"That was my courtship. That minute's exchanged look"* [132]) or the less than time it takes Henry to deny Sutpen's assertion of Bon's paternity ("'They cannot marry because he is your brother' and Henry said 'You lie' like that, that quick: no space, no interval, no nothing between like when you press the button and get light in the room" [235]). Quicker than the eye can see, or the brain comprehend: the temporality of capitalist materialization and dematerialization.[29]

The prominence of the *future perfect* tense in Faulkner registers a second mode of financial temporality: the expectation that assets will come to profitable issue over time. One could call this the temporality of investment. Diagram the syntax of capitalist speculation: investment predicates profit. The future already exists as the consummation of the present, a period set by the cap. In the credit-crazed cotton frontier of the 1830s, "whites financed slave purchases as they did anything of great value—by borrowing against anticipated cotton production" (Rothman, "The Contours of Cotton Capitalism," 130). One wonders how much Shreve has gleaned of this history given his joking about the "Creditor" in charge (see *Absalom* 145–47). Expected rises in crop prices as well as the value of land and slaves meant that capital poured into the region, from Europe as well as New York and Boston.[30] The tense was future, the expectation perfect. Sutpen imagines the ancestral obligations of his design as having "to fix things right so that he would be able to look in the face not only the old dead ones but all the living ones that would come after him when he would be one of the dead" (178). Sutpen thinks through the speculative temporality of capitalism to realize his future worth in terms of its justification of the past and present, as the already waiting redemption of that past. Charles

Bon, prospective fulfillment of Jefferson's planter aspirations, arrives as "*Charles Husband-soon-to-be*" (119). For all that, however, the future anterior tense as often delineates the folly of such confidence as its fruition: "and so," Shreve observes, mocking the hubris of dynastic time, "in a few thousand years, I who regard you will also have sprung from the loins of African kings" (302).[31]

Counting on profit in the future also assumes its continued exploitability in the past. "[E]lapsed and yet elapsing time" (15), as Rosa puts it once, the *past imperfect* measures the strange capacity of dead or absent things to keep generating income. This is the temporality of assets. The elements of such financial "necromancy," as a report in the *Emancipator* put it in 1840 (Rothman, "The Contours of Cotton Capitalism," 144n54), meant that a "slave's commodification lingered long after he or she had been buried" (Beckert and Rockman, "Introduction," 16): "enslaved people were understood as human capital long before they were born and well after they were dead. As slaves remained commodities even after their death, they created ghost values that confounded the standard temporality of slavery and forced a rethinking of a given slave's 'life-cycle.'" No expiry on work; a slave could be physically dead yet fiscally alive. Slave capitalism's hauntology amplifies the Gothic in Faulkner: the spectrality of Clytie, Charles Bon's first wife as the "supreme apotheosis of chattelry" (89), Eulalia as a figment of reparations, Bon himself ("*One day he was not. Then he was. Then he was not*" [122]), and finally Jim Bond, the unreconciled ledger entry, a disembodied voice whose name designates the fate of goods to be transformed into financial instrument: bon to bond. All these point to an economy in which Blacks function as the living dead, absent resources that remain ghost donors to the profits of the living. Where in Faulkner are descriptions of the actual work of slaves? Where are depictions of fields and soil and planting and plowing? Kenneth Pomeranz has used the term "ghost acres" to characterize colonized land around the world from which, without ever seeing it, European economies extracted food and raw materials.[32] The unseen of slave capitalism haunts national prosperity as that which has been erased, forgotten, disavowed from national history, even as it continues to enrich owning classes: the past imperfect having disembodied a great many as they lay dying.

## "*incredulous (and shocked) speculation*"

Faulkner contrives fictional forms that at once replicate and resist the deformations of personhood and time inflicted by the ontology of the modern, a modernity whose genealogy I have sought to extend here to slave capitalism. In *Absalom, Absalom!* the novel has become as much a dispersal of knowledge as an accumulation of it—or, rather, it is accumulation *as* dispersal. Each narrator's recounting invests in a particular rendering of events, of sense-making, while insisting on the uncertainty of interpretive profit. Failure is made the condition of narrative production, speculation a risk that will not yield predictable results, negation rather than representation the product of literature's confrontation with the real. Nothing arrives at timely conclusion: we learn the story's climax repeatedly before we need or want to; we wait for other information that never comes. Shreve listens to Quentin's recounting of Sutpen's disposition of his last child under a mistaken inference of its gender—the overdue revelation, oddly, both decisive and not mattering.[33] There's literally no time for the novel to recount the acquisition of long-awaited information: Quentin learns what Henry has to say about the murder of Bon, but the narrative itself makes the completion of the transaction something that for Quentin and Shreve at once never takes place and always seems to have taken place. Time dissolves backward, so that we return repeatedly to more narratively impoverished circumstances, as if we might find the origins of a future we have already encountered without being sure we know what it is or ever will be. Each successive narrative is an act of creative destruction; the narratives do not build on former ones so much as compete inconclusively with them. Gains made in comprehension demand the liquidation of earlier certainties, as when Mr. Compson's recounting of Bon's wounding and Henry's saving him gets reversed by Shreve. Both accounts are true. Truths we come into possession of later become abandoned property. The novel refuses to capitalize detail—the image in Bon's cameo is of his white fiancée, his octoroon wife, either, both. Rival assessments are all "true enough" (268). The narrators *make* sense, they don't deduce it. Theirs is the sort of speculation that renounces profit. Manifest in this aesthetic is Adorno's conviction that modern art absorbs and critically negates the forms of advanced capitalism—the means of rational abstraction and the extraction of profit.

Faulkner's writing on slavery returns us to the scene of human labor commodified under plantation bondage, but he also displays the machinery of financialization that further abstracted humans into instruments of paper profit. Faulkner's aesthetic bears witness to the refusal to forget what cannot be profitably remembered under such toxic logic. His indulgence of time-sprung prose, of lapsed and yet elapsing event, of ludic narrative without conclusion rewrites the demands of financialized time and person that were embedded so deeply in the history of a modern world made by slave capitalism.

NOTES

I wish to thank Jenna Sciuto, Nina Silber, and Richard Godden for their insightful comments on a draft of this paper, and Garry Bertholf, Bob Jackson, Julie Beth Napolin, Scotti Parrish, Stephanie Rountree, Myka Tucker-Abramson, and Jay Watson for enlightening questions and conversations about it before and after its presentation at the conference.

1. Piketty himself discusses the capitalization of slaves in connection with the extreme disproportion of national wealth that slave-owning planters in the New World possessed, since only under the conditions of total ownership could slaves be counted as assets (Thomas Piketty, *Capital in the Twenty-First Century*, trans. Arthur Goldhammer (Cambridge, MA: Harvard University Press, 2014), 158–63.

2. Sven Beckert and Seth Rockman, "Introduction: Slavery's Capitalism," in *Slavery's Capitalism: A New History of American Economic Development*, ed. Beckert and Rockman (Philadelphia: University of Pennsylvania Press, 2016), 7. Hereafter cited parenthetically in the text.

3. Sven Beckert, *Empire of Cotton: A Global History* (New York: Knopf, 2014); Edward E. Baptist, *The Half Has Never Been Told: Slavery and the Making of American Capitalism* (New York: Basic Books, 2014); Greg Grandin, *The Empire of Necessity: Slavery, Freedom, and Deception in the New World* (New York: Holt, 2014); Sven Beckert and Christine Desan, eds., *American Capitalism: New Histories* (New York: Columbia University Press, 2018); Craig Steven Wilder, *Ebony & Ivy: Race, Slavery, and the Troubled History of American Universities* (New York: Bloomsbury, 2013); Stephen M. Best, *The Fugitive's Properties: Law and the Poetics of Possession* (Chicago: University of Chicago Press, 2007); Tim Armstrong, *The Logic of Slavery: Debt, Technology, and Pain in American Literature* (New York: Cambridge University Press, 2012); Ian Baucom, *Specters of the Atlantic: Finance Capital, Slavery, and the Philosophy of History* (Durham, NC: Duke University Press, 2005); and Walter Johnson, *River of Dark Dreams: Slavery and Empire in the Cotton Kingdom* (Cambridge, MA: Harvard University Press, 2013). Hereafter cited parenthetically in the text.

The scholarship about the relations of cotton capitalism and slavery published over the last few years by Beckert, Baptist, and Johnson has been understood as exemplifying the "New History of Capitalism," or NHC. Influential as its general claims have become, substantial dispute has developed over a number of the principal conclusions drawn about the cotton plantation regime and the growth of Euro-American capitalism. The economists Alan L. Olmstead and Paul W. Rhode, who have published extensively on the economics of plantation agriculture in the antebellum South, take issue with elements of all three of the flagship books on cotton capitalism and slavery. They argue that in *Empire of Cotton*, Beckert exaggerates the role of European state involvement in cotton commerce, fails to account for the turn against slavery in Great Britain (a complaint other critics lodge as well), miscalculates the relative expensiveness of slave labor in the United States, and does not account for the increase in post-Emancipation cotton productivity (also a repeated criticism). Olmstead and Rhode fault Johnson's *River of Dark Dreams* for underestimating the importance of innovations in cotton plant varieties to increasing yield (an even larger problem in Baptist's *The Half Has Never Been Told*, they claim), for misconstruing the factors that impeded overspecialization in cotton agriculture, and for exaggerating the riskiness of riverboat commerce on the Mississippi. The two economists are especially severe in their criticism of Baptist, charging him with quoting selectively and misleadingly from primary sources to support his claims about torture within "the pushing system" as the primary factor in increases in cotton productivity. A related influential critique by John Clegg concentrates on the absence of a working theoretical definition of capitalism in much NHC analyses. He points out that the new historians of capitalism, tired of historiographic trends toward the study of agency and affect, are as a result in danger of replicating the limitations of statistical analysis, or cliometrics (even if its continued significance must be acknowledged). Clegg raises an important question about whether it might not be the case instead that capitalism preceded slavery, thus making Great Britain uniquely receptive among European states to the investment possibilities and yields of colonial speculation and domestic manufacture. See also Stephanie McCurry's critique of the absence of race in NHC's account of slavery as fundamentally a form of commoditized labor that functioned like any other. The reproach of NHC's comparative obliviousness to matters of race informs one other major kind of critique. In a joint review of the monographs by Johnson, Beckert, and Baptist, as well as of Nicholas Draper's *The Price of Emancipation: Slave-Ownership, Compensation and British Society at the End of Slavery* (New York: Cambridge University Press, 2010), Peter James Hudson argues that the NHC fails to acknowledge the extent of its indebtedness to earlier Black radical historians of capitalism and slavery. In neglecting an historiographic tradition that Hudson traces to Jean Jaurès's Marxist history of the French Revolution, the influence of which may be followed through C. L. R. James, W. E. B. Du Bois, and Eric Williams, some work of the NHC, instanced for Hudson in Baptist and Beckert, isolates itself as an analytical project indifferent to political commitment. Hudson charges that such a position replicates, without challenging, the forces of "neglect, erasure, and absence" that constituted the very absence of scholarship on slavery and capitalism the NHC bids to address. By contrast, Hudson finds Johnson's emphasis on slave resistance to "dishumanization" and commoditization, as well as Draper's focus on British compensation policies to owners upon their slaves' emancipation, both to reinforce contemporary activist programs—for resistance to resurgent white supremacy and for continued agitation for reparations. See Alan L. Olmstead and Paul W. Rhode, "Cotton, Slavery, and the New History of Capitalism," *Explorations in Economic History* 67 (2018): 1–17; John Clegg, "Capitalism and Slavery," *Critical Historical Studies* (Fall 2015): 281–304; Stephanie McCurry, "The Problem of Connecting the History of Slavery to the Economics of the Present," *Times Literary Supplement*, May 19, 2017, n.p. (www.the-tls.co.uk/articles/private/slavery-economics [accessed July 26, 2017]); and Peter James Hudson, "The Racist Dawn of Capitalism: Unearthing the Economy of Bondage," *Boston Review*, March 14, 2016, n.p. (http://bostonreview.net/books-ideas/peter-james-hudson-slavery-capitalism [accessed December 14, 2018]). For an argument that recent studies of capitalism and slavery suffer from neglecting earlier historiography on the subject, see Scott Reynolds Nelson, "Who Put Their Capitalism in My Slavery," *Journal of the Civil War Era* 5, no. 2 (June 2015): 289–310.

4. Bonnie Martin, "Neighbor-to-Neighbor Capitalism: Local Credit Networks and the Mortgaging of Slaves," in *Slavery's Capitalism: A New History of American Economic Development*, ed. Sven Beckert and Seth Rockman (Philadelphia: University of Pennsylvania Press, 2016), 108.

5. Beckert and Rockman summarize the historiographic division of views about the relation between slavery and capitalism ("Introduction," 9ff). That owners extracted value from slaves financially as well as in the form of their labor may qualify the Marxist view that slavery must be distinguished from waged labor. The differentiation held that chattel slavery involved the owner's mastery of the *totality of relations*, while an employer controls only partial relations with the worker, whose labor has been commodified as labor power for the expropriation of its "surplus" value. This distinction governs Eugene Genovese's once influential view of US southern slaveholding as precapitalist.

6. For a sample of such new scholarship see Martin, "Neighbor-to-Neighbor Capitalism," along with the following essays in *Slavery's Capitalism*: Joshua D. Rothman,

"The Contours of Cotton Capitalism: Speculation, Slavery, and Economic Panic in Mississippi, 1832–1841" (122–45); Daina Ramey Berry, "'Broad is de Road dat Leads ter Death': Human Capital and Enslaved Mortality" (146–62); Calvin Schermerhorn, "The Coastwise Slave Trade and a Mercantile Community of Interest" (209–24). See also the following essays in *American Capitalism*: Christopher Tomlins, "Revulsions of Capital: Slavery and Political Economy in the Epoch of the Turner Rebellion, Virginia, 1829–1832" (195–220); Michael Ralph, "Value of Life: Insurance, Slavery, and Expertise" (257–81); Kris Manjapra, "Plantation Dispossessions: The Global Travel of Agricultural Racial Capitalism" (361–87).

7. William Faulkner, *Absalom, Absalom!*, rev. ed. (1936; repr., New York: Vintage International, 1990), 196. Hereafter cited parenthetically in the text.

8. Beckert and Rockman refer to "inattentiveness" and "erasure" ("Introduction," 5) and Martin to recovering national memory ("Neighbor-to-Neighbor Capitalism," 121).

9. This material account may add another dimension to Pascale Casanova's mapping of the value of Faulkner's peripheral subject matter as it is alchemized for European consecration as modernist aesthetics. See Casanova, *The World Republic of Letters*, trans. Malcolm DeBevoise (Cambridge, MA: Harvard University Press, 2004), especially 336–45.

10. Mr. Compson imagines how Ellen Coldfield must have understood that the mob has something to do with "the entire business which had come to a head when the vigilance committee followed him to Mr Coldfield's gate that day two months before" and that the unfamiliar faces head back toward the "taverns twenty and fifty and a hundred miles further on along nameless roads" (44).

11. Frederick Douglass, *Selected Speeches and Writings*, ed. Philip S. Foner (Chicago: Lawrence Hill, 1999), 197.

12. Mississippi planters purchased so many slaves to fuel the boom cotton economy of the opening decades of the nineteenth century that by 1832 a new state Constitution prohibited new importation via interstate trade (international importation having been outlawed federally by 1807, with the exception of New Orleans, which was granted an exemption to continue to merchandise Africans [Baptist, *The Half Has Never Been Told*, 55]). Worries leading to the interstate ban included the rapid expansion of a Black population, the destabilizing economic effects of easy credit, and increasing reliance on trade with individuals held to be of degraded morals and manners. The paper ban went largely unenforced. See Rothman, "Contours of Capitalism," especially 126–33.

13. Richard Godden has written on the significance of Charles Bon's name as the encryption of his status as goods. See Godden, *Fictions of Labor: William Faulkner and the South's Long Revolution* (Cambridge, UK: Cambridge University Press, 2007), 69–73. (Hereafter cited parenthetically in the text.) The generational transformation of Bon to (Jim) Bond may limn the course of financial capitalism. In "Toxic Debt, Liar Loans, and Securitized Human Beings: The Panic of 1837 and the Fate of Slavery" (*Commonplace* 10, no. 3 [April 2010], http://www.common-place-archives.org/vol-10/no-03/baptist/ [accessed June 4, 2018]), Edward E. Baptist explains that

> enslavers had already—by the end of the 1820s—created a highly innovative alternative to the existing financial structure. The Consolidated Association of the Planters of Louisiana (despite its name, the "C.A.P.L." was still a bank) created more leverage for enslavers at less cost, and on longer terms. It did so by securitizing slaves, hedging even more effectively against the individual investors' losses—so long as the financial system itself did not fail. Here is how it worked: potential borrowers mortgaged slaves and cultivated land to the C.A.P.L., which entitled them to borrow up to half of the assessed value of their property from the C.A.P.L. in bank notes.

To convince others to accept the notes thus disbursed at face value, the C.A.P.L. convinced the Louisiana legislature to back $2.5 million in bank bonds (due in ten to fifteen years, bearing five percent interest) with the "faith and credit" of the people of the state. The Great British merchant bank Baring Brothers agreed to advance the C.A.P.L. the equivalent of $2.5 million in sterling bills, and market the bonds on European securities markets.

The bonds effectively converted enslavers' biggest investment—human beings, or "hands," from Maryland and Virginia and North Carolina and Kentucky—into multiple streams of income, all under their own control, since all borrowers were officially stockholders in the bank. The sale of the bonds created a pool of high-quality credit to be lent back to the planters at a rate significantly lower than the rate of return that they could expect that money to produce. That pool could be used for all sorts of income-generating purposes: buying more slaves (to produce more cotton and sugar and hence more income) or lending to other enslavers. Clever borrowers could pyramid their leverage even higher—by borrowing on the same collateral from multiple lenders, by also getting unsecured short-term commercial loans from the C.A.P.L., by purchasing new slaves with the money they borrowed and borrowing on them too. They had mortgaged their slaves—sometimes multiple times, and sometimes they even mortgaged fictitious slaves—but . . . this type of mortgage gave the enslaver tremendous margins, control, and flexibility. It was hard to imagine that such borrowers would be foreclosed, even if they fell behind on their payments. After all, the borrowers owned the bank.

Using the C.A.P.L. model, slaveholders were now able to monetize their slaves by securitizing them and then leveraging them multiple times on the international financial market. This also allowed a much wider group of people to profit from the opportunities of slavery's expansion. Perhaps it was no accident that the typical bond issued by the C.A.P.L. and the series of copycat institutions that followed was denominated at $1,000, which was roughly the price of a field hand. For the investor who bought it from the House of Baring Brothers or some other seller, a bond was really the purchase of a completely commodified slave: not a particular individual, but a tiny percentage of each of thousands of slaves. The investor, of course, escaped the risk inherent in owning an individual slave, who might die, run away, or become rebellious (Baptist, n.p.).

14. Following the Hegelian dialectic of lord and bondsman, Godden reads the image as an expression of the master's dependence on the slave, an exhalation of the master's breath into the slave's body—a capsule summary that does no justice to the subtlety and extensiveness of Godden's explication (*Fictions of Labor*, 56–61).

15. Don H. Doyle does not find Sutpen's delay unusual per se in that planters typically got on with planting before they took the time to finish their houses. See Doyle, *Faulkner's County: The Historical Roots of Yoknapatawpha* (Chapel Hill: University of North Carolina Press, 2001), 77.

16. Johnson formulates this situation as the "slaveholding contradiction between not knowing and claiming knowledge expressed along the juncture of the unfathomable and the incomprehensible, the lived experience of slaves and the efforts of planters to explain what they themselves only half knew" (*River of Dark Dreams*, 165).

17. See the story of Jesse Mabry, a merchant determined to acquire planter status, recounted by Rothman in "The Contours of Cotton Capitalism" (122–25).

18. It is the allegorical openness of Sutpen's having converted slaves into money and money into the furnishing of plantation prosperity—whether the result of a second trip to

the West Indies or larcenous trickery in riverboat commerce—that makes the locals realize he is "forcing the town to compound" the original "felony" (33).

19. Such gyrations around disavowed benefit resemble Buck and Buddy McCaslin's schizoid solution to being slaveholders who disapprove of slavery.

20. See Kathryn Boodry, "August Belmont and the World the Slaves Made," in Beckert and Rockman, *Slavery's Capitalism*, 166, on the Rothschilds' avoidance of slave finance.

21. Natalie J. Ring, "Massachusetts and Mississippi: Faulkner, History, and the Problem of the South," in *Faulkner and History*, ed. Jay Watson and James G. Thomas, Jr. (Jackson: University Press of Mississippi, 2017): 192–209. Ring discusses Hart's teaching at Harvard and his scholarship on the South. Hart's *Slavery and Abolition 1831–1841* (New York: Harper & Brothers, 1906) contains lengthy discussions of the economics of slavery.

22. Bon is said to realize the lawyer has "been plowing and planting and watering and manuring and harvesting him" "since before he could remember" (245).

23. On reparations for ex-slaves, see Miranda Booker Perry, "No Pensions for Ex-Slaves: How Federal Agencies Suppressed Movement to Aid Freedpeople," *Prologue Magazine* 42.2 (Summer 2010).

24. Shreve's luminous Caucasian flesh is repeatedly remarked in *Absalom*: "his naked torso pink-gleaming and baby-smooth, cherubic" (147).

25. William Faulkner, *The Sound and the Fury*, rev. ed. (1929; repr., New York: Vintage International, 1990), 82.

26. C. S. Manegold tells the complete story in *Ten Hills Farm: The Forgotten History of Slavery in the North* (Princeton, NJ: Princeton University Press, 2010).

27. See, for example, Eric Kimball, "'What have we to do with slavery?' New Englanders and the Slave Economies of the West Indies," in Beckert and Rockman, *Slavery's Capitalism*, 181–94.

28. Curiously, the chief engineer responsible for efforts to straighten the Mississippi River and facilitate commercial traffic from midwestern states sending goods downriver to supply the plantations of the Deep South and Caribbean was named Henry Shreve (Johnson, *River of Dark Dreams*, 90).

29. It is a capitalist fantasy that commodities can be changed into money form instantaneously and completely by owners, the more so in the case of human goods. The precipitous change in financial status is opposed by a process of struggle to convert resistant human bodies to chattel. Baucom characterizes the instantaneous creation of paper value represented by insured bodies in *Specters of the Atlantic*, while in *Saltwater Slavery: A Middle Passage from African to American Diaspora* (Cambridge, MA: Harvard University Press, 2007), Stephanie Smallwood elaborates on the uneven temporality of conversion to chattel status (34–35); the effects of prolonged liminality, suddenness of shipboard death, brutality of commodification, and violence of permanent relocation (61 and *passim*); and the power of this alchemy to alter lives (63).

30. Beckert summarizes: "Few if any places in the world drew such concentrated capital investments as the plantation belt of the United States—and few places were the source of such massive profits" (*Empire of Cotton*, 220).

31. Best comments on the way the law evolved to try to insure the predictability of the future: "Within an emerging market of infinite abstraction, interminable speculation, and miraculous profits, property served as a synonym for certainty, and property law became a means of proscribing actions in such a way that the future remained consistent with current calculations" (*The Fugitive's Properties*, 33). As such, property law represented "a formalization of a way of thinking about future actions."

32. Kenneth Pomeranz, *The Great Divergence: China, Europe, and the Making of the Modern World Economy* (Princeton, NJ: Princeton University Press, 2000), 275–77.

33. Not only does Quentin ignore Shreve's pleas for clarification about the gender of Sutpen's child with Milly Jones, he as much as lies by replying to Shreve's explicit inference—"You mean that he got the son he wanted . . . ?"—with "Yes" (234). Only when Shreve insists that Quentin "wait" is the confusion resolved: "It wasn't a son. It was a girl." Quentin's narration in effect robs Sutpen of a son a second time, "giving" it to Shreve, then taking it back. The narrative structure imitates as well as mocks the willfulness of the plantocratic narrative to overvalue "a son" and discard "a girl." Quentin's heedless construal apes Sutpen's monomaniacal self-construction, even as Shreve's "wait" demands stoppage, a disruption of onrushing linear temporality. The surprise of Quentin's belated correction jolts *chrononormativity*, the term Elizabeth Freeman proposes for the "logic of time-as-productive" (*Time Binds: Queer Temporalities, Queer Histories* [Durham, NC: Duke University Press, 2010], 5). Against such "homogeneous time" stand "wayward temporalities" such as asynchrony, anachronism, belatedness, delay, ellipsis, flashback, pause, repetition, reversal, and surprise (xxii).

# Loosh

## Michael Gorra

We first meet the enslaved man known as Loosh, for Lucius, on the second page of William Faulkner's *The Unvanquished* (1938), when he breaks up the game that two twelve-year-old boys are playing with woodchips and water. One of those boys is the book's narrator, young Bayard Sartoris, the son of Loosh's owner, a Confederate colonel named John Sartoris; the other is Bayard's best friend, and slave, called Ringo for Marengo. The two of them have scratched a trough in the ground and filled it to make the Mississippi River, and are enacting the siege of Vicksburg, with Bayard getting two turns as the southern defenders for every one of Ringo's; neither of them want to be General Grant. They explain the game to Loosh, who then stoops and sweeps the chips away. "There's your Vicksburg," he says, as if his knowledge ran in advance of the news, and then tells them a little more about the Rebels' reverses as well.[1]

This chapter falls into three parts. The first asks about the conditions of slavery on the Sartoris plantation, just outside the town of Jefferson in Faulkner's imagined Yoknapatawpha County: what he shows us about the lives of the enslaved, and what he just as crucially doesn't. The second looks at the moment of transition—the moment when Loosh leaves the place and indeed the page in the wake of the Union army. And I will then ask what happens to him afterward, or what might have happened, looking at some of the conditions that governed the lives of the newly freed. Yoknapatawpha's world is a violent one, and yet Faulkner never depicts a slave auction or a family broken by sale. Nor does he describe a whipping, still less the salt and pepper that were often rubbed into the skin the leather had broken; none of his people have a tree of scars upon their back. Certainly nothing like that happens on the Sartoris place. Slavery there seems barely a burden, and that's not only because it's seen from a white child's point of view. Faulkner depicts the plantation as though it were a well-run manor house, something almost English and with master and servants bound together by affection and loyalty. Everyone knows his or her job and place, a sense of order seems innate, and the people there are presented as if they formed an extended family, with the Colonel at its head.

In drawing on that patriarchal image, Faulkner is absolutely in accord with the dominant beliefs of young Bayard's time—or rather, perhaps, the dominant beliefs of the white historiography of his own. We don't and probably never will know enough about what Faulkner read. But maybe he didn't actually have to open the work of the Georgia-born historian Ulrich B. Phillips in order to absorb its argument. Phillips's 1918 *American Negro Slavery* stood for a generation as the canonical view of its subject, one that presented a benign image of its subject: labor on a human scale and with "little of that curse of impersonality and indifference which too commonly prevails in the factories of the present-day."[2] For Phillips, master and slave lived in a realm of mutually understood obligations. They knew what to expect of each other, and their relations were a matter of custom in which each found meaning and purpose.

Phillips believed that each white family provided a model of conduct to emulate, one reinforced by a "vigor of discipline which democracy cannot possess" (343). Just let that euphemism sink in. Such views are easy to caricature. The ideological screen through which Phillips saw his material kept him from consulting African American sources; and indeed W. E. B. Du Bois gave the book a devastating review.[3] Nevertheless it has endured, even as its every judgment has been challenged: a point of departure for later scholars, an old understanding forever in need of correction. And it survives for another reason, too, though not as an account of how slavery worked. It stands instead as a picture of how the slaveholders' descendants believed that it worked: of how, half a century on, they hoped and wanted and imagined it to have functioned.

And that at times includes Faulkner himself—who in other books and even in other parts of this one knows better. But he has to handle his material carefully in order to present it that way. John Sartoris is depicted as a substantial planter, one of Yoknapatawpha's leading men; and he would need to be, in order to pay, as we're told, for his regiment's initial outfit. Look closely, however, and it seems that there are just six slaves on his place: an older couple, Joby and Louvinia; their two sons, Loosh and Simon, along with Loosh's wife Philadelphia; and Simon's son Marengo, Bayard's playmate. I say six, but Simon himself appears only for two sentences in the book's last chapter, one set long after the end of the war. He's described as having gone north with Sartoris, as his body servant, and yet he doesn't ride back through the gates on the Colonel's visits home, and Faulkner never thinks to include him in Sartoris's reunion with his family in 1865. His wife, Ringo's mother, never has a name or even a sentence devoted to her. The only reason for Simon's almost entirely nominal existence is to keep us from wondering about Ringo's parentage, to stop us from asking if he might be Bayard's brother as well as his friend.

These characters all work around the house, with Loosh the only one who resembles a field hand, though he's more commonly found with the horses. There are a couple of slave cabins, but Faulkner never suggests that there's a separate set of quarters, another body of men and women whose labor produces the cotton and the corn to pay for Sartoris's soldiers. This isn't a plantation—it's a farm. The details of Sartoris's military service are often taken to resemble those of Faulkner's own great-grandfather, Col. William Clark Falkner, a lawyer in the northern Mississippi town of Ripley. What's less commonly noted is that Sartoris also resembles his model in the relatively modest size and scale of his prewar property; census records show that in 1860 Falkner owned six slaves, all of them living in the town itself.[4]

One mark of that modest scope is in the fact that there's no man on the place—that is, no adult white male. The Confederacy feared its slaves, feared their potential for unrest and disorder, for violence. Somebody needed to stay home and keep rebellion down, and an 1862 conscription act exempted one white man for every twenty slaves a plantation might hold, somebody to act as its overseer. The Sartoris land does without one, however, and seems instead to run on its own, with the crops made and the smokehouse full. The Colonel's mother-in-law—Rosa, Granny, Grandmother Millard—exercises a gentle and evenhanded discipline. She gives her orders calmly, expecting the obedience she receives, and puts up with a reasonable amount of grumbling in return. All this helped keep the initial readers of *The Unvanquished* firmly on the Sartoris side, and Faulkner's depiction of slaveholder paternalism finds its counterpart here in the myth of the faithful servant, the slave who stands by his or her master, and resists the Yankee temptations.

But Loosh is not faithful, and the Colonel knows it. He tells Bayard to watch him, because Loosh knows things, he's part of a network by which the news spreads from place to place, and if he starts to act odd . . . well, that's when Bayard should start expecting the Yankees to arrive. Moreover, Loosh knows the Sartoris family secret. He knows where Granny has buried the family silver, and at the end of the book's second section he will indeed show the raiding Union troops just where that silver lies. The house of the Rebel Colonel foams with yellow smoke, and the sky is full of noise, as the northerners' flames take the Sartoris place down to its chimneys. Then Bayard sees Loosh walking up from his cabin, a bundle on his shoulder, ready to go off with his liberators, and with his wife Philadelphia following.

"Fore God, Miss Rosa," Philadelphia says. "I tried to stop him. I done tried" (75). And Loosh himself will say that "I dont belong to John Sartoris now." It's interesting that Granny doesn't dispute that—she concentrates on the silver instead. That's not yours, she says, that's the Colonel's, and who are you to give it away? Loosh's reply has all the eloquence of a spiritual. Bayard may not hear it that way, but the contemporary reader does, and the man's words retain their force even if we share the young narrator's sorrow at the loss of the house. "Let God ax John Sartoris who the man name that give me to him," Loosh cries. "Let the man that buried me in the black dark ax that of the man what dug me free." Rosa Millard is one of the most tenderly seen characters in all of Faulkner's work; nevertheless this moment makes me want to tell her something: *How dare you.*

But those are our words, not Faulkner's, and still less those of his characters. Not even Loosh would ask that, not quite, for all that we feel, and are intended to feel, the justice of his claim. "I belongs to me and God," he says, not to John Sartoris, and Grandmother Millard knows that she cannot keep him from going, from taking title to himself (75). Her concern lies only with the silver, a form of property that can't walk off on its own. Still, newly freed slaves did often claim a right to the products of their labor: to the land they had cleared and planted, the cotton and the livestock, and sometimes to the master's house as well. Why not the silver? Their work had created the white man's wealth, and they knew that one of the things freedom offered was the right—and perhaps the retrospective right—to be compensated for that work. They knew that their bondage was a form of theft. Their ancestors had been stolen from Africa, and in America their own lives and labor; as he walks into freedom Loosh is simply taking what should always have been his already.

Not that Rosa Millard can see it that way. Loosh may claim himself but no more, and yet he does walk off with something besides the bundle on his shoulder, for he is accompanied by his wife, Philadelphia. "Dont you know he's leading you into misery and starvation?" Granny asks, and Philadelphia replies that indeed she does. She doesn't believe what the Yankee soldiers have said about the new world ahead of them. "But he my husband. I reckon I got to go with him." Traditional marriage has its own conceptions of mastery and obedience, and she will not escape from those. Nevertheless she decides to obey that law rather than the one that binds her to Sartorises. She determines her own fate, as a slave cannot; she may submit but she will no longer be owned.

At this point we must step into the world that Faulkner only half-imagined. "God's own angel proclamated me free and gonter general me to Jordan," Loosh says (75), and yet where is Jordan, and how does one get there? Rivers provide barriers to cross and places in which to be washed clean. Joshua had led the Israelites over the Jordan into the Promised Land, its waters had been the first baptismal font, and the Biblical river figures in any number of spirituals. Its rolling current held the irresistible force of Christian faith, and its very name marked the border between servitude and freedom; crossing it would lead to some blessed home on the other side, however fraught the journey. Yet Jordan was also the flowing columns of the Union army itself, an army on the move and with physical rivers of its own to cross.

*The Unvanquished*'s third episode, "Raid," takes us from the ruins of the Sartoris plantation to Hawkhurst in Alabama, the home of Bayard's cousin Drusilla Hawk. Grandmother Millard has decided she must try to recover Loosh and Philadelphia, along with some mules and the silver the Yankees have taken; Hawkhurst lies near the spot where the units that swept through Jefferson are now camped. The burnt-out houses on their way show that the Federals have passed, but Bayard can't at first make sense of the dust clouds they see in the distance, not until he wakes one night to what sounds like "about fifty of them; we could hear the feet hurrying, and a . . . kind of gasping murmuring chant and the feet whispering fast in the deep dust" of the road (83). Drusilla will tell him what they are doing, these people singing in the road. They are "going to Jordan" (91). Going, that is, to the flowing columns of the Union Army itself, a place of relative safety, and yet one that is also on the move, with physical rivers to cross, and imperatives of its own.

"Negroes coming in by wagon loads," General Grant had cabled to Washington in November 1862—men and women who believed that freedom could be found wherever the Federals were. "What will I do with them?"[5] But he didn't wait for instructions and ordered a regimental chaplain named John Eaton to establish a system of relief. In civilian life Eaton had been superintendent of the Toledo schools, and he wrote, in his posthumous 1907 memoirs, that many of the army's new followers were in desperate circumstances. They were filled with terror and hope alike, they believed that their own interests were identical with those of the invading forces, and there were so many of them their arrival "was like the oncoming of cities" (Eaton, *Grant, Lincoln and the Freedmen*, 2). They needed food and shelter and especially doctors, but Eaton's job wasn't purely humanitarian. For the very presence of those freedpeople threatened an army in which deaths from disease always outnumbered those in battle.

Eaton met that emergency by establishing a series of settlements that effectively protected and quarantined the freedpeople at once. Today we would call them refugee camps, and they would be served by an array of well-established organizations and procedures. Nothing like that existed in 1862. The contrabands, as they were called, numbered in the tens of thousands, and there were more each day as Grant's army moved into new territory. No private charity could meet that need, and no army, as the historian Chandra Manning has argued, had ever tried to do the work that now fell to the Federal troops.[6] None of the camps Eaton set up in Tennessee or Mississippi was especially healthy. Infection spread freely, mortality rates were high, and food at times ran short; in some cases, he admitted, "the slaves . . . met prejudices against their color more bitter than any they had left behind" (2). It was better than being on the road, however, where many people starved, and the settlements were garrisoned for safety from marauding Confederates, even as they also gave the Federals the freedom to move without their trailing columns.

If Loosh and Philadelphia were lucky they would have gotten to the camp in Corinth, the rail junction in the state's northeast. It was large, with between three and four thousand people, fairly administered, and well-supplied with clean water. The people at Corinth built houses along with a school and a church, and planted hundreds of acres of fresh vegetables for both themselves and the market. Loosh himself probably wouldn't have stayed there, though, not after the start of 1863, when Lincoln authorized the enlistment of Black soldiers. The government put many men and women back to work in the cotton fields of abandoned plantations, and the camps also provided recruits for the United States Colored Troops. Loosh would soon have found himself with a musket; I suspect he wanted it. But armies rarely stand still. The war moved elsewhere, and by January 1864 the Union no longer needed its base in Corinth. Most of the contrabands went by rail to new camps near Memphis, and the Rebels came back to re-enslave those Black people who remained. The Federals marched on, with more runaways in their wake and Eaton's work needing to be done all over again as they entered Alabama and then Georgia.

Let's go back to *The Unvanquished*. After a night at Hawkhurst, Bayard takes to the road again, with Granny and Ringo in the wagon and a cloud of dust in the road ahead, dust thrown up by men and women marching on. "We never did overtake them," he says, "just as you do not overtake a tide. You just keep moving, then suddenly you know that the set is about you, beneath you, overtaking you," a force that gathers you in and pushes you on (102). People step out of the woods behind them, alongside, in front, and soon they are themselves a part of that crowd, the wagon "enclosed by a mass of heads and shoulders . . . [and] breasting slowly and terrifically through them" as the wave carries them on to the river (102–3). A river where disaster waits, for the Union army plans to blow up the bridge across it as a way of cutting off Confederate pursuit, and not everybody trying to get over will be clear when the explosion comes.

The sequence that Faulkner begins with the sound of those feet in the dust is exhilarating, disturbing, and finally sublime. None of the Black people Bayard sees on this journey acquires a name or even a face, and yet the more one reads in the literature of the war the less it seems possible to forget them. "I been in the storm so long," the old song goes, and Leon Litwack has used those words for his great history of slavery's end.[7] How free is free? Nobody in this world quite knows, not yet. But that storm certainly won't end with Emancipation alone, and the men and women following Bayard's wagon now live in a world of confusion, its rules uncertain and ever changing. Few of them would want their old lives back, but freedom is a hard school, and in Eaton's words, "the law, to the Negro, took any form of caprice" (*Grant, Lincoln, and the Freedmen*, 136). Some people will be lost in that freedom; some will be lost to it.

In his memoirs Eaton writes that he wanted to provide "some definite and reliable notion of . . . a task which is all but forgotten by the present generation" (123). He offers deeply admiring portraits of both Grant and Lincoln, but the book's heart lies in its minute account of a job that needed to be done, one that "represented an important phase in the National policy, and one closely associated with the principles of the Union cause." By the time he wrote, the white South had, however, functionally replaced the Civil War Amendments to the US Constitution with Jim Crow, and the white North no longer worried much about it. Reunion seemed to require amnesia, and accounts of the conflict instead looked to constitutional questions on the one hand and military ones on the other. Yet the role of Black soldiers, the story of the contrabands, or indeed of those people who simply stayed put in a land that, as the armies swept back and forth, was neither quite slave nor quite free— those who lived through the war felt that these were among its major issues. They were, in the end, what the struggle was about, and today these questions seem utterly compelling once more.

It was very different in Faulkner's time, when few scholars were willing to view slavery itself as the fighting's motive force. There were exceptions, and Eaton himself must have been among the first to cite Du Bois's newly published *Souls of Black Folk* (*Grant, Lincoln, and the Freedmen*, 47). Yet the major historians of the American South, such as

Phillips, preferred to write of the antebellum world, and the critics of Reconstruction were hardly interested in the lived experience of Black people.[8] That would begin to change in the years of Faulkner's maturity, but his account of Loosh's self-emancipation doesn't fit the dominant historiography of his own day, Du Bois aside, so much as it anticipates that of ours. Bayard's understanding may be strictly limited, but he does at least acknowledge what's happening around him. Another way to put that is to say that at his best Faulkner couldn't keep from remembering what other people wanted to forget.

And Loosh? We need to speculate a bit. After the fighting stopped, he and Philadelphia might have gone north to St. Louis or south to New Orleans. Maybe they farmed on shares in another county—or maybe they simply found their way back to Jefferson, where they still had family. Whatever happened, by the mid-1870s Loosh is back on the Sartoris place once more. He returns to the text of *The Unvanquished* for just a few sentences in "An Odor of Verbena," which describe him as tending the horses at the time of the Colonel's death. What would have driven him back there? What might his experience have been, in what Douglas Egerton has called the wars of Reconstruction?[9] We can only imagine the events that would have sent this once-determined man back to those who had held him in bondage. Still, any reader of Faulkner gets used to filling an absence, to sketching the shape that defines it. We brush back on what we're told, we listen to the silence and read for what goes unsaid; we think our way inside a postwar experience that never quite gets on the page. But that would be material for another essay.

## NOTES

1. William Faulkner, *The Unvanquished*, rev. ed. (1938; repr., New York: Vintage International, 1991), 5. Hereafter cited parenthetically in the text.

2. Ulrich Bonnell Phillips, *American Negro Slavery* (1918; repr., Baton Rouge: Louisiana State University Press, 1966), 307. Hereafter cited parenthetically in the text.

3. Du Bois's review of Phillips appeared in *American Political Science Review* 12 (November 1918): 722–26.

4. See Joel Williamson, *William Faulkner and Southern History* (New York: Oxford University Press, 1993), 24.

5. Grant to Henry Halleck, November 15, 1862, quoted in John Eaton, *Grant, Lincoln, and the Freedmen* (1907; repr., New York: Negro Universities Press, 1969), 12. Hereafter cited parenthetically in the text.

6. Chandra Manning, *Troubled Refuge: Struggling for Freedom in the Civil War* (New York: Knopf, 2016). See especially chapter 2, "Constant Turbulence: Experiencing Emancipation in Western Contraband Camps."

7. Leon Litwack, *Been in the Storm So Long: The Aftermath of Slavery* (New York: Knopf, 1979).

8. See, for example, William Archibald Dunning, *Reconstruction, Political and Economic, 1865–1877* (New York: Harper and Brothers, 1907), or Claude Bowers, *The Tragic Era* (Cambridge, MA: Riverside Press, 1929). The counterargument is, of course, put by Du Bois in *Black Reconstruction in America* (New York: Harcourt, Brace, 1935).

9. Douglas Egerton, *The Wars of Reconstruction* (New York: Bloomsbury, 2014).

# Beyond the Door of the Big House: Slavery and Poor Whites in Faulkner and the Slave Narratives

## Andrew B. Leiter

As perceptive as Faulkner's fiction may be regarding some aspects of slavery, it does not offer readers particularly valuable insight into the enslaved condition. At an early iteration of the Faulkner and Yoknapatawpha conference, Darwin T. Turner accurately summarized Faulkner's general presentation of slavery: "He insists that slavery as a system was a sin, but he implies that slavery in practice was no more severe than other burdens God has placed on people whom he plans eventually to reward."[1] Faulkner does occasionally address slaves' dissatisfaction with their situations at various points in his fiction: the mass exodus of slaves during the Civil War in *The Unvanquished* (1938); Loosh's passionate defense of his actions after aiding Union soldiers in the same novel; the enigmatic Percival Brownlee or Eunice's suicide in *Go Down, Moses* (1942); and so on. These occasional moments of slave resistance notwithstanding, to understand slavery as it was lived one should turn to the historical records, the slave narratives, and the neo-slave narratives as they reimagine the psychological and narrative blank spaces of the slave narratives. Faulkner's fiction is far more revelatory regarding slavery's legacy in white minds struggling with the implications of southern history and a sense of a racial burden or curse, whether it be Joanna Burden, Quentin Compson, Isaac McCaslin, or Chick Mallison. In response to a question about the problems of the South, Faulkner even asserted that "the curse is slavery."[2] Criticism attending to this notion begins with Irving Howe's early pronouncement that "the curse is the inescapable mold of life for Faulkner's characters" and extends through generations of scholars elucidating the nuances of Faulkner and his characters grappling with slavery's legacy.[3] Similarly, we have robust critical assessments of slavery's impact on the young Thomas Sutpen in

*Absalom, Absalom!* (1936) from such scholars as Philip Weinstein, Dirk Kuyk Jr., Erin Sweeney, Ramón Saldívar, Scott Romine, John Rodden, Gretchen Martin, and others. This body of criticism approaches slavery primarily as a demarcation for white class issues in Faulkner's antebellum world, addresses the economics of class and mobility in southern society, argues the extent to which Sutpen challenges or simply joins the planter aristocracy, and so on.[4]

Given the complexity of Faulkner's fiction, evolving avenues of critical inquiry, and the insightful chapters of this collection, I would not argue that these areas—the impact of slavery on white characters, broadly speaking—are exhausted, but rather that they illuminate the underdeveloped nature of work considering what Faulkner's prioritization of whiteness means for slavery as conceptualized in his work. A comparative analysis of Faulkner's fiction and African American slave narratives, this essay contextualizes the presentations of slaves and poor whites within the historical record in an effort to reverse the traditional critical considerations of poor whites and slavery in Faulkner's imagination. Those considerations address what the slave economy means for the condition of poor whites in the antebellum South. They do not, however, address how the poor-white presence defines Faulkner's construction of slavery. The slave narratives not only reveal the reductive antipathy between poor whites and slaves in Faulkner's fiction; they also reveal how the poor-white presence mitigates the condition of slavery in his work by displacing the brutalities of slavery with poor-white suffering.

Fraught relations between poor whites and slaves appear throughout Faulkner's fiction. Poor whites' animosity toward slaves extends from their economic and social displacement in the slave economy, while the slaves in turn scorn the poverty of those displaced whites. In Faulkner's fictive antebellum world, this dynamic is most familiarly encapsulated with the image of Thomas Sutpen being turned away from the front door of a Tidewater plantation home by a well-dressed slave who "told him, even before he had had time to say what he came for, never to come to that front door again but to go around to the back."[5] The humiliating dismissal awakens Sutpen to his debased condition, and his realization is not unique within the novel. The moment crystallizes for Sutpen the same racialized class resentment that his sister exhibits "throwing vain clods of dirt" at a slave-driven carriage and that his father exults in after beating a slave because he is "that goddamn son of a bitch Pettibone's nigger" (187). Similar class antagonism plays out against a racial background for Wash Jones, who resents Sutpen's slaves because they "were better found and housed and even clothed than he and his granddaughter" but who takes solace in his identification with Sutpen and the notion that Blacks "had been created and cursed by God to be brute and vassal to all men of white skin" (226). Such antagonism is not limited to *Absalom, Absalom!* The short story "Mountain Victory" (1932) features the genteel Confederate soldier Saucier Weddel and his slave Jubal who are homeward bound in the wake of the Civil War and stop at the home of a poor-white Tennessee family. The daughter of the family and the youngest son want to escape their poverty by joining Weddel and partaking of his plantation bounty, but another who fought for the Union murders Weddel and Jubal, an act imbued with the racial and class tensions of the story.

Faulkner's fictional slaves offer, arguably, an even more monolithic contempt for poor whites that focuses on a combination of poverty and character. In *Absalom, Absalom!* this derisive scorn shapes Sutpen's seminal moment when he perceives the house slave who orders him to the back door as "a child's toy balloon with a face painted on it, a face slick and smooth and distended and about to burst into laughing" (186). In the same novel, as well as in its precursor short story "Wash" (1934), the Sutpen slaves openly mock Wash and his claims of taking care of the plantation in Sutpen's absence: "they would ask him why he wasn't at the war and he would say, 'Git outen my road, niggers!' and then it would be the outright laughing, asking one another (except it was not one another but him): 'Who him, calling us niggers?' and he would rush at them with a stick and them avoiding him just enough, not mad at all, just laughing" (226). Again, such antagonism is not limited to *Absalom, Absalom!* Ringo's refusal to address Ab Snopes as "Mister" in *The Unvanquished* is a minor but suggestive detail highlighting his contempt for that novel's analog to Wash Jones. Likewise, in "Mountain Victory" Jubal immediately and dismissively sizes up the mountain family's poverty when he sees the wife "standing barefoot in her faded calico garment" and "the bleak and barren interior of the cabin hall."[6] He later remonstrates with his master for getting them mixed up with "[h]illbilly rednecks" (771). Throughout Faulkner's fiction, slaves' perceptions of and interactions with poor whites amount to little more than Mammy's dismissal of the Slatterys in Margaret Mitchell's *Gone with the Wind* (1936) as "po' w'ite trash."[7]

This mutually antagonistic presentation of poor-white and slave relations is, arguably, as reductive and one-dimensional as any aspect of Faulkner's widespread engagements with race or class. It receives relatively sparse critical attention—at least beyond race as a demarcator for white class issues—perhaps because of that lack of nuance, but also, I believe, because it reflects a traditionally widely accepted version of poor white–slave relations, one of unremittent acrimony and strife.

According to Jeff Forret, this animosity reflects the prevailing historical conception of Faulkner's day: "When historians acknowledged contact between slaves and poor whites at all, they offered only a perfunctory comment that mutual hatred and animosity characterized their relationships."[8] Keri Leigh Merritt has argued that these reductive treatments of the topic were developed by "historians who have based their analyses on Jim Crow–era race relations" rather than on the historical record.[9] Faulkner may have been familiar with some of these historical assessments of poor white–slave relations, or he may have similarly developed his antebellum presentation from his segregation-era perspective on the contemporaneous conflict between poor whites and Blacks, a conflict that he explores most fully with *Intruder in the Dust* (1948). At the very least, Ab Snopes's infamous confrontation with the Black servant at the front door of Major de Spain's house in "Barn Burning" (1939) suggests a distinct continuity in Faulkner's rendering of antebellum and postbellum racialized class resentment.[10]

This is not to say that the historical record or slave narratives are bereft of examples of such conflict between poor whites and slaves. Readers of *Narrative of the Life of Frederick Douglass* (1845) will recall the white working-class resentment of slave labor that Douglass encounters in a Baltimore shipyard and the brutal beating he receives from the white workers who rage at "'niggers' taking the country."[11] He also alludes to the slaves' sense of white class distinctions when he writes, "It was considered as being bad enough to be a slave; but to be a poor man's slave was deemed a disgrace indeed!" (37). In *Incidents in the Life of a Slave Girl* (1861), Harriet Jacobs bitterly recalls, in the wake of the Nat Turner revolt, the invasion of her home by deputized poor whites: "It was a grand opportunity for the low whites, who had no negroes of their own to scourge."[12] She blames the slave system for their "poverty, ignorance, and moral degradation" (64) while characterizing them as illiterate and envious of her relative comfort, with one patroller complaining in heavy dialect, "you seem to feel mighty gran' 'cause you got all them 'ere fixens. White folks oughter have 'em all" (65). Such moments in the slave narratives appear to validate Faulkner's artistic rendering of slaves' relations with poor whites; however, the narratives also offer a more complex pattern of relations that belie a one-dimensional antagonism and that historians have only recently begun to investigate in earnest.

In *Slavery in Black and White: Class and Race in the Southern Slaveholder's New World Order,* Elizabeth Fox-Genovese and Eugene Genovese study the widespread development and implications of the antebellum argument for "Slavery in the Abstract—the doctrine that declared slavery or a kindred system of personal servitude the best possible condition for all labor regardless of race."[13] This doctrine "flowed from a confluence of three commonly held premises: Southern slaves fared better than most peasants and wage-workers in free societies; slavery was proving a more humane, stable, and morally responsible social system than its free-labor rival; and Christians had to accept responsibility to succor fellow human beings" (8). Readers of *The Unvanquished* will likely recognize reflections of these premises, particularly the last one, in that novel's uncomfortable apologist tendencies, but I am more interested here in their relevance for poor white and slave relations. "Slavery in the Abstract" obviously expresses a paternalist contempt for working classes of all races, but in the antebellum South, according to Fox-Genovese and Genovese, the doctrine was used to justify Black slavery as the means of sparing the white working classes (68–69). One of numerous nonsensical defenses of slavery, this perspective contends that servitude represents an idealized state for laborers while simultaneously implying that whites need to be protected from reduction to such a state.

The reality, of course, is that the slave economy, rather than protecting poor whites, devalued their labor to such an extent that historians estimate, "by 1860, at least one-third of the Deep South's white population consisted of the truly, cyclically poor."[14] Merritt argues that "poor white Southerners not only possessed class consciousness, but as the antebellum period wore on, they became overtly resentful of slaveholders" and that elite whites, concerned over potentially dangerous alliances between poor whites and slaves, relied on "a Southern legal system dominated by slaveholders who generally incarcerated [poor whites] for behavioral, non-violent 'crimes' such as trading, drinking, and other social interactions with slaves and free blacks" (8). Although poor white–slave socialization varied by region, community, family, and individual, Jeff Forret has detailed the extensive nature of those interactions in the most thorough study to date of poor white–slave connections, *Race Relations at the Margins: Slaves and Poor Whites in the Antebellum Countryside*. While acknowledging that lower-class whites participated in the subjugation of African Americans by contributing to the policing of slave populations, Forret demonstrates that

> at other times, slaves and poor whites . . . worked side by side in a state of mutual dependence. They fraternized and socialized with one another, drinking, gambling, and attending church, and they conducted an informal underground network of trade to the detriment of the master. Potentially more subversive to the racially based slave society, slaves and poor whites sometimes consented to interracial sex. Poor whites also appeared to undermine the southern social structure when they aided fugitive slaves.[15]

Evidence of these types of cordial and symbiotic relationships between poor whites and slaves are sprinkled throughout the slave narratives, but I will highlight just two of them here. The first example occurs as part of Frederick Douglass's famous struggle for literacy after Sophia Auld begins to teach Douglass to read and is subsequently forbidden from doing so. When the fount of knowledge dries up at home, Douglass takes his educational efforts to the streets, where he allies himself with sympathetic poor-white children: "I used also to carry bread with me, enough of which was always in the house, and to which I was always welcome; for I was much better off in this regard than many of the poor white children in our neighborhood. The bread I used to bestow upon the hungry little urchins, who, in turn would give me that more valuable bread of knowledge" (53–54). This economic exchange also entailed friendship that crossed racial divides, with Douglass describing his "gratitude and affection" for the youths who in turn "would express for me the liveliest sympathy, and console me with the hope that something would occur by which I might be free" (54).

The second incident occurs in the less widely read narrative of Charles Ball. While Ball was enslaved on a South Carolina plantation, the overseer accused a neighboring poor-white man of receiving stolen cotton from slaves. The man lived in a decrepit cabin, and according to Ball,

> [t]he appearance of the man and his wife was such as one might expect to find in such a dwelling. The lowest poverty had, through life, been the companion of these poor people, of which their clayey complexions, haggard figures, and tattered garments, gave the strongest proof. It appeared to me that the state of destitution in which these people lived, afforded very convincing evidence that they were not in possession of the proceeds of the stolen goods of any person. I had often been at the cabin of this man in my trapping expeditions, the previous autumn and winter; and I believe the overseer regarded the circumstance, that black people often called at his house, as conclusive evidence that he held criminal intercourse with them.[16]

The accusers burned down the man's cabin as punishment for being a "white negro dealer" (196), and the gentlemen of the community determined to drive off the "many white men who, residing in the district without property, or without interest in preserving the morals of the slaves, were believed to carry on an unlawful and criminal traffic with the negroes." In both of these examples, we see poor whites and slaves engaged in transgressive actions that undermine the dominance of the master class. We might understand the economic interdependence as mere utilitarianism of the desperate—significant in itself—but the slave narrators specifically highlight the friendly relations suggestive of personal identification and sympathy. These and other such moments in the slave narratives highlight white degradation, interracial shared humanity, "true" Christianity, childhood innocence, and so on as part of a multifaceted understanding of marginalized lives in the antebellum world.

I do not want to suggest that novelists have an obligation to historical accuracy, but when an author is as influential in our conception of American history as Faulkner, the historical discrepancies warrant attention. If Faulkner's emphasis on poor-white dislocation and their corresponding animosity toward slaves fails to reflect the complexity of the relationship between poor whites and slaves in the antebellum South, what, then, are the implications for the role of slavery in his historical imagination? I would like to suggest that Faulkner presents a conjoined racialized degradation of poor whites and class-oriented elevation of slaves that is accompanied by a twofold displacement regarding the brutality of slavery, particularly in the case of *Absalom, Absalom!*

The racialized degradation of poor whites materializes routinely in their interactions with better-clothed and presumably more comfortable slaves. When Sutpen is turned away from the front door of the plantation house by the slave in "broadcloth and linen and silk stockings" (189), the boy becomes conscious for the first time of "his patched made-over jeans clothes" (188). Likewise, the daughter of the poor-white family in "Mountain Victory" notes the slave's footwear that his master has cut and crafted from his own coat, and when she imagines life with Weddel at his plantation, she wonders if "the girls there wear shoes all the time" (757). Such instances emphasize white poverty, but in doing so, they imply an inverse degree of physical comfort for slaves that reflects the traditional mythology of the extended plantation family more than the reality. The reality for the vast majority of slaves was something more akin to the "torture" Booker T. Washington experienced when wearing "the cheapest and roughest" flax shirts.[17] And while Douglass may have bread to share with poor-white children in Baltimore, he regards his time in Baltimore as a blessing because it spares him from the harsher conditions that are endured by the majority of the underfed, underclothed, and overworked slaves on the plantations. We might simply understand the juxtaposition of poor white and comfortable Black servant as Faulkner's fictive device to highlight poor-white exclusion from the extended plantation "family" and slave economy, but the corresponding animosity also reconfigures the traumatic violence of slavery in two crucial ways.

First, the animosity removes the planter class from association with the physical violence of slavery. When Sutpen's father and the other poor-white men beat Pettibone's slave, for example, this is not the violence of slave control; rather, it is violence enacted on an emblem of poor-white exclusion. Sutpen asks his father what the slave had done to deserve the beating, and the elated, drunken elder Sutpen pointedly identifies the slave's offense as simply being the property of Pettibone, "that goddamn son of a bitch Pettibone's nigger" (187). Similarly, the labor revolt in Haiti, in addition to being removed from American soil, is cast primarily as a conflict between the poor-white Sutpen and the Black Haitians. Here, Sutpen decidedly acts on behalf of the planter aristocracy as his entry point to that class: "on the eighth night the water gave out and something had to be done so he put the musket down and went out and subdued them . . . and when he returned he and the girl became engaged to marry" (204). In both instances, the interracial violence exists primarily as a class demarcation rather than a physical condition of enslavement.

A second and more troubling displacement occurs regarding racial violence in these instances as well: the poor-white body supersedes the slave body as the site of traumatic antebellum violence. Physical violence enacted on slaves is remarkably rare in Faulkner's fiction considering the widespread and shocking brutalization of bodies throughout his oeuvre. This absence looms even more significantly when we consider how compellingly perceptive and rich *Absalom, Absalom!* is in terms of the legal, spatial, architectural, and economic contours of slavery, as various essays of this collection demonstrate.[18] Faulkner was certainly aware of the violence associated with slavery, and Mr. Compson describes slavery in the West Indies as "a theatre for violence and injustice and bloodshed and all the satanic lusts of human greed and cruelty" (202). Yet Faulkner seems to willfully avoid addressing the same sort of abuses on American soil, abuses that are central to the slave narratives. Even the beating of Pettibone's unnamed slave is dismissed textually through Sutpen's perspective: "no actual nigger, living creature, living flesh to feel pain and writhe and cry out. . . . Maybe the nigger's hands would be tied or held but that would be all right because they were not the hands with which the balloon face would struggle and writhe for freedom" (187). In Sutpen's imagination the beaten slave is not a tortured victim but rather a reminder of poor-white insignificance that releases "roaring waves of mellow laughter" (188).

Proper critical etiquette should here distinguish Sutpen's perspective from Faulkner's perspective, but the text as a whole not only mirrors Sutpen's dismissal of such violence, it appropriates that violence as a marker of poor-white identity. When Sutpen quells the insurrection at the Haitian plantation, the act presumably requires substantial violence against the Black bodies in rebellion, the sort of "counterrevolutionary violence" that Richard Godden identifies in *Absalom, Absalom!* as "necessary to the workings of the plantation system."[19] According to General

Compson, however, the violence in this conflict is enacted upon Sutpen's body as opposed to the conquered Black bodies. As Compson explains, Sutpen "bear[s] more than they believed any bones and flesh could or should . . . maybe at last they themselves turning in horror and fleeing from the white arms and legs shaped like theirs and from which blood could be made to spurt and flow" (205). The battle leaves him badly scarred as we know from his later physical unveiling for General Compson, who notes that one wound nearly castrated him. Here, the disfigured former poor-white body is on display in ways reminiscent of the scarred slave body so frequently displayed in abolitionist discourse as evidence of slavery's violence.[20] We might understand Sutpen's body on display in much the same way that the whip-scarred body of an antebellum slave speaks to the violence of the slave system as a whole. In Sutpen's case, however, his unveiled, abused body marks him as the survivor of a savage Black-enacted violence broadly associated with the Haitian Revolution in southern white imaginations and specifically materialized in *Absalom, Absalom!* through the body of the "half breed" who is so badly mutilated that Sutpen will not describe it: "there were some things which a man who pretended to be civilised saw when he had to but which he did not talk about" (204).[21] The racial violence of the West Indies does not similarly characterize Faulkner's portrayal of a more domesticated slavery in the antebellum South. Rather, as I have suggested, such violence is largely absent, or perhaps more accurately, transfigured onto the bodies of the marginalized poor whites.

The murdered genteel Charles Bon with his invisible Blackness and its symbolic resonance notwithstanding, the most horrifying violence of *Absalom, Absalom!* is done to the poor-white body; furthermore, despite the class-determined nature of the brutality, the various white deaths resonate with the violence of slavery and its immediate aftermath. Wash Jones, for example, dies at the hands of the elite white vigilantes who restore the social order Wash threatens when he murders Sutpen. If we understand this moment of vigilantism as the primary scene of Reconstruction violence in the novel, it clearly displaces the widespread historical violence against freedmen that the white South resorted to as a means of ensuring white supremacy. Likewise, it is the sexually victimized Millie and her newborn daughter who are decapitated with a butcher knife because their grandfather/great-grandfather would rather see them dead than enduring longer in their poor-white condition. This horrific act of nihilistic despair has much in common with the motifs of infanticide that appear throughout slave narratives and abolitionist literature, as well as in later fiction. The infanticide of *Absalom, Absalom!* is disturbingly similar to Sethe's murder of her infant daughter to protect her from slavery in Toni Morrison's *Beloved*, and it is even more similar to the actions of Margaret Garner, Sethe's historical prototype. Garner fled slavery in 1856 with her family, was overtaken by slavecatchers in Cincinnati, and "seeing that her hopes for freedom were vain seized a butcher knife that lay on the table, and with one stroke cut the throat of her little daughter, whom she probably loved the best."[22] I would like to suggest that such similarities are not happenstance; rather, when we consider them in conjunction with Faulkner's reversal of slavery's violence in the West Indies and his avoidance of depicting violence against slaves more generally, Faulkner appears consciously to appropriate the historical brutalities of enslavement and use them to establish the parameters of poor-white existence in the antebellum world.

The persistence with which the poor-white condition displaces the enslaved condition raises the question to what extent Faulkner might have in mind other motifs of slavery discourse in his presentation of poor whites. Faulkner is clearly comfortable recasting some of the standard elements of slave literature, such as the hunt for the escaped slave. *Absalom, Absalom!* pointedly reverses the racial dynamics of the antebellum manhunt in its presentation of the French architect's flight and pursuit on Sutpen's Hundred. The (essentially) enslaved architect is tracked by Sutpen's slaves while other whites of the planter class join Sutpen in the sport. More specific to poor whites, however, could Faulkner's presentation of Sutpen's class awakening at the door of the big house be considered analogous to a common feature of the slave narratives, the slave's awakening to his or her enslaved condition? For Frederick Douglass, witnessing the savage whipping of his aunt serves as "the blood-stained gate, the entrance to the hell of slavery" (25), while Harriet Jacobs explains that upon the death of her mother, "for the first time, I learned, by the talk around me, that I was a slave" (6). Sutpen's class awakening is followed by a flight that is not dissimilar to the flight of fugitive slaves to the North, although Sutpen flees Virginia to the West Indies, not toward freedom but toward a region that offers escape from his impoverished condition, a land where "poor men went in ships and became rich" (195). Likewise, might Millie Jones be understood as the violated slave girl dismissed with her offspring as were so many slave women, such as the sexual victims of Dr. Flint whom Harriet Jacobs describes or Jacobs herself who was impregnated and abandoned by Mr. Sands?

How should we understand Faulkner's adoption of the brutalities of slavery—as well as, perhaps, the tropes of antislavery discourse—to address the poor-white condition in a novel purportedly about slavery but that largely ignores the enslaved condition? At the very least, to reiterate bluntly, virtually every aspect of the poor-white presence in

Faulkner's antebellum fiction mitigates the conditions of slavery. The transposition of racially coded suffering illustrates poor-white debasement, but conversely poor-white debasement ameliorates slavery. For every Sutpen or Wash turned away from the plantation door, we have a laughing house servant or the enigmatic but faithful Clytie separating the quality from the "trash." For Ab Snopes and his betrayal of Granny in *The Unvanquished*, Faulkner gives us the faithful Ringo to deride Snopes and remain unbothered by his own enslavement. For the poverty-stricken children of "Mountain Victory," there is the well-cared-for and content slave Jubal to scoff at their condition. Exclusion from the slave economy, as Faulkner represents it, is an exclusion from the patriarchal family in which we are constantly reminded that the slave has a place, and by extension Faulkner infers through the juxtaposition of poor white and slave that this exclusion is worse than being the commodified element of the economy, however disguised as family.

## NOTES

1. Darwin T. Turner, "Faulkner and Slavery," in *The South and Faulkner's Yoknapatawpha: The Actual and the Apocryphal*, ed. Evans Harrington and Ann J. Abadie (Jackson: University Press of Mississippi, 1977), 65–66.

2. Frederick L. Gwynn and Joseph L. Blotner, eds., *Faulkner in the University: Class Conferences at the University of Virginia, 1957–1958* (1959; repr., Charlottesville: University Press of Virginia, 1995), 79.

3. Irving Howe, *William Faulkner: A Critical Study* (1952; repr., New York: Vintage, 1970), 151.

4. Philip M. Weinstein, *What Else But Love? The Ordeal of Race in Faulkner and Morrison* (New York: Columbia University Press, 1996); Dirk Kuyk Jr., "Sutpen's Design," in *William Faulkner's* Absalom, Absalom! *A Casebook*, ed. Fred Hobson (Oxford, UK: Oxford University Press, 2003), 189–217; Erin Sweeney, "Landless Whites, Dual-Class Identification, and Sutpen's Sub-Design," *Mississippi Quarterly* 68, no. 1–2 (Winter-Spring 2015): 99–118; Ramón Saldívar, "Looking for a Master Plan: Faulkner, Paredes, and the Colonial and Postcolonial Subject," in *The Cambridge Companion to William Faulkner*, ed. Philip M. Weinstein (New York: Cambridge University Press, 1995), 96–120; Scott Romine, "Designing Spaces: Sutpen, Snopes, and the Promise of the Plantation," in *Faulkner's Geographies: Faulkner and Yoknapatawpha, 2011*, ed. Jay Watson and Ann J. Abadie (Jackson: University Press of Mississippi, 2015), 17–34; John Rodden, "'The Faithful Gravedigger': The Role of 'Innocent' Wash Jones and the Invisible 'White Trash' in Faulkner's *Absalom, Absalom!*," *Southern Literary Journal* 43, no. 1 (Fall 2010): 23–38; Gretchen Martin, "Vanquished by a Different Set of Rules: Labor vs. Leisure in William Faulkner's *Absalom, Absalom!*," *Mississippi Quarterly* 61, no. 3 (Summer 2008): 397–416; Dorette Sobolewski, "The 'Grand Design' of Southern Class: Race and Class Constructs in Southern Society and William Faulkner's Literature," in *Bonds and Borders: Identity, Imagination, and Transformation in Literature*, ed. Rebecca DeWald and Dorette Sobolewski (Newcastle upon Tyne, UK: Cambridge Scholars, 2011), 63–72.

5. William Faulkner, *Absalom, Absalom!*, rev. ed. (1936; repr., New York: Vintage, 1990), 188. Hereafter cited parenthetically.

6. William Faulkner, "Mountain Victory," in *Collected Stories of William Faulkner* (1950; repr., New York: Vintage, 1977), 746. Hereafter cited parenthetically.

7. Margaret Mitchell, *Gone with the Wind* (1936; repr., New York: Avon, 1973), 41.

8. Jeff Forret, *Race Relations at the Margins: Slaves and Poor Whites in the Antebellum Southern Countryside* (Baton Rouge: Louisiana State University Press, 2006), 4.

9. Keri Leigh Merritt, *Masterless Men: Poor Whites and Slavery in the Antebellum South* (Cambridge, UK: Cambridge University Press, 2017), 28.

10. For an engaging analysis of the repetition of this scene in *Absalom, Absalom!*, "Barn Burning," and *The Hamlet* (as V. K. Ratliff retells the incident from "Barn Burning"), see Richard C. Moreland, "Compulsive and Revisionary Repetition: Faulkner's 'Barn Burning' and the Craft of Writing Difference," in *Faulkner and the Craft of Fiction: Faulkner and Yoknapatawpha, 1987*, ed. Doreen Fowler and Ann J. Abadie (Jackson: University Press of Mississippi, 1989), 48–70. Moreland argues that Faulkner revises the scene to bring out specific social implications: "It is now a primal scene not for compulsive repetition but for humorous appreciation and elaboration as an exemplary scene of critical escape from oppressive social categories and oppositions, a scene that points a way out for others without pretending to point the one new way" (54).

11. Frederick Douglass, *Narrative of the Life of Frederick Douglass, an American Slave* (1845; repr., New York: Signet, 1968), 101. Hereafter cited parenthetically.

12. Harriet Jacobs, *Incidents in the Life of a Slave Girl, Written by Herself* (1861; repr., Cambridge, MA: Harvard University Press, 1987), 64. Hereafter cited parenthetically.

13. Elizabeth Fox-Genovese and Eugene Genovese, *Slavery in White and Black: Class and Race in the Southern Slaveholder's New World Order* (Cambridge, UK: Cambridge University Press, 2008), 1. Hereafter cited parenthetically.

14. Merritt, *Masterless Men*, 16. See also Forret, *Race Relations at the Margins*, 11.

15. Forret, *Race Relations at the Margins*, 16.

16. Charles Ball, *Fifty Years in Chains* (1837; repr., Mineola, NY: Dover, 1970), 193. Hereafter cited parenthetically.

17. Booker T. Washington, *Up from Slavery*, ed. William L. Andrews (1901; repr., New York: Norton, 1996), 11.

18. See the essays in this volume by Chappell, Foley, Johnson, and Matthews.

19. Richard Godden, *Fictions of Labor: William Faulkner and the South's Long Revolution* (Cambridge, UK: Cambridge University Press, 1997), 53.

20. Celeste-Marie Bernier contends that this display entails a complex "intellectual, historical, and cultural relationship between the experimentation with rhetoric and the spectacle of the slave body"; see "'Iron Arguments': Spectacle, Rhetoric and the Slave Body in New England and British Antislavery Oratory," *European Journal of American Culture* 26. no. 1 (2007): 57.

21. For discussions of the Haitian Revolution relative to *Absalom, Absalom!* see, among others, Godden, *Fictions of Labor*, 49–79; and John B. Padgett, "Language and the Volcano: The Haitian Revolution and Historical Allegory in Faulkner's *Absalom, Absalom!*," in *Faulkner and Hurston*, ed. Christopher Rieger and Andrew B. Leiter (Cape Girardeau: Southeast Missouri State University Press, 2017), 183–97.

22. Levi Coffin, *Reminiscences of Levi Coffin, the Reputed President of the Underground Railroad* (Cincinnati: Robert Clarke & Co., 1880), 559–60, www.docsouth.unc.edu/nc/coffin/coffin.html (accessed October 10, 2019).

# Ritual Architectures: Doorless and Makeshift Boundaries in Faulkner's Slave Quarters

## Amy A. Foley

In "Knight's Gambit" Benbow Sartoris, from a train upon entering Jefferson, observes the town's buildings both as montage and in acute distinction:

> The first Negro cabins weathered and paintless until you realised it was more than just that and that they were a little, just a little awry: not out of plumb so much as beyond plumb: as though created for, seen in or by a different perspective, by a different architect, for a different purpose or anyway with a different past . . . each in its fierce yet orderly miniature jungle of vegetable patch . . . having a quality flimsy and make-shift, alien yet inviolably durable like Crusoe's cave.[1]

It is this "difference" in both building and dwelling between masters and slaves, later white and Black inhabitants, to which Faulkner returns repeatedly. Specifically, open doorways and windows or the lack thereof, as with a cave, signify this difference to the white onlooker. Particularly in *Go Down, Moses, Absalom, Absalom!*, and "Red Leaves," slaves live in cabins entirely without doors[2] or with doors of a crude design as do the "domiciled"[3] slaves of Thomas Sutpen and the McCaslins. Faulkner suggests that Sutpen is an honorary tribal member in his adamant preference for a mansion without decoration, which operates in contrast to Faulkner's association of windows and modern décor with femininity. For the McCaslin slaves, the doorless back exit is a tacit allowance and contract between master and slave for the slave to roam freely without the masters' interference. Throughout his fiction, Faulkner's suggestions of European ornamentation in buildings as both an excess and a lack contribute to a discourse on racialized civilization and the relationship between building and being. His spare architectures are cavelike, not only indicating the demands of raw survival but also proposing an alternative to the collective values of the mansion. The door is an ornamental ritual in Faulkner's world, a sign of European maturation and an unfulfilling promise of the "Spartan shell" (39) that would be refined.[4]

In the following essay, I describe how Faulkner's fluid slave architectures emphasize the complex power dynamics of the slave environment, with special attention to the McCaslin slave quarters. I discuss three implications or effects of Faulkner's fluid slave boundaries. First, I demonstrate how his representations of slave quarters are preserved and distinct products of African architectural concepts, reflecting a materially accurate and historically resonant colonial transference of culture between Africa and the Americas. Even in the aforementioned excerpt, Faulkner identifies the builder of African American cabins as a "different architect." Second, the dislocation and ambiguous sense of place for the McCaslin slaves correlates with the ambiguity of slave ontology; the unclear distinction between insides and outsides mirrors the confused status of one who is owned as property and yet able to act. In place of the term *freedom*, which assumes a political and social agency totally denied to slaves, I apply the concept of *exemption* to the fluid movements and pathways of slaves in Faulkner's fiction. Finally, Faulkner's slave architecture importantly highlights a culture of spatial confusion between owners and slaves, drawing our attention to the alienation inherent to white architectures. The following section describes how Faulkner's doorless architectures signify a rejection of the boundaries and ornamentation essential to imperial architectures, thereby refusing an inherited European concept of civilization.

## Civilizing Architectures

Architecture in Faulkner's fiction both facilitates particular practices and also demonstrates cultural attitudes at play in the politics of the South, specifically reflecting ideologies about civilization. Faulkner's imperialist architectures are broadly conceptualized in Taylor Hagood's *Faulkner's Imperialism* (2008), Thomas S. Hines's *William Faulkner and the Tangible Past* (1996), and William T. Ruzicka's *Faulkner's Fictive Architecture* (1987). Architectural design in general, while often hierarchical and articulating vertical power relations, can also express horizontal, resistant, and alternative relationships.[5] Many of Faulkner's contemporaries, though not necessarily read by Faulkner, provide adjacent and parallel theories to his own fictional representations of the relationship between civilization, boundaries, and architectural ornament.

In his original 1930 publication of *Civilization and Its Discontents*, Sigmund Freud expresses the architectural practices and signs of Western civilization that have been embedded in Euro-American visual landscapes for centuries. Freud understands the façade and features of building boundaries as a social contract. He repeatedly identifies mastery over space and time as a function of civilization. Architecture figures in his categories of the instincts of the individual versus those of the group. Freud theorizes the difference between an instinctual individual, whom he calls "primal man," and a collectivist, ego-sacrificing "other man,"[6] who is part of civilization:

> Human life in common is only made possible when a majority comes together which is stronger than any separate individual and which remains united against all separate individuals. The power of this community is then set up as "right" in opposition to the power of the individual. . . . This replacement of the power of the individual by the power of the community constitutes the decisive step of civilization. (740)

Freud points to architectural "uselessness" as one sign of civilization, writing that "we welcome it as a sign of civilization as well if we see people directing their care too to what has no practical value whatever, to what is useless" (738). Freud gives the example of windows adorned with flowerpots and playgrounds. As secular rituals, boundaries signify the contract of the individual with the group and secure the individual's interests of self and family unit. The boundaries of buildings, whether imagined as decorative or functional, are at once signs of personal affectation and a language with which we communicate a general will to order.

The useless space of civilization referred to by Freud is associated, by Faulkner and certainly by the wider culture, with femininity, which Sutpen resists along with the society of the town until he realizes the need for a woman to continue his legacy:

> So it was finished then, down to the last plank and brick and wooden pin which they could make themselves. Unpainted and unfurnished, without a pane of glass or a doorknob or hinge in it, twelve miles from town and almost that far from any neighbor . . . in masculine solitude in what might be called the half-acre gunroom of a baronial splendor. He lived in the Spartan shell of the largest edifice in the county . . . whose threshold no woman had so much as seen, without any feminized softness of window-pane or door or mattress . . . in the naked rooms of his embryonic formal opulence. . . . He now had a plantation; inside of two years he had dragged house and gardens out of virgin swamp. (39–40)

For Faulkner the windowpane, doorknob, and garden are mythic signs of useless, civilized space. Eventually, Sutpen "and his now somewhat tamed negroes had installed the windows and doors and the spits and pots in the kitchen and the crystal chandeliers in the parlors and the furniture and the curtains and the rugs" (44). We may consider how, for Faulkner, the "primal man" and his primal architectures are individualizing and desirable circumstances, as well as how the "ego sacrificing man" who strives for civilization may signify a lack. His representations of civilized and individualistic architectures must be received in the context of white male supremacy as a cultural dominant.

Aliyyah I. Abdur-Rahman cites Gail Bederman's racialized and gendered cultural concepts of civilization and primitivism as essential to Faulkner's philosophy of progress.[7] Bederman, speaking to the complex, multiple, and contradictory discourses of "civilization" during the early 1900s, writes: "[h]uman races were assumed to evolve from simple savagery, through violent barbarism, to advanced and valuable civilization. But only white races had, as yet, evolved to the civilized stage. . . . The discourse of civilization linked both male dominance and white supremacy to a Darwinist version of Protestant millennialism."[8] Manliness, a construct solely applied to white men willing to protect and provide for the traditional family unit, defines and directs civilization in Faulkner as well. While white manliness is arguably central to his idea of civilization, it is often Faulkner's ideal of rugged individualism and separation from civilization that surpasses and contrasts white manliness as defined by Bederman. Faulkner's search for civilization beyond the strict boundaries of Protestant white manhood is thematically prevalent throughout his fiction, but perhaps most evident in the architecture of Sutpen and as modeled by characters of African descent.

Doorlessness for Sutpen is an emblem of an ideal civilization. As much as Sutpen's trajectory is completely driven by what he sees as the tacit challenge of inserting himself behind the door so as to retrieve and redeem his former excluded self as a "boy at the door," he also sees doors and the treatment of façades as a concession. Sutpen's own architecture illustrates Faulkner's wider rejection or challenge to "civilized manliness" in his fiction and his embrace of what Bederman calls a "primitive masculinity" (23).[9] His noted lack of "feminine softness" foreshadows the entrance of Ellen Coldfield. The narrative arc of *Absalom, Absalom!* concretizes Faulkner's alignment of women with civilization and social contract, since Sutpen's search for marriage is entirely prompted by his desire for legacy and power in the wider southern social strata. Sutpen's architecture is one of many examples of his conflict between brute individualism and accommodation to civilization in order to get what he wants.

Civilizing architectures, for Sutpen and Faulkner's other slaveholders, are both a burden and a ritual, illustrating Freud's concept of a "useless" and also socially contractual building. This uselessness is a cornerstone of white civilization; the presence of a door shows slaves and other owners that a tacit set of rules has been agreed upon. Faulkner repeatedly illustrates the arrangement whereby slaves occupy the main quarters while the master sleeps in the slave cabin, as in *The Unvanquished*[10] and *Go Down, Moses*. The McCaslin sleeping arrangement, combined with their allowance for the slaves to run free by an open back door, only securing the front door for show, makes the reader think that the entire institution is only for show, a tired ritual for both slave and master. In *The Unvanquished*, Faulkner presents primal architecture in the form of the cave, doorless and without civilizing features, as the home of slaves "who had followed the Yankees away and then returned, to find their families and owners gone, to scatter into the hills and live in caves and hollow trees like animals I suppose, not only with no one to depend on but with no one depending on them, caring whether they returned or not or lived or died or not" (177–78). This primal architecture is also aligned with individualism and the rejection of the white social contract. In order fully to describe the philosophical challenge of Faulkner's slave architectures to white civilization, we must consider to what extent his representations are verified by historical accounts and their relationship to African diasporic notions of civilization and architecture.[11]

W. E. B. Du Bois and Booker T. Washington, despite their divergent racial politics, were both concerned with slave housing during the late nineteenth and early twentieth centuries. Similar to Faulkner, both writers relate the crudeness of slave cabins to the alienation of a people and the breakdown of former African communal relations. Both refer to architectures as indicators of "civilization." In his 1909 sociological study *The Negro American Family*, Du Bois draws on many nineteenth-century historical records to characterize typical slave homes. He writes, "The Negro home practically disappeared, and the house was simply rude, inadequate shelter."[12] He recognizes the slave home's "lack of comfort":

> The Negro knew nothing of the little niceties and comforts of the civilized home—everything of beauty and daintiness had disappeared with the rude uprooting of the African home, and little had been learned to replace them. Thus, even to this day, there is a curious bareness and roughness in the ordinary Negro home. . . . There were, for instance, few chairs with backs, no sheets on the beds, no books, no newspapers, no closets or out-houses, no bed-rooms, no table-cloths and very few dishes, no carpets and usually no

floors, no windows, no pictures, no clocks, no lights at night save that of the fire-place, little or nothing save rough shelter.

In *Up from Slavery*, Washington recounts the following:

> I was born in a typical log cabin, about fourteen by sixteen feet square. In this cabin I lived with my mother and a brother and sister till after the Civil War, when we were all declared free.... The cabin was without glass windows; it had only openings in the side which let in the light and also the cold, chilly air of winter. There was a door to the cabin—that is, something that was called a door—but the uncertain hinges by which it was hung, and the large cracks in it, to say nothing of the fact that it was too small, made the room a very uncomfortable one.[13]

Washington emphasizes the estrangement among his family members and the lack of centralized family life. He recalls never having eaten at a table with his family "in a civilized manner" or having slept in a bed until after Emancipation; instead, he slept "in and on a bundle of filthy rags laid upon the dirt floor" (3). In the accounts of both Du Bois and Washington, "civilization" is an aesthetic largely influenced by the gaze of the white onlooker and by nineteenth-century European standards of ornateness, with the door as a central fixture of ornamentation.

In his other writings, Du Bois establishes the integral relationship between architecture and the contrasting ideologies of African and European civilizations. The mobilization of ideology through architecture is significant to his Marxist interpretation of civil rights for Africans and African Americans.[14] Du Bois's study of the African village unit corroborates his theory of African subjugation. He writes that development of the modern city-state is an underlying reason for our respective changes from individualistic to group-oriented communities (41). Du Bois understands slavery, capitalism, modernization, and industrialization as forces that work against individual freedom, genuine community, and human connectedness (636). In "Africa, Colonialism, and Zionism" (1919), Du Bois equates European civilization with "exploitation" (639) and imagines Africa as a new civilization without the "rush" of machinery (647). African building is the highest form of cultivation in "What is Civilization?" (1925), where Du Bois describes Africans as the "only group of human beings successfully advancing from animal savagery toward primitive civilization" (647–48).

Most importantly, Du Bois observes the form of the African village unit in its distinction from European ideologies. Du Bois's study of African architecture in his later travels and writings is very similar to his study of African American urban living and of African American slave quarters in *The Negro American Family*. He relates several key concepts to African village building. One is that the African unit is expansive and connected, allowing a distinct form of cross-continental communication from village to village. Second, the village unit uniquely "socialized the individual completely" (649), yet because of its size and structure "did not submerge and kill individuality." The differences between the European modern city-state and African village have two major consequences. On one hand, the African experience is the cultivation of an individualized collective; on the other hand, Du Bois believed that because the village concept lacked the city-state's consolidation of power and ideology, it provided an environment in which Africans were more easily dominated and enslaved by colonial powers. Still, Du Bois insists that African building fosters equality, "depth and personal knowledge" (650). He illustrates how African formal and cultural attitudes toward building were transferred to the New World, becoming part of postcolonial resistance and incorporated into twentieth-century Marxist philosophy.

A distinguishing feature between Euro-American and African structural boundaries is the specific feature of the door, its role in defining boundaries, and the relative expansiveness of the home territory as a result. The doorless structure, though imposed by the master in the case of Faulkner's McCaslins, resists white southern ideals of civilization and reminds us of African spatiality with its individualizing and socializing effect on Tomey's Turl. Closer to African patterns of socialization, the path of Tomey's Turl takes him beyond the boundaries of his own household and toward Tennie on a neighboring plantation. The absence of a physical barrier preventing exit from the slave house enables an exchange with residents of other houses, subverting conventions of group and individual identification both within and beyond the group. The family unit created by the enclosed house as an essential device of imperial ideology is not enforced for Tomey's Turl, which allows him to imagine a more extensive social network. Slave boundaries in Faulkner's fiction present an individualistic and communal personal philosophy inherited from African materiality.

## Boundaries, Dialectics, and Postcolonial Recovery

Boundaries or the perception of boundaries figure in many nonfiction writings by American plantation owners. Architectural historians Clifton Ellis and Rebecca Ginsburg insist there is evidence that, particularly in the 1830s, slaveholders began instituting more nightly patrols of slave quarters as a "ritual" motivated by fear and by a "suspicion on the landscape they created. Each day when the sun set, a new landscape emerged in which slaves moved more freely and not always with benign intent. . . . Slaveholders often found themselves constricted by the very environments they so diligently arranged and commanded."[15] Eliza Bruce, the wife of a Virginia plantation owner of over one hundred slaves, wrote to her husband, who was away on business, "I have not seen a white face in over a month. . . . I frequently feel uneasy at night." She asked him for a "good strong lock for the door" (qtd. in Ellis and Ginsburg, 3). In the case of Faulkner's McCaslin slaves, the lack of any segregative boundary, let alone a preventative one such as a lock, allows a spatial promiscuity between master and slave that perpetuates the already promiscuous trading of big house and slave cabin. The absence of doors, and therefore boundaries, in and among Faulkner's slave dwellings allows different pathways and ranges of movement for their inhabitants.

Faulkner's permeable slave housing signifies the transference and preservation of African architectures in America. Du Bois describes the early dwellings built by slaves for themselves using construction methods from their tribes and the later dominance of European over African architectures as masters directed their slaves to build additional European cabins for slave use (*The Negro American Family*, 45–46). Other scholars have written on the combination of both building methods in slave housing. We have extensive knowledge of the building of colonial cabins and their architectural roots, especially German, Scottish, and Irish methods of rural construction in Mississippi.[16] More recently, architects and archaeologists have studied how slaves asserted agency over their environments in relation to African architectures and also how those intentions translated to European configurations. Architectural historian Dell Upton, for example, emphasizes that the slave "quarter extended beyond its walls. The space around buildings was as important as the building itself."[17] Archaeologist Garrett Fesler, in his examination of slaves sweeping the yards of their quarters on Virginia plantations, contrasts African and European strategies of spatial occupation:

> Whereas Europeans congregated inside their houses, closely bunched around the hearth, Africans spread out in the yard, segregating various activities in different zones around their home. In African cultures, dwellings often were grouped into compounds with a shared central space. . . . The dwellings, often a single room, were considered just one of many venues at the home site. Thus, Africans moved outward in a corporate manner, blending nature and culture, whereas Europeans drew inward within the house, forming a barrier between themselves and nature. These opposite modes of existence collided during the African Diaspora. ("Excavating the Spaces," 31)

Some important differences in lifestyle surface from these architectural distinctions. The fluidity between insides and outsides in slave housing, rooted in African attitudes toward mobility and dwelling, suggests a view of place alternative to Euro-American capitalist-driven definitions of property and borders, a point to which I will return.

The differences between Anglo and African American architectures determine and allow for contrasting movements among slaves and masters, as well as among Blacks and whites. The inherited architectural fluidity of slave life lies in opposition to the many rituals and rules of white architectures from which slaves were exempt. Processional architecture is a key figure in southern plantation houses, particularly as a legacy of Greco-Roman design. Upton illustrates the extent to which "the common white planter . . . was part of the intended audience of the processional landscape, and it served to affirm his *lack* of standing in it."[18] Upton retraces the prescribed route for slaves through the big house, beginning at the street and passing through the back door, usually connected to the kitchen, and through other internal doorways leading to the dining room. Upton observes that "in this kind of landscape, blacks could pass almost at will, while whites from outside had to observe the formalities."[19] Joe Christmas of *Light in August* and Tobe of "A Rose for Emily" are just two characters who travel a path through the back door, indicating both a segregated lifestyle and an exemption from the rituals and boundaries of the white world. The respective memorable scenes of Sarty Snopes and Thomas Sutpen intimidated and overwhelmed with desire at the front door of wealthy white plantation owners illustrate the processional intention.

In addition to the distinction between slave and master housing and the preservation of African culture through the formal elements of slave cabins, Faulkner's flexible boundaries and the absence of "civilizing" embellishments illustrate an architectural logic of personal agency. The European formal opposition between insides and outsides has a history rooted in ritual and myth. In *The Poetics of Space*, Gaston Bachelard explicates Jean Hyppolite's "first myth of outside and inside" as a philosophy of being and nonbeing in which "simple geometrical opposition becomes tinged with aggressivity."[20] Hyppolite writes, "you feel the full significance of this myth of outside and inside in alienation, which is founded on these two terms. Beyond what is expressed in their formal opposition lie alienation and hostility between the two."[21] Bachelard understands insides and outsides as commands of language, observing that each "has the sharpness of the dialectics of *yes* and *no*, which decides everything. Unless one is careful, it is made into a basis of images that govern all thoughts of positive and negative" (211). I propose that the dialectics of space as imperialized by white masters is one geographic restriction that slaves often evaded. When interiors and exteriors are fluidly linked, no hierarchy exists between the two.

An African spatial logic, which embraces a singular ubiquity rather than a binary concept of place, also shapes plantation decorum in Faulkner. Spatial mobility affects the rules and rituals of the McCaslin plantation, particularly in "Was." Using Bachelard's concept of insides and outsides as a language of "yes" and "no," we understand that for Buddy McCaslin, land ownership (for Buddy, a "yes") is always in opposition to Hubert Beauchamp's land, which for Buddy is a "no." Whoever and whatever belongs to Buddy cannot belong to Hubert and vice versa; hence their decision to settle the question of ownership of Tomey's Turl and Tennie through their poker game, significantly defined by rules and decorum. In *The Unvanquished*, Bayard Sartoris observes of the McCaslin system of doors, "it was like a game with rules" that the brothers "played . . . between themselves" (53). While the two landowners must restrict their slaves to one property or another, respecting the distinction between insides and outsides, Tomey's Turl and his fellow slaves are in many ways exempt from the ritual boundaries imagined by the McCaslins in their act of nailing the animal skin to the plantation house doorway each night. More importantly, they are exempt from rules applied to owners. They are pawns, not players. Tomey's Turl's inability to own grants him exemption from the rules and restrictions of ownership, which includes the obligation to respect borders and boundaries.[22] Bachelard quotes poet Ramon Gomez de la Serna: "Doors that open on the countryside seem to confer freedom behind the world's back" (*The Poetics of Space*, 224). While the word "freedom" does not apply to the life of any slave, the open back door of the McCaslin house does confer an exemption from European dialectics of space.[23]

Finally, Faulkner's architectures communicate a spatial confusion between master and slave. Without the hard distinction between insides and outsides, the slave is perhaps both homeless and dwelling everywhere. One cannot help but think that the permeability and promiscuity of slave housing is linked to the breakdown of separate slave and master spaces. Slaves inhabit their masters' spaces intimately, sleeping in slaveholders' own homes and bedrooms, as in *Go Down, Moses* and *The Unvanquished*. Scholars theorize how the slave occupation of master spaces functioned as a method of surveillance and control;[24] however, it also demonstrates how spatial ambiguity became an institutional ritual. Faulkner's slave architecture shows African American living and movement as distinct from Anglo American lifestyles. His slave architectures and boundaries also mark white values and attitudes, drawing our attention to the entrenched and dominant ritualism, mythmaking, and alienation inherent in Euro-American architectures. Most importantly, Faulkner's amalgamated structures point toward a postcolonial recovery. In the end, it is the spatial ritual and contract of European civilization that keeps the master in his house and places the slave, in the words of Faulkner, "beyond."

NOTES

1. William Faulkner, *Knight's Gambit* (1949; repr., New York: Vintage International, 2011), 252–53.

2. "The two Indians crossed the plantation toward the slave quarters. Neat with whitewash, of baked soft brick, the two rows of houses in which lived the slaves belonging to the clan, faced one another across the mild shade of the lane marked and scored with naked feet and with a few home-made toys mute in the dust.... There was no door in the door frame. There were no doors in any of the cabins" (William Faulkner, "Red Leaves" [1930], *Collected Stories of William Faulkner* [1950; repr., New York: Vintage International, 1995], 313, 316).

3. "[T]he two brothers who as soon as their father was buried moved out of the tremendously-conceived, the almost barn-like edifice ... which the two of them built themselves and added other rooms to while they lived in it ... domiciled all the slaves in the big house some of the windows of which were still merely boarded up with odds and ends of plank or with the skins of bear and deer nailed over the empty frames: each sundown the brother who superintended the farming would parade the negroes as a first sergeant dismisses a company, and herd them willynilly, man woman and child.... [H]e would call his mental roll and herd them in and with a hand-wrought nail as long as a flenching-knife and suspended from a short deer-hide thong attached to the door-jamb for that purpose, he would nail to the door of that house which lacked half its windows and had no hinged back door at all, so that presently and for fifty years afterward, when the boy himself was big to hear and remember it, there was in the land a sort of folk-tale: of the countryside all night long full of skulking McCaslin slaves dodging the moonlit roads and the Patrol-riders to visit other plantations, and of the unspoken gentlemen's agreement between the two white men and the two dozen black ones after that, after the white man had counted them and driven the home-made nail into the front door at sundown, neither of the white men would go around behind the house and look at the back door, provided that all the negroes were behind the front one when the brother who drove it drew out the nail again at daybreak" (William Faulkner, *Go Down, Moses*, rev. ed. [1942; repr., New York: Vintage International, 1990], 250–51).

4. William Faulkner, *Absalom, Absalom!* (1936; repr., New York: Vintage, 1964), 39. Hereafter cited parenthetically in the text.

5. See Jill Stoner, *Toward a Minor Architecture* (Cambridge, MA: MIT Press, 2012).

6. Freud refers to "primal man" and the "other man" in contrast. See Freud, *Civilization and Its Discontents*, ed. Peter Gay (New York: W. W. Norton, 1989), 742–43. Hereafter cited parenthetically in the text.

7. Aliyyah I. Abdur-Rahman, "White Disavowal, Black Enfranchisement, and the Homoerotic in William Faulkner's *Light in August*," in *Faulkner and Whiteness*, ed. Jay Watson (Jackson: University Press of Mississippi, 2011), 146.

8. Gail Bederman, *Manliness and Civilization: A Cultural History of Gender and Race in the United States, 1880–1917* (Chicago: University of Chicago Press, 1995), 25. Hereafter cited parenthetically in the text.

9. Just as Freud correlates architecture with the civilizing social contract, so does Faulkner in his 1955 essay "On Privacy." It is noteworthy that in this essay, Faulkner's ideas about boundaries and privacy are more conservative and conform more fully to the values of white manliness than do those of the characters of his fiction. Faulkner describes the American dream as an apotheosis of individuality reacting against the "Old World which existed as nations not on citizenship but subjectship, which endured only on the premise of size and docility of the subject mass." See William Faulkner, "On Privacy" (1955), in *Essays, Speeches, and Public Letters*, ed. James B. Meriwether (London: Chatto & Windus, 1966), 62. His spatial metaphor for America's individual equality is a "warm and airless bath . . . like the yet-wombed embryo" (65). Readers may notice that Faulkner describes both the American individual ideal and Sutpen's house as embryonic, primal in formation rather than late, and protecting the individual rather than the collective. He insists that America is "destroying man's individuality as a man by . . . destroying the last vestige of privacy without which man cannot be an individual. Our very architecture itself has warned us. Time was when you could see neither from inside nor from outside through the walls of our houses. Time is when you can see from inside out though still not from outside in through the walls. Time will be when you can do both. Then privacy will indeed be gone; he who is individual enough to want it even to change his shirt or bathe in, will be cursed by one universal American voice" (72–73). Faulkner defines the American past by boundaries that fulfill a social contract of individual privacy and the national present by increased surveillance and diminishing boundaries.

10. In "Raid," Granny and Bayard stay in a slave cabin (William Faulkner, *The Unvanquished* [1938; repr., New York: Vintage, 1965], 106. Hereafter cited parenthetically in text).

11. It is arguable that Faulkner's emphasis on primal form in his architectures without doors is both a response to the specific imperialist building and dwelling milieu of the South and to contemporaneous modernist design discourses. The goal of greater fluidity and interrelationality between insides and outsides is part of late modernist and postmodern architectural movements. Le Corbusier and Adolf Loos both champion "folk culture" as a sign of cultivation and argue that the more ornamental a culture, the less developed it is. Faulkner would have been aware of these aesthetic politics, even if only indirectly. In particular, we know that Faulkner was exposed to folk aesthetics through his friend and traveling companion William Spratling, an architect famous for his use of Taxco Mexican folk designs in silver. The combination of spareness and folk aesthetics informs a Faulknerian architecture that thwarts existing European values and espouses a way of imagining a future out of a past that has been interrupted by colonialism.

12. W. E. B. Du Bois, *The Negro American Family* (Atlanta: Atlanta University Press, 1908), 48. Hereafter cited parenthetically in text.

13. Booker T. Washington, *Up from Slavery: An Autobiography* (Cambridge, MA: Riverside Press, 1901), 2. Hereafter cited parenthetically in text.

14. In Du Bois's theoretical writings on racial identity, civilization is defined by group power instead of individual power, by "primitive" cultures as opposed to those deemed as modern Western powers, and also by the independence of African cultures from white leadership. In his early pamphlet "The Conservation of Races" (1897), Du Bois theorizes that the future of civilization depends on the ability of each race to develop itself "not as individuals, but as races." See Eric J. Sundquist, ed., *The Oxford W. E. B. Du Bois Reader*

(Oxford, UK: Oxford University Press, 1996), 42. Hereafter cited parenthetically in text. Later, in his travels to West Africa, Du Bois understands the "primitive man" as progressive and as an example to the modern man: "primitive men are not following us afar, frantically waving and seeking our goals; primitive men are not behind us in some swift foot-race. Primitive men have already arrived. They are abreast, and in places ahead of us; in others behind. But all their curving advance line is contemporary, not prehistoric" (127). He also describes African civilization apart from white dominance as the group's "self-realization" of "its highest cultural possibilities" (70).

15. Clifton Ellis and Rebecca Ginsburg, introduction to *Cabin, Quarter, Plantation: Architecture and Landscapes of North American Slavery*, ed. Ellis and Ginsburg (New Haven, CT: Yale University Press, 2010), 3–4. Hereafter cited parenthetically in text.

16. See Thomas S. Hines, *William Faulkner and the Tangible Past: The Architecture of Yoknapatawpha* (Berkeley: University of California Press, 1996), 24; and J. Frazer Smith, *White Pillars: Early Life and Architecture of the Lower Mississippi Valley Country* (New York: Bramhall House, 1941), 227.

17. Upton quoted in Garrett Fesler, "Excavating the Spaces and Interpreting the Places of Enslaved Africans and Their Descendants," in *Cabin, Quarter, Plantation: Architecture and Landscapes of North American Slavery*, ed. Clifton Ellis and Rebecca Ginsburg (New Haven, CT: Yale University Press, 2010), 31. Hereafter cited parenthetically in text.

18. Dell Upton, "White and Black Landscapes in Eighteenth Century Virginia" in *Cabin, Quarter, Plantation: Architecture and Landscapes of North American Slavery*, ed. Clifton Ellis and Rebecca Ginsburg (New Haven, CT: Yale University Press, 2010), 133.

19. Upton, "White and Black Landscapes in Eighteenth Century Virginia," 133.

20. Gaston Bachelard, *The Poetics of Space*, trans. Maria Jolas (1958; repr., Boston: Beacon Press, 1994), 212. Hereafter cited parenthetically in text.

21. Hyppolite quoted in Bachelard, *The Poetics of Space*, 212.

22. See Thadious M. Davis, *Games of Property: Law, Race, Gender, and Faulkner's Go Down, Moses* (Durham, NC: Duke University Press, 2003). Davis similarly frames Tomey's Turl "as a subject with both a will and rights" (8) in a complex system of power involving rules and rituals.

23. The historical importance of the distinction between interiors and exteriors for European architectures is thoroughly analyzed by twentieth-century architectural and cultural theorists like Le Corbusier, Fredric Jameson, Henri Lefebvre, David Harvey, and Edward Soja. This spatial distinction came under interrogation and subversion for many postmodern architects, who sought to transform architecture according to a principle of anti-hierarchy.

24. See Robert K. Fitts, "The Landscapes of Northern Bondage," in *Cabin, Quarter, Plantation: Architecture and Landscapes of North American Slavery*, ed. Clifton Ellis and Rebecca Ginsburg (New Haven, CT: Yale University Press, 2010), 193–222.

# Race, Family, and Architecture at Faulkner's Rowan Oak

## Edward A. Chappell

Speaking as an architectural historian, I suggest to the reader that an excursion into the world lived in by William Faulkner reveals things about him and his conception of race and slavery that you will not find in his writing. The physical evidence is bound up with that for his evolving attitude toward the whole household at Rowan Oak. It is richly informative.

### Paper Houses

Scholars and common readers widely recognize Faulkner's powerful use of architectural and landscape description to define his varied characters' place in Mississippi society as well as to advance his narratives about the place.[1] He especially focused description on the houses of southern whites, where he saw a greater range than for homes of rural or town-dwelling Blacks. While that reflected a partial reality, he avoided anything approaching middle-class Black life.

His description in *The Hamlet* of the house to which sharecropper Mink Snopes retreats after he murders Jack Houston is more evocative, to me, than his frequent and relatively generic descriptions of the ruinous mansion at Frenchman's Bend.[2] Poorly built and essentially unfinished, the tenant house resembles more than a dozen houses Ab Snopes occupied, all deteriorating as soon as they were completed.[3] Faulkner establishes Houston's status and character when referring to his spartan but sizable house (not a mansion because it had no columns [*Snopes*, 205]; columns were as totemic to Faulkner as they were more briefly to rich antebellum Mississippians).[4]

The author was adept at establishing much in a few words about a white individual and her family's shifting position in the community as when he set the scene in "A Rose for Emily" by describing Emily Grierson's large, once-painted house "decorated with cupolas and spires and scrolled balconies in the heavily lightsome style of the seventies, set on what had been our most select street." Now only her house was left, "lifting its stubborn and coquettish decay above the cotton wagons and the gasoline pumps—an eyesore among eyesores."[5]

Realistically or otherwise, Faulkner assumed readers shared his perception that postwar Black Mississippians simply lived near the bottom of peasant housing in the South and that deeper architectural characterization was unnecessary. The cabin was his set stage-piece for the Black home, whether he used the term or not. In "That Evening Sun," the narrator Quentin Compson introduces Aunt Rachel's house as simply where she smoked a pipe all day in the doorway. Quentin describes her daughter-in-law Nancy's cabin only by mentioning its smell, its oil lamp, and a bar for the door.[6] Elnora's cabin is simply downhill behind her half-brother Bayard Sartoris's gentry house.[7] Faulkner describes Dilsey Gibson's cabin in *The Sound and the Fury* only as having a worn spot before the door, as well as standing beside mulberry trees and within shouting distance of the Compsons' house. The houses she passes in route to church sit low beside the road, and their yards are scattered with castoff possessions.[8] Faulkner occasionally toyed with the then common paternalist argument that slaves lived better than poor southerners after the Civil War, as when unnamed Black characters needle Wash Jones. Jones himself feels that Thomas Sutpen wouldn't have allowed them to occupy the dilapidated fishing shack that shelters him on Sutpen's land.[9] The author generally avoided portraying slave housing, and when he engaged the subject he could do so idiosyncratically. In "Red Leaves" (1930), Faulkner envisioned slaveholding Chickasaw Indians housing enslaved African couples in doorless soft-brick cabins aligned along a lane through the quarter. Such single-couple houses could represent improvement over spaces occupied by unrelated individuals in eighteenth-century Chesapeake, but the author imagined these Mississippi pairings as assigned by their captors solely to promote reproduction.[10] He described the slave quarters at John Sartoris's plantation and Hawkhurst in *The Unvanquished* only after Yankee soldiers burn the mansions, leaving whites to occupy and partition the cabins with quilts hung from overhead framing. A scattering of subsequent details, such as floorboards and a mantel, hint that these were somewhat better than the thousand or so dirt-floored cabins his son Bayard reckoned poor white farmers occupied in the hills.[11]

Exceptions in *Light in August* underscore the general pattern in Faulkner's novels, especially given the indeterminate nature of Joe

**Fig. 1:** African American sharecroppers' house, Washington County, Mississippi, 1937. Photo by Dorothea Lange, Farm Security Administration photo, Library of Congress Prints and Photographs Division.

Christmas's racial identity. This contributes to the current perspective that the author cast his Black characters less three-dimensionally than his white ones, more acted against or upon than asserting their own wishes/intentions with any success until the 1940s.[12] It is not as though poor Black housing was felt an inappropriate topic for white delectation. Indeed, handmade houses with wooden chimneys and crazy roofs were popular objects for white photographers in the in the 1920s and '30s, and paintings of picturesque African American poverty by artists such as South Carolina's William Aiken Walker have remained popular for affluent collectors harboring romantic affection for an earlier time in the South. These too make assumptions about the unprogressive limits of Black material accommodation. Why, then, Faulkner? Was Faulkner turning away from scrutinizing the topic of how Black people actually lived, as less appropriate for his penetrating gaze?

Jay Watson informs the analysis by observing that Faulkner's writing began addressing slavery and enslaved characters in earnest at or just before the moment in 1930 when he bought the property he would rename Rowan Oak.[13] It was at that point when he began to engage with Black Mississippians and their history in ways that materially affected their lives and his.

A decade later the author used the word *house* rather than *cabin* when introducing the home of Lucas Beauchamp in *Go Down, Moses*, and in 1948, *Intruder in the Dust* refers to "the house, the cabin" of this unusually independent-minded Black character. Faulkner describes the house in ways that reflect both domestic order and ethnicity. Molly Beauchamp and/or a daughter sweeps the fenced yard into ornamental patterns; lines the axial walk with bricks, glass, tin cans, and broken china; and grows flowers in reused containers edging the porch. Inside, the family occupies a front room whose hearth never goes cold and a kitchen with cookstove and dining table. There is a dark hall and a bedroom with a colorfully quilted and canopied bed. A gilt-framed photo on a gold-colored easel shows the couple, Molly's normal head cloth removed because Lucas forbids any seeming field-worker picture in his house. Faulkner's attention to the appearance of the house as well as to Lucas's dress gives substance to the development of the character, before most of his story unfolds.[14] The author ascribes much of Lucas's pride to his descent through the male line from planter Carothers McCaslin. On the other hand, presumably for more practical reasons, his daughter Nathalie demands a stove, a well, and porch repair before she will marry George Wilkins (*Go Down, Moses*, 67, 71–75).

Scholars have viewed Faulkner's own buildings at Rowan Oak in light of his literary constructions, but one can interpret them much more effectively, especially when considering the buildings he maintained, in the broader architectural context of their region.[15] Comparing what he built or repaired with what he wrote offers a new perspective on his views about race and African American influence in Mississippi.

## Housing Enslaved Mississippians

First, some brief architectural background is useful. Most of the slave quarters surviving in the South in Faulkner's lifetime were what

**Fig. 2:** Riverview kitchen-quarter, Columbus, Mississippi. Photo by Edward Chappell.

slaveholders and their apologists saw as model worker housing, especially intended for enslaved domestic workers, located close to elite owners' houses. They should be recognized as rhetorical constructions, conceived in contrast to roughly built frame or log cabins and intended as a defense of slavery and an expression of owners' expendable wealth.[16]

Generally called "Negro houses" by whites, and sometimes "servant rooms," the buildings constituted sufficient substance to be enumerated, usually after owners' houses and kitchens, in advertisements to sell or rent urban and town properties. In 1849, for example, J. E. Matthews advertised a brick building with apartments on the edge of Jackson having a "brick negro house with four rooms" and another property with "one other comfortable negro house with brick chimney and shingled roof."[17] The previous year, George Scoval offered a property near the Alabama capitol including "a large Negro House with two fire places."[18] These differ from plantation ads, which, though inconsistent, tend to list "Negro cabins" and occasionally Negro or servant quarters, the latter commonly referring to multiple houses at a single site. Claremont plantation in Wilkinson County, Mississippi, was advertised in 1828 as having a "good Overseer's house [and] negro cabins for 120 negroes."[19] Anna S. McComs held a plantation near Woodville, Mississippi, with a dwelling for whites and "Negro Cabins" in 1851.[20] A plantation below Meridian was offered in 1862 with "Negro Cabins enough to accommodate seventy or eighty negroes."[21] Primrose Place near Clinton had "quarters for

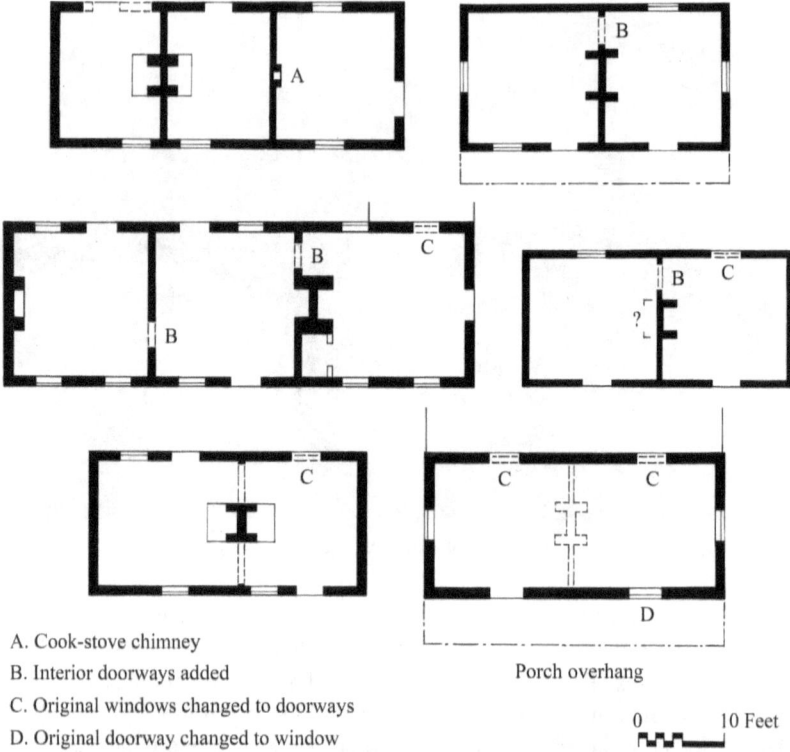

A. Cook-stove chimney
B. Interior doorways added
C. Original windows changed to doorways
D. Original doorway changed to window

Porch overhang

0  10 Feet

**Fig. 3:** Antebellum slave quarters and kitchens layouts in northern Mississippi towns. Clockwise from upper left: Featherston, Holly Springs; McCarroll House, Holly Springs; Wakefield, Holly Springs; White Arches, Columbus; Montrose, Holly Springs; Riverview, Columbus. Plans by Chappell after Carl R. Lounsbury.

40 servant[s]" in 1857.[22] Especially euphemistic when applied to houses of field laborers, owners' use of the appellation *servants' quarters* was a coy effort to assume a more humanitarian pose by borrowing the term widely employed elsewhere, as in Britain and northern states, for spaces assigned to non-enslaved workers.

From Maryland to Texas, the improved buildings, most dating from the 1840s and '50s, had certain recognizable standards, usually including a single room with independent access for a family or non-family group, a masonry fireplace, and one or two windows.[23] Glass windows, plaster or sheathed walls, and wood flooring were optional features. Probably a majority of the professionally constructed quarters had only shuttered windows, inwardly exposed wall and roof structures, and clay or dirt floors. Both rooms in the two-family quarter that Robert Sheegog built between 1855 and 1860 at Faulkner's Rowan Oak, for example, seem to have had two glazed windows and very low wooden floors but no plaster on the roughly built brick walls or on overhead joists.[24] (Sheegog had built his large frame house roughly a decade earlier, 1845–48.)

In spite of a broad geographic pattern that owners created pursuing what they considered acceptable late-antebellum model slave housing, there was certain regional variation, economy-based or otherwise. The Mississippi cotton boom coincided with the era of increased international emphasis on minimum standards of housing for workers, encouraging wealthy slaveholders to construct large domestic quarters near their big new mansions. Together, these owner and worker houses constituted much of the planter's architectural image in the short-lived Old South of northern Mississippi.

Clearly, the outward character of the buildings was substantially intended for show. The kitchen-quarter at the Hugh Craft House in Holly Springs is a respectable, picturesque-looking board-and-batten cottage with deep overhanging eaves and exaggeratedly tall doors, but its rooms are rough and unfinished. The ca. 1855–60 quarters at Rowan Oak have oversized doors and ornamentally sawn boards on the deep eaves, but again the rooms are unfinished. The rough interior was common in brick-walled quarters, sometimes when those builders' own houses were wooden but finely finished, as at Rowan Oak and a number of Holly Springs and Columbus sites. Double quarters at an elaborate house now called White Arches in Columbus had well-executed Flemish bond walls facing the main house and plainer brickwork facing away from it. Cost was always a concern, even at the showiest houses, exemplified by rich Mississippians building thin board partitions rather than brick or stud-and-plaster walls in otherwise finished spaces. Pairing fireplaces in chimneys located on the partitions was so widely practiced as a means of economizing in construction that center-chimney houses were associated with slavery throughout most of the antebellum South. More economical still was to omit fireplaces in rooms of certain workers. At Concord in Natchez, for example, columned quarters beside the Minor family's grand house had four rooms with fireplaces and two without, all six intended for different families or individuals. In the two-room 1850s quarters at Wakefield in Holly Springs, one group had a fireplace, the other did not. This saved costs in both construction and firewood.

Slaveholders presented improved housing as an ameliorative alternative in the face of increased calls for emancipation, and it is essential to recognize that provision of purported model housing was highly selective, even within properties owned by very rich planters. It was seldom

**Fig. 4:** Residential room in Craft kitchen-quarter, Holly Springs. Photo by Edward Chappell.

a predictable investment, illustrated by the fact that some quarters, including Sheegog's and those at Concord, followed construction of the main house by a decade or more, the uncertainty appealing to owners as an effective means of regulation. Owners could use such inequality in accommodation as incentives when negotiating for labor, just as they could shift individuals and families between domestic work and field toiling or threaten to limit their freedom of movement. What appeared as improvements in these buildings, such as finished walls and wood floors, could also increase surveillance and control, when combined with the absence of access to attics, cellars, and cuddies that would have given co-residents opportunities to separate sleeping spaces and to store their possessions out of sight. Given the extent of miscegenation involving southern slaveholders and enslaved women, one can read improved housing as an inducement as well as a setting for forced sexual relations, erasing some of the binary distinction between well-finished mansions and rude, unfinished cabins.[25] Especially in Mississippi, white families and judges resisted the more compelling incentive of promised manumission.[26] Living at owners' houses generally brought increased contact and surveillance, by whites and Blacks.

Model quarters had some appeal for residents as well as owners. The choices reflected enslaved workers' own expectations, particularly a desire for private space assigned to themselves or their family, a state of affairs seemingly more valued than heat, superior windows, or finished interiors.[27] As archaeologist Fraser Neiman has argued, the character of enslaved workers' housing can reflect the residents' resistance or demands, often now constituting the only evidence of that influence.[28] In Oxford, Columbus, Holly Springs, and elsewhere, this was handled simply by giving each room its own exterior door and avoiding internal circulation. The concern for relative privacy is emphatically illustrated by the varied means created to reach rooms in multistory quarters. In Natchez and other cities, rooms were often individually reached from porches, the upper ones by way of stairs housed in lobbies or passages or by way of steps open to the air on the porches themselves. Concentration of antebellum wealth in Natchez made for more residential rooms of enslaved people and therefore more complex means of access.

The assumption is that most single rooms were assigned to a family group or a group of individuals, although the reality of slavery was that families had little assurance of remaining together at a single site. Sheegog's Oxford property offers a glimpse of housing for domestic workers. An old photo of the rear yard captures the end of a wooden building that may have been the Sheegogs' kitchen, located east of the quarters, and there had to have been a kitchen prior to construction of the quarter. An 1860 slave census lists two "houses" other than the main residence, potentially the present quarters and a lost second building.

In 1860 Robert Sheegog owned seven or eight people at his "home place": three adult men, named Dave, George, and Simon, ranging in age from 35 to 40; two women, Frances, 37, and Nancy, 40; as well as two or three young people aged 10 to 14.[29] An 1870 ad in the *Oxford*

**Fig. 5:** Sheegog quarter at Rowan Oak. Photo by Edward Chappell.

*Falcon* offering the property for rent claimed it included "comfortable improvements, including kitchens [and] servants rooms."[30] Again, there is evidence that there was once a kitchen separate from both the quarter and the main house. The relationships among the five enslaved adults are unrecorded, but it is possible that in 1860 Sheegog had two enslaved couples and one man occupying two rooms in the quarter and a now lost kitchen.

## After the War

After the Civil War, Black workers ensured that some change came with freedom. However tied to domestic or agricultural drudgery, freed African Americans acted on new expectations, more evident in the buildings themselves than in Faulkner's portraits of postbellum Black southerners. For all his searing critique of northern Mississippi society, one questions how much visiting he actually did in Black people's houses beyond those associated with Caroline Barr and her family.[31]

The long lives of surviving slave quarters in Mississippi reflect their continued use over a century following their short period of habitation by enslaved people. Many, including the brick quarter at Rowan Oak, housed the enslaved for less than a decade, but African Americans continued to occupy many of them into the 1960s. It was not unusual that Black workers still cooked in the detached kitchen for Ellen Bailey at the Sheegog place within a decade or two of Faulkner's purchase.[32]

Property owners and workers remodeled many of these quarters, in varying degrees, after the Civil War. Changes commonly included combining two rooms from a duplex into a single-family house, the addition of a porch, and sometimes provision for a wood stove and separate space for cooking. The product of such changes was often occupation of a two- or three-room house rather than a single room, a pattern representing the strengthened agency of free Black families rather than increased white perception of decency in accommodation outside their own houses. Reflecting limited improvement in some northern Mississippi housing, changes to the Sheegog quarter before Faulkner were very modest, including addition of a cupboard in the cook-room but no internal circulation, perhaps to keep separate the work room and living space. Wood floors seem to have disappeared there after 1865, leaving the surfaces uneven and often wet.

## Servants' Quarters at Rowan Oak

Faulkner weighed his words carefully. He ignored the complexities of African American housing in his fiction, relying almost exclusively on the term *cabin*. What Faulkner meant by cabin was a roughly built small house, often with log walls. Not all cabin residents were Black. Driven from his father's workable farm, young Anse Holland lived a hermit's life in a dirt-floored cabin in the Yoknapatawpha hills.[33] The twins Buck and Buddy McCaslin built their own cabin using their enslaved workers only to hoist logs too heavy for them alone. They further overturned convention by then housing the workforce in their father's unfinished mansion.[34] The poverty of the Tennesseans who are tragically visited by patrician Saucier Weddel and his servant Jubal in 1865 is expressed in their rustic mountain cabin with "bleak and barren" hall, main room, and kitchen, poorly sealed.[35] He wryly observed in "Knight's Gambit" that whites would fight anyone applying the term cabin to their own houses, identical but for being less clean than those of Blacks.[36] Faulkner deliberately avoided such rustic images by calling his own workers' house by the term "servants' quarters," emphasizing class over race. Interestingly, he called it a cabin only when writing to Estelle dismissively about Andrew Price, his gardener and helper, in 1960.[37]

Faulkner bought the Sheegog-Bailey property in 1930—a year after marrying Estelle Oldham Franklin—and made substantial improvements to modernize the shopworn buildings in 1933, when he briefly had significant Hollywood income from MGM.[38] The old buildings at Rowan Oak charmed Faulkner, who harbored romantic beliefs about

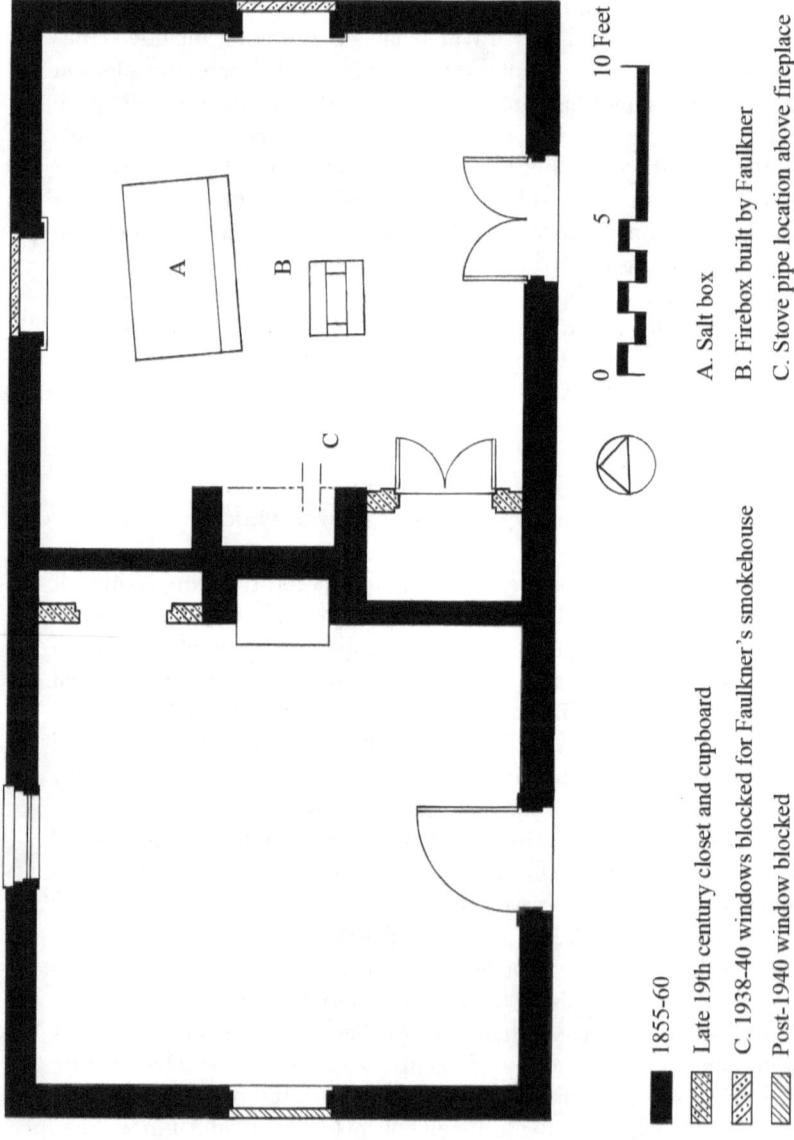

**Fig. 6:** Sheegog quarter at Rowan Oak with late nineteenth-century additions and William Faulkner's changes. Photo by Edward Chappell.

their great age. Chickasaw Indian E-Ah-Nah-Yea had built the old barn, he suggested, and the slave quarter predated the house (in a common but usually false modern claim about antiquity).[39] It is notable, in this context, that Faulkner chose to build a new house for Black employees Narcissus McEwen, Jack Oliver, Caroline Barr, Ned Barnett, and other domestic workers.

Faulkner can be seen, then, as engaged in 1933 in his own effort at improvement of domestic workers' accommodations. Many of his better-off but blinkered white contemporaries in north Mississippi towns chose to continue housing their cooks, housekeepers, gardeners, butlers, and nannies in old slave quarters, however marginally improved. Faulkner might have done likewise, sparing the cost of entirely new housing. Noel Polk and others have suggested that Faulkner was more attentive to the condition of Black individuals from a humanitarian standpoint, as evidenced, for example, in his handling of Greenfield, the farm he bought in 1938, and of the funds from his Nobel Prize, than to national policy affecting race in the South, as expressed in his unfortunate public statements in the 1950s.[40] In spite of the Sheegog quarter's brick walls, glazed windows, and other details lifting its finish somewhat above that of rough cabins, it unsettled Faulkner's vision for life at Rowan Oak. Without apparent public comment, he chose to employ resident Black workers but to remove them by 1933 from slave-tainted space to an improved house.

What he called the servants' quarters at Rowan Oak—and what Jill Faulkner Summers and others called "the cabin"—stood with a porch at the end of a near-axial path, without the vessel fragments and tin cans marking the fictional Beauchamp landscape as independent of a white owner's house. Faulkner had the servants' quarters built as two rooms, well-lighted with large glass windows and provided with elevated floors, board wall and ceiling finish; a porch; and a partially open breezeway (now enclosed) giving access to the rooms. Placement of the windows was also significant. Smaller windows in Sheegog's quarter were located on the end and rear, indicating status and offering no unnecessary visual connection with the rear yard of the main house. Faulkner's plan was like that of Mink Snopes's last tenant house (*Snopes*, 210) rather than like the old slave-associated form with central chimney and separate front doors. Faulkner made the sizable circulation space possible by having his builders construct two end chimneys, using the same bricks he employed on the main house.

With wood floors raised above the mud, rooms in the servants' quarters could be cleaner and somewhat more comfortable than those in the old quarter.[41] More than one non-family resident usually co-occupied

**Fig. 7:** Servants' quarters built by Faulkner at Rowan Oak about 1933. Photo by Edward Chappell.

the new house. In 1940 Faulkner wrote to Caroline Barr's daughter saying that she occupied one room and a young couple (Ben and Evelyn Pegues) the other, so the amount of private space was about the same as in the 1850s quarter.[42] Nevertheless, the windows, central doorway, and end chimneys signaled improvement over the Sheegogs' quarter and countless other two-door duplexes. If not in 1933 then soon afterward, Faulkner added a rear kitchen, so that later residents like the Prices occupied at least two rooms, and eventually the house grew to four rooms, the last space as a toilet and bath.

Faulkner had several objectives beyond providing improved worker accommodations. Significant among them was a desire to escape the specter of Black workers occupying a scruffy slave quarter and of those people moving conspicuously back and forth between the house and quarter. His and Estelle's Rowan Oak was to be a modern 1930s home, however dressed as an antebellum plantation. By 1933, at least, Rowan Oak was both modern and romantically old-fashioned. Strengthening this distinction was Faulkner's choice to build the servants' house farther from the main house and to buffer it visually by garden plantings. In other words, he made Rowan Oak structurally more segregated, however integrated it was functionally.

## William and Estelle Faulkner at Rowan Oak

Buying the property placed the Faulkners deeply in the context of southern elites living in two-story houses with white pillars, a cedar-lined approach, outbuildings, and gardens—and more specifically in the 1930s context of affluent middle-class restorers of old and refined houses, particularly southern mansions. In Mississippi, the favored model set the columned house in the countryside or on a large wooded property at the edge of town, with an extended processional approach from the road. Here the model also favored a sheltered balcony rather than a second floor to the porch, tightening the privileged, axial view of that approach. A prosperous Oxford landowner might proudly appear on such a balcony, imagining himself as Lafayette, or later as Charles de Gaulle—or envision being greeted by belles there in hoop skirts when he rode home from the war/golf course. For Faulkner, the aligned cedars both controlled the approach of visitors and screened their view, so that observers could see the white house only in tantalizing fragments, even at close range. In the common Greek Revival arrangement, panes of glass around the front doorways offered teasing glimpses of inside without physical access.

Jill Summers plausibly observed that her father bought Rowan Oak to establish himself and his immediate family as significant, to appear more substantial than his ill-fated father to fellow Mississippians. Signing at least once in 1932 as "William Faulkner of Rowanoake," Faulkner privately cast himself as southern gentleman.[43] The property transaction had deeper contexts, however. Buying, naming, and selectively restoring Rowan Oak associated William and Estelle Faulkner with the Colonial Revival, with its affection for the preindustrial past and respect for the buildings and furnishings of a more tasteful old regime.[44] That regime itself drew connections with the classical past. Regional architectural revivals extended from eastern Europe to California in the 1920s and '30s, but the Colonial Revival in the Deep South cultivated a particularly strong romantic focus on antebellum mansions, their owners, and especially their enslaved workers. Most revivals have some political motivation, and the one in the South was strongly racialized, romanticizing an era before the perceived loss of white gentry dominance in the Civil War and Reconstruction. As historian Joel Williamson has put it, "the New South in the turn-of-the-century years levered up the Old South and made it beautiful."[45] It was a striking choice for the Faulkners to buy and restore the old Sheegog place instead of living in a convenient 1930s suburban house, as his parents chose to do in 1930–31 on South Lamar

Avenue.[46] Faulkner celebrated such "old obsolete columned" survivors standing among the new houses, "like old horses surged suddenly out of slumbering in the middle of a flock of sheep."[47] The common setting for photos of both Faulkners was the front walk or steps, with the portico as the backdrop.

As Thomas Sutpen's plantation also demonstrates, such residences needed more than self-contained mansions. Gardens carried refined reflection beyond the house, stables housed spirited horses to be ridden, not worked, and smokehouses expressed the self-sufficiency of the estate, even if situated at the edge of town. All these elements increased the need for workers, who were inevitably Black. Faulkner further chose to have his employees primarily live on site rather than to be day-workers, though Rowan Oak's Oxford location made it unnecessary.

I suspect the novelist was never a very productive hog-farmer, but he sealed up the old slave cook-room in the Sheegog quarter, built a hefty firebox, and made it his smokehouse. More brickwork is attributed to Faulkner than he was actually responsible for at Rowan Oak, I also imagine, but parts of the converted smokehouse are so uneven that they must reflect his own hands.

Mitigating Faulkner's ironic architectural dress as a Mississippi planter backed by his Greek-pillared mansion and supported by a plantation ensemble with Black workers, then, was a second pose, at least initially: as a modern American homeowner, prepared to make house repairs himself by jacking up the building along with a fellow alcoholic carpenter, and painting and laying recycled bricks collected by his stepson when intrusive visitors made a yard wall necessary.[48] Slightly reminiscent of author Charles Lummis in Los Angeles, the handy repairman-builder pose distanced Faulkner from the old elites whose slaveholding histories had bred disdain for manual labor.

Williamson observes that Faulkner played many roles in his life, one being that of a plain Mississippi farmer, working with laborers at Greenfield Farm from 1938 to the early 1950s. (On learning he had won the Nobel Prize for literature, he first responded that, as a farmer, he wouldn't be able to travel to Stockholm to receive it.)[49] T. J. Jackson Lears reads Faulkner's respect for hand craftsmanship more deeply, as a "productionist critique" of modern consumption.[50] Working thoughtfully at joinery, for instance, lifts Cash Bundren above the indignity of his father and siblings.

Mitigating his mansion-owner role, too, was his choice to leave it in relatively scruffy condition. Like most rural southern houses in the 1930s and '40s, Rowan Oak was usually in need of a fresh coat of paint. The author was generally short of cash, but patina also bespoke rugged self-reliance, free of money's infatuation. Reflecting Flaubert's view that high living cost writers their independence in the 1930s, Faulkner professed teaching his family how to live poor.[51] He chopped wood for the fireplaces, but his reputation for yard maintenance was spotty.[52] Unlike many restoration-minded twentieth-century couples, William and Estelle collected few antiques. Especially beyond the parlor, they finished the rooms simply. His friend and Random House editor Saxe Commins confided that "[t]he rooms are bare and what they do contain is rickety, tasteless, ordinary."[53] Bookcases, for example, were plain boarded affairs, not showy joinery creations. Faulkner's self-fashioning was complex, and he harbored no uncritical pretentions to gentility in this phase of his life.

## House Restoration and Expansion

Nevertheless, returning with income from Hollywood and with his great *Light in August* in production in 1932, Faulkner was ready to work with Estelle in remaking their home. Not content with an old six-room house, they created an upper-middle-class residence with a parlor, dining room, library, kitchen and pantry, guest room, and three family bedrooms.[54] Once new central heating made selective wood burning possible, Faulkner remarked with pride that he was opening up all the fireplaces.[55] The intended use of open-hearth fireplaces for domestic pleasure and nurturance in the restored house was in contrast to the burning of wood fuel in fireplaces as the sole source of heat in the servants' quarters.

The changing character of the Faulkners' additions to the main house is revealing. The architectural quality and purpose of their 1933 expansion are strikingly different from what came later. Upstairs, the couple spent substantial funds to create a refined fourth bedroom with symmetrical walls, a fireplace, and woodwork made specifically to match existing 1840s mantels and trim in the house. For flooring, they bought wide boards of old-growth heart pine resembling the 1840s floors.

One can always ask just how interested resident-builders were in such details of woodwork, but the fact that Faulkner's fiction confers significance on things as minor as the wall molding on which Flem Snopes rests his feet between farm foreclosures reveals that he was paying attention. Stately old Bayard Sartoris lays a hand on his walnut newel when pausing to speak with Elnora.[56] Faulkner most potently interpreted refined woodwork as both civilized and feminine in Thomas Sutpen's big house, left raw for three years until he finished it in preparation for acquiring a wife.[57] Contrast between the refined woodwork at Rowan Oak and that

**Fig. 8:** Estelle Faulkner's bedroom, Rowan Oak, dating from 1933. Photo by Edward Chappell.

in the service space makes clear the qualitative difference. Below the new bedroom the couple built a modern kitchen, separated by a butler's pantry from the dining room. The finish there has a backstage quality, built with cheaper stock woodwork and inexpensive flooring. Little effort was made at visual order; the spaces were better than those in the servants' quarters, but comparable.

Outwardly, the 1933 expansion created a second impressive façade on the east, providing an orderly backdrop to open-air sitting space for the family and guests. Two Greek-styled doors were cut from the dining room onto the new porch and patio, so it could be comfortably reached and politely served.[58] Single-story but mimicking details from the arrangement of the old front porch, the new porch sheltered doorframes that the Faulkners capped with tall, plain Grecian friezes. William Faulkner repeatedly looked askance at arrivistes grossly re-orchestrating old Yoknapatawpha houses, making them, as he remarked, appear "about five times as big and ten times as Southern" ("Knight's Gambit," 155). But the Rowan Oak recasting was within the bounds of the couple's taste.

This first expansion was a collaborative restoration, one expressing the couple's shared interest in 1933 in creating a workable home in which

**Fig. 9:** East side of Rowan Oak, with the Faulkners' 1933 addition to the north (*right*). Photo by Edward Chappell.

they could live and entertain gracefully, however tempestuous the marriage already had become. There is no known evidence for the help of an architect. Rather, the Faulkners worked together, simply relying on the old regional grammar of house arrangement, which commonly added kitchens at the rear of linear wings and bedrooms above.[59] Conceptually simple but structurally somewhat complex, the addition involved demolishing an earlier twentieth-century kitchen, digging a furnace cellar, and doing surgery on original wall framing to create a lobby and generous closet for Estelle's bedroom.[60]

It also graded the spaces by race. Like pantries commonly found in elite American houses of the 1920s, the Faulkners' pantry marked a physical transition between predominately Black and white sections of the house, the model being that domestic labor took place to the rear and refined life characterized by leisure and hospitality was centered in the front. Again, the Faulkners used plain, lumber-supply finish in the rear, contrasting with historic and new Greek Revival finish in the front.

Yet the reality was that racial zones overlapped and the barrier was constantly penetrated. Faulkner portrayed this truth in *The Sound and the Fury*, having the steady and wise Dilsey Gibson in nearly constant contact at home with the tortured Compsons, her white employers.

Sometimes more comically, Simon Strother moves throughout the Sartoris house, serving and cajoling its landed denizens. Whether or not he had spent time in many Black households, by 1928 the author clearly had experienced such integrated owners' houses. At Rowan Oak, workers like Narcissus McEwen cleaned, Caroline Barr tended to Jill, and Ned Barnett served the Faulkners in the front of the house. At the most formal, presentational times, Black domestics like butler Barnett were essential actors in a genteel scene. The iconic if joking tableau of William and Estelle Faulkner in hunting dress at the front door of Rowan Oak places Barnett between them with a platter of drinks. Black servants patrolling just such front doors set tragic stories in motion in both *Absalom, Absalom!* and "Barn Burning." Faulkner chose to hold Caroline Barr's funeral service in the parlor. For quiet service, personal interaction, guard duty, or public show, then, Blacks occupied all of the house.

The white family also lived backstage, like the fictional Compsons. William Faulkner fixed his own breakfasts in the kitchen, and he cooked game when it was brought to the house. Estelle cooked certain meals, and young Jill was entertained there as well as in the "servants' quarters." Jill retreated to Barr's house when her parents fought. The only telephone in the household was located in the pantry, where servants usually answered it. This is where Faulkner took the call saying he'd won the Nobel Prize and received racist threats after his public comments on the murder of Emmett Till.

## Isolating Faulkners

Later additions, primarily in 1952, blurred the architectural distinctions between front- and backstage.[61] With them, Faulkner made Rowan Oak a far more gendered house, segregating spaces among the family members. The 1933 addition had aligned three family bedrooms without independent access, soon occupied separately by baby Jill and her parents. Both parents passed through the daughter's (front) room to reach their own, and Estelle walked through her husband's (middle) room to reach her own, which was therefore the most private. Directed by Faulkner alone and begun while Estelle and Jill were away, 1952 construction was principally intended to create rear passages giving independent access to the two adult bedrooms as well as to the dining room, to the kitchen, and indirectly to Faulkner's new office. Family members later recalled Estelle being angered by the additions, deeming them ugly and the construction work destroying much of her flower garden and an antebellum cistern.[62]

Previously Faulkner wrote in the library and occasionally his bedroom. The 1952 office, which he used for his writing and for solitude, was further buffered from the genteel core of the house by a lobby and his bathroom on the east and by a second passage on the south that recessed it from the library.[63] It separated him from the household behind often locked doors while providing an exterior door that gave Black workers outside, such as Andrew Price, more direct daytime access to the author than the family had. A bed and sizable private closet allowed him to rise early, dress, and ride a horse without attention from Estelle and Jill. Outwardly the 1952 additions were awkward, with none of the visual order the 1933 alterations created.

Faulkner also chose to execute all the post-1933 additions in stock materials, with little of the restoration-grade work used in the first expansion. He installed a fireplace in the office with its own diagonally set chimney and mantel, but he left the walls plain, without the wallpaper Estelle favored in the house. Plain plaster allowed him further to mark the office as his private place for writing, most emphatically by inscribing his outlines for his intended masterwork, *A Fable*, on the walls.

## William Faulkner, Architect

The 1933 restoration/remodeling represented a familial partnership, focused on crafting an identity together and defining the couple's intended status in the community. It structured race within the household, however ephemerally, just as building the servants' quarters was intended to do in the landscape. The '33 adjustments to the house followed domestic arrangements as well as a taste for antebellum appearance common among affluent southerners of the mid–Jim Crow era, however much Faulkner professed poverty. An uninformed visitor would not have recognized Rowan Oak as a home of a great writer based solely on its spatial arrangements and finish. Race and taste are less evident in Faulkner's 1950s additions. Those subsequent efforts favored privacy and marital separation while omitting the architectural refinements that sought to distinguish white from Black.

In conclusion, Faulkner was among the most perceptive white southern critics when exploring the heritage of slavery and racism, though his public utterances were inconsistent over time. Architecturally, confronting real people, he made an effort as early as 1933 to avoid placing Black workers in old slave quarters. This choice may well have reflected those workers' expressed preferences as well as his consent—a racial relationship that he seldom if ever explored in his writing, where Blacks other than the Beauchamps say little about their material lives. He and Estelle Faulkner created a refined Colonial Revival house for themselves with Black and white zones, and his construction of the servants' quarters extended that architectural division. Yet Black members of the household variously occupied all the spaces in both houses, in a pattern that characterized families of the Faulkners' economic status throughout most of the South during their lifetimes. It represented a degree of negotiation that is hard to recognize in Faulkner's fiction, a background for the more assertive (if still contested) racial advances of the last half-century.

NOTES

The author thanks Jennifer Baughn, Susan L. Buck, Cary Carson, Jack Elliott, William Griffith, Jeffrey T. Jackson, Carl R. Lounsbury, David Person, Chuck Ross, Robert Saarnio, Jodi Skipper, James G. Thomas, Jr., and Jay Watson. Architectural fieldwork for this paper was supported by a 2017–18 project at the University of Mississippi to study slavery-related buildings and landscapes in northern Mississippi.

1. William T. Ruzicka, *Faulkner's Fictive Architecture* (Ann Arbor, MI: UMI Research Press, 1987).

2. The Frenchman's Bend place comes alive in *Sanctuary*, but with its spaces hollowed out beyond description by its prior abandonment. William Faulkner, *Sanctuary* (New York: Random House, 1931).

3. William Faulkner, *Snopes: The Hamlet, The Town, The Mansion* (New York: Modern Library, 1994), 210–11. Hereafter cited parenthetically in text. William Faulkner, "Barn Burning," *Collected Stories of William Faulkner* (New York: Random House, 1950), 8.

4. V. K. Ratliff comments on Flem Snopes's addition of oversized columns after buying Manfred de Spain's house in Jefferson (Faulkner, *Snopes*, 654). Greek-inspired columns were widely admired by North Mississippi slaveholders in the last two decades of slavery.

5. William Faulkner, "A Rose for Emily," *Collected Stories of William Faulkner*, 119.

6. William Faulkner, "That Evening Sun," *Collected Stories of William Faulkner*, 294, 301, 303.

7. William Faulkner, "There Was a Queen," *Collected Stories of William Faulkner*, 727.

8. William Faulkner, *The Sound and the Fury: An Authoritative Text, Backgrounds and Contexts, Criticism*, ed. Michael Gorra (New York: W. W. Norton, 2014), 173–74, 189.

9. William Faulkner, "Wash," *Collected Stories of William Faulkner*, 537–38.

10. William Faulkner, "Red Leaves," *Selected Stories of William Faulkner* (New York: Modern Library, 1961), 101–5.

11. William Faulkner, *The Unvanquished* (New York: Vintage Books, 1966), 88, 106, 121, 141, 185.

12. See, for example, Philip M. Weinstein, "Marginalia: Faulkner and Black Lives," in *Faulkner and Race: Faulkner and Yoknapatawpha, 1986*, ed. Doreen Fowler and Ann J. Abadie (Jackson: University Press of Mississippi, 1987), 170–91.

13. Jay Watson, opening remarks, Faulkner and Slavery conference, July 23, 2018. *The Sound and the Fury* was published in October 1929. One could argue that the Dilsey character, and perhaps the Gibsons as a whole, occupying a freestanding cabin on the Compson place, might be considered bridge figures into the more conscientious engagement with chattel slavery that Faulkner begins in 1930.

14. The Beauchamp house is introduced in William Faulkner, *Go Down, Moses*, rev. ed. (1942; repr., New York: Vintage International, 1990), 107, 110, 115. Hereafter cited parenthetically in text. The house is further described in William Faulkner, *Intruder in the Dust* (New York: Random House, 1948), 8–15.

15. Thomas S. Hines, *William Faulkner and the Tangible Past: The Architecture of Yoknapatawpha* (Berkeley: University of California Press, 1997).

16. Evidence of older and once far more common housing for enslaved fieldworkers and many house servants is now primarily found archaeologically and in rare written accounts such as an 1825 contract to build fourteen "Negro cabins" at Bruinsburg in northern Mississippi. All fourteen were to be identical, measuring eighteen by twenty feet, built of wood, with wood and clay chimneys, wood floors, and a single unglazed window. Only the fireplaces were to be lined with brick. Many quarters were much worse, but the Bruinsburg house specifications offer a contrast with superior quarters and work buildings that now survive. Adams County Probate Records, box 13, Packets for Estate of Lewis Evans, item 50.

17. *Mississippian* (Jackson), May 4, 1849, 3. Also see *Mississippi Free Trader & Natchez Gazette*, December 30, 1836, 3; *Hinds County Gazette* (Raymond, Mississippi), April 21, 1858, 3.

18. *Tri-Weekly Flag & Advisor* (Montgomery, AL), January 20, 1848, 3.

19. *Statesman & Gazette* (Natchez), June 26, 1828, 4. Also see *Hinds County Gazette*, December 6, 1854, 2; *Semi-Weekly Mississippian* (Jackson), July 19, 1859, 4.

20. *Natchez Courier*, October 21, 1851, 3.

21. *Daily Mississippian* (Jackson), October 10, 1862, 3.

22. *Mississippian and State Gazette* (Jackson), December 2, 1857, 1. Also see *Mississippi Free Trader* (Natchez), November 13, 1835, 4, and April 21, 1837, 3; the *Mississippian*, December 13, 1839, 3. Plantation quarters were not without some claims of improvement. O. B. Cobb sought to sell his plantation and its people in Louisiana, characterizing their houses as "excellent frame Negro Cabins lined with brick and brick chimneys" (*Natchez Daily Courier*, April 18, 1839, 1). The *Daily Mississippian* offered a plantation with "good negro cabins" (November 18, 1859, 2).

23. Edward A. Chappell, "Housing Slavery," *The Chesapeake House*, ed. Cary Carson and Carl R. Lounsbury (Chapel Hill: University of North Carolina Press, 2011), 156–78; and Chappell, "Architecture of Urban Domestic Slavery in the Chesapeake and Jamaica," *Slavery in the City*, ed. Clifton Ellis and Rebecca Ginsburg (Charlottesville: University of Virginia Press, 2017), 19–51.

24. Brick construction of Rowan Oak's surviving quarter, behind a frame mansion, is paralleled by a similar combination at ca. 1857 White Arches in Columbus and at the McCarroll house in Holly Springs, Mississippi. The McCarroll quarter dates to 1855–60, a decade or more following the initial house construction. Some ca. 1820–60 Lowcountry quarters held two small sleeping rooms appended to the residents' main living space, and enslaved fieldworkers in Jamaica appear to have built two-room wooden houses for themselves in the decades before emancipation in the 1830s.

25. "That anybody white could take your whole self for anything that came to mind. Not just work, kill, or maim you, but dirty you . . . so bad you forgot who you were and couldn't think it up." Toni Morrison, *Beloved* (New York: Alfred A. Knopf, 1987), 251.

26. Bernie D. Jones, *Fathers of Conscience: Mixed Race Inheritance in the Antebellum South* (Athens: University of Georgia Press, 2009).

27. James O. Breeden, ed., *Advice among Masters* (Westport, CT: Greenwood, 1980), 125.

28. Fraser D. Neiman, "The Lost World of Monticello: An Evolutionary Perspective," *Journal of Anthropological Research* 64, no. 2 (Summer 2008): 161–93.

29. Inventory list, November 1, 1860, Lafayette County Probate File 852 (Robert Sheegog Estate), Lafayette County Chancery Clerk's Office. The 1860 MS Lafayette County Slave Census lists the adults, some with slightly different ages, and a second ten-year-old, without naming him.

30. *Oxford Falcon*, December 24, 1870, 3.

31. Judith L. Sensibar, *Faulkner and Love* (New Haven, CT: Yale University Press, 2009).

32. Lucy Bailey is listed as Black, aged thirty, and a cook in the Bailey household in the 1880 Lafayette County Census.

33. William Faulkner, "Smoke," *Knight's Gambit* (New York: Vintage Books, 1978), 5, 16.

34. Faulkner, *Go Down, Moses*, 6, 44, 250–51.

35. William Faulkner, "Mountain Victory," *Collected Stories of William Faulkner*, 746, 748, 751.

36. Faulkner, "Knight's Gambit," *Knight's Gambit*, 241.

37. Joseph Blotner, ed., *Selected Letters of William Faulkner* (New York: Random House, 1977), 440–41.

38. Faulkner's initial work was underpinning and painting parts of the house in 1930. See Joseph Blotner, *Faulkner: A Biography*, vol. 1 (New York: Random House, 1974), 657–58; and John Faulkner, *My Brother Bill* (New York: Trident Press, 1962), 162.

39. Malcolm Franklin, *Bitterweeds: Life with William Faulkner at Rowan Oak* (Irving, TX: Society for the Study of Traditional Culture, 1977), 24.

40. Noel Polk, "Man in the Middle: Faulkner and the Southern White Moderate," in *Faulkner and Race: Faulkner and Yoknapatawpha, 1986*, ed. Doreen Fowler and Ann J. Abadie (Jackson: University Press of Mississippi, 1988), 130–51.

41. Low wooden floors and their supports had probably disappeared from both 1855–60 rooms by 1930, replaced by paving in the east room and dirt in the west.

42. Blotner, *Selected Letters*, 117–18. MS Lafayette Oxford Ward 3 Census, enumerated April 8–9, 1940, lists Ben Pegues, aged thirty-five, as houseboy, wife Evelyn, thirty-one, maid, and cousin Lydia Jones, thirty-five, cook, residing on the property with the Faulkners and Malcolm Franklin. Jones probably occupied Barr's former room.

43. Blotner, *Faulkner: A Biography*, vol. 1, 791.

44. Blotner reports that Sallie Bailey Bryant chose to sell the property to Faulkner because he was sympathetic to restoring the deteriorating house (*Faulkner: A Biography*, vol. 1, 652).

45. Joel Williamson, *William Faulkner and Southern History* (New York: Oxford University Press, 1993), 356.

46. Blotner, *Faulkner: A Biography*, vol. 1, 662.

47. William Faulkner, *Requiem for a Nun* (New York: Vintage Books, 1975), 215. Also see Faulkner, *Intruder in the Dust*, 119–20, on Jefferson's unpainted old columned houses peering over the shoulders of "new one-story houses designed in Florida and California set with matching garages in their neat plots of clipped grass and tedious flowerbeds."

48. As late as 1945, Faulkner wrote to Estelle that he was eager to leave Hollywood so he could fix Jill's room and paint the house at Rowan Oak (Blotner, *Selected Letters*, 194–95).

49. Williamson, *William Faulkner and Southern History*, 272–73, 330–32.

50. T. J. Jackson Lears, "True and False Things: Faulkner and the World of Goods," in *Faulkner and Material Culture: Faulkner and Yoknapatawpha, 2004*, ed. Joseph R. Urgo and Ann J. Abadie (Jackson: University Press of Mississippi, 2007), 142–43.

51. Karl F. Zender, "Two Unpublished Letters from William Faulkner to Helen Baird," *American Literature* 63, no. 1 (September 1991): 538. Gustave Flaubert quoted in Elizabeth Pochoda, "An Author's Artifacts," *The Nation*, August 12/19, 2019, 4. Faulkner read Flaubert and cited him as early as 1924. Blotner, *Faulkner: A Biography*, vol. 1, 331, 459, 606, 812.

52. John Faulkner, *My Brother Bill*, 163, 207.

53. Louis Daniel Brodsky and Robert Hamblin, eds., *Faulkner: A Comprehensive Guide to the Brodsky Collection, II: The Letters* (Jackson: University Press of Mississippi, 1984), 89–90.

54. Faulkner wrote Bennett Cerf on December 16, 1932, that he was squeezing every nickel he could to fix up his house (Blotner, *Selected Letters*, 68–69). Two months later he wrote Ben Wasson that he had "enough money now to finish my house," which he described simply as adding a bedroom, bath, and heat as well as painting (70–71).

55. Faulkner wrote to W. C. Bryant on May 18, 1933, "I am res[t]oring all the fireplaces to wood hearths in brick of soft red color." Sally Stone Trotter, *Rowan Oak* (Oxford, MS: Nautilus Publishing, 2017), 94–95. Faulkner later installed gas burners in all the fireplaces except those in the two front rooms, kept open for wood fires.

56. William Faulkner, *Flags in the Dust* (New York: Vintage Books, 1974), 12.

57. William Faulkner, *Absalom, Absalom!* (New York: Random House, 1936), 39–52.

58. Without questioning the dates, Blotner recounts the now-famous story that Estelle Faulkner commented on the distinctive quality of light in August while sitting on the east porch in 1931, unintentionally providing her husband with the title for the novel he then had underway (*Faulkner: A Biography*, vol. 1, 702).

59. The house is what folklorists call an I-house: symmetrical-fronted, two stories high, with a room on either side of a stair passage on both floors. Built by the hundreds of thousands across the South and much of the Midwest, especially in the nineteenth century, I-houses were commonly expanded (both originally and as additions) with a single off-center rear wing much like the one the Sheegogs built and the Faulkners extended. In northern Mississippi, most antebellum houses of Rowan Oak's scale had exterior kitchens. Kitchens occupied by enslaved cooks were located at the rear of the wings in selected sub-regions but became far more common after 1865, in smaller houses as well as I-houses. The kitchens Faulkner had built at the rear of the servants' house and at Greenfield Farm illustrate the latter plan.

60. In *Faulkner and Love*, Sensibar portrays Estelle and William Faulkner's emotional dependence and argues for her influence on his writing but, like most Faulkner scholars, she does not consider the architectural evidence for their evolving relationship.

61. Joseph R. Urgo, introduction to *Faulkner and Material Culture: Faulkner and Yoknapatawpha, 2004*, ed. Joseph R. Urgo and Ann J. Abadie (Jackson: University Press of Mississippi, 2007), xiii. Faulkner asked Saxe Commins at Random House to send him $15,000 soon after January 1, 1952, much of it for the additions (Blotner, *Faulkner: A Biography*, vol. 2, 1404).

62. James Murry Faulkner to William Griffith, ca. 1999–2002; also confirmed by Jill Faulkner Summers to Griffith, 2002. Griffith, personal communication to the author, July 2, 2019.

63. William Griffith to author, December 3, 2017. Faulkner favored the term *office* as the traditional name of the room in which planters and lawyers worked, over the affected term *study*, with its taint of unproductive space in contemporary middle-class, often suburban houses. He did allow county attorney Gavin Stevens a study in "An Error in Chemistry," *Knight's Gambit*, 111, 116, 129.

# Faulkner, Slavery, and the University of Mississippi

## W. Ralph Eubanks

William Faulkner's *Absalom, Absalom!* is not a novel known for its tidy plot or linear story line. The story of Thomas Sutpen and his sons Henry Sutpen and Charles Bon is told from multiple points of view, as well as from several perspectives in time, which makes it incredibly complex and layered. Yet underneath all these various narrative threads *Absalom Absalom!* tells a story of the intersection of race, identity, and history, since the novel's characters and the story that unfolds around them is propelled by those forces. The issue of race turns up throughout the novel, whether it is in the slow reveal of Charles Bon's one drop of Black blood or Sutpen's racist behavior, which in time leads to the destruction of his family. Questions of identity arise with the character of Charles Bon, who looks completely white, lacks even the "parchment colored" skin of his mother, attends the University of Mississippi—where Blacks were forbidden until 1962—and volunteers for the University Greys, a part of the Army of the Confederacy. Bon even tells Henry Sutpen, *"if you haven't got honor and pride, then nothing matters,"* even though one could argue that his desire to be a cosmopolitan white gentleman and to deny his African ancestry shows both a lack of both honor and pride.[1] If American Blackness—not merely as a racialized category, but as a cultural, political, and economic identity—has a history that is largely southern, Charles Bon's denial of his Blackness and his embrace of whiteness is also southern in its origin, with the one-drop rule used as the ultimate means of social control, determining who was enslaved and who could be free. But it is history that drives the narrative of *Absalom, Absalom!* In this novel, history is about the impact of choices and the cycle that history creates, a cycle that can be difficult, if not impossible, to escape.

Although *Absalom, Absalom!* is a novel driven by history, its primary character, Thomas Sutpen, arrives in Jefferson, Mississippi, as a man with no history: "a man who so far as anyone . . . knew either had no past at all or did not dare reveal it—a man who rode into town from out of nowhere" (10). Sutpen, through his son Henry, seeks to create a history for himself yet fails to realize how the past is not so easily discarded. So while this narrative is about the cycle history creates, it is also about the ghosts of history—particularly the ghosts of Thomas Sutpen's history—and how those ghosts cannot be escaped.

An essential part of any writer's toolkit in constructing a narrative is to withhold and gradually reveal information. In *Absalom, Absalom!* Faulkner slowly unspools the story of Thomas Sutpen and his family to keep the reader engaged with this complex allegory of the South and to build tension in the novel's nonlinear narrative. This same technique is now driving a new story about Faulkner, his home of Rowan Oak, and the University of Mississippi. As the story begins to unfold, a closer connection between Faulkner's fiction, his longtime home, and the university becomes apparent. *Absalom, Absalom!*, as well as a few historical documents, is helping this connection come into closer focus.

When Faulkner purchased Rowan Oak in 1930, he purchased a property with direct links to slavery and to the story of the University of Mississippi. Robert Sheegog, the original owner of Rowan Oak, was an early settler in Oxford, Mississippi, as well as a merchant, cotton producer, and slaveowner. Payment records from the 1840s in the archives of the University of Mississippi indicate that Sheegog, along with other local slaveowners, loaned slaves to the university.[2] The university records characterize the use of slaves as "servant hires," slaves who would have labored to build the university, which was founded in 1848. Of the eight enslaved individuals living at Rowan Oak in 1860, records indicate the first names of six: Simon, George, Dave, Lila, Frances, Phillis. Records also include a runaway slave ad dated August 9, 1845, and posted by Sheegog for "George" (a slave name that is also included in the 1860 probate documents for Rowan Oak).

It is difficult to say whether Faulkner gained any literary inspiration for *Absalom, Absalom!* from his knowledge that slaves once housed on the grounds of the home he then occupied helped construct the University of Mississippi. In the early twentieth century the prevailing cultural view was that slavery was a relatively benign institution, even one that led to civilizing slaves by lifting them from the barbarism of Africa. It was not until the 1933 publication of Charles Sydnor's *Slavery in Mississippi* that historians began to question what slavery as an institution did to slaves. Sydnor was a faculty member of the University of Mississippi at the time of the publication of his book, and pioneering African American historian Carter G. Woodson admitted in an unsigned review in the *Journal of Negro History*—after questioning whether whites could write about Negroes without bias—that the author "apparently endeavored to write with restraint and care, but he does not adhere to this standard throughout the work."[3] While Sydnor outlined the cruelties of slavery in his text, he also still maintained the prevailing paternalistic view of the institution of slavery.

Sydnor's *Slavery in Mississippi* drew on some of the same documents, including university faculty and trustee minutes, that are now being used to show the close relationship between the University of Mississippi and the economic and cultural institution of slavery.[4] Whether Faulkner was aware of this at the time cannot be proven, yet it is important to note that the history of slavery was being debated at the university that is near his home around the time he was writing *Absalom, Absalom!* In fact, in a 1934 letter to his agent, Faulkner never mentions slavery as part of *Absalom, Absalom!*; instead he said the novel was meant to be "the story of a man who wanted a son through pride, and got too many of them and they destroyed him."[5]

In his outline of *Absalom, Absalom!*—which can be found in his papers at the University of Virginia—Faulkner notes facts about his characters and the shape of his narrative, and you can see how owning slaves was merely a component of Sutpen's wealth. "Col. Sutpen, his daughter Judith, his son Henry. The family is well-to-do in land and slaves, but still provincial country aristocracy of that period: simple, honorable, proud, of good stock."[6] What this outline reveals is the influence of Faulkner's work as a screenwriter, since it seems to be part narrative structure and part dramatis personae. So, for Faulkner, slavery was simply part of the architecture of the antebellum South. The story of any ambitious white man in the antebellum South involved the institution of slavery in one way or another.

Yet *Absalom, Absalom!* is a novel about history, and it is the South's history of slavery and miscegenation—and the shame sometimes associated with that history—that contributed to the destruction of the Sutpen family. Thomas Sutpen may be framed in the narrative as a man with no past, but he is actually a man with a hidden past, and Charles Bon stands as evidence of that past. Cleanth Brooks believed that Faulkner saw "the past as a living force in the present, a force that molds our sense of the present."[7] So the past can never be escaped.

That is why the narrative of *Absalom, Absalom!* is propelled by history's ghosts, by what is hidden. Like the ghosts of history of the American South Faulkner confronts in *Absalom, Absalom!*, the history of American universities is tied to the institution of slavery, which once only had a ghostlike presence but now is real and present. Given

Faulkner's belief that the past is a living force in the present, slavery at the University of Mississippi is something that we must now examine in its connection with the narrative of *Absalom, Absalom!* At the University of Mississippi, as well as at Harvard, where Quentin Compson tells the story of the Sutpen family to his Canadian roommate, Shreve McCannon, slavery was used to raise buildings, maintain campuses, and enhance institutional wealth. As Craig Steven Wilder notes in his book *Ebony & Ivy*—a study of the intertwined history of slavery, race, and higher education—American colleges and universities also "trained the personnel and cultivated the ideas that accelerated and legitimated the dispossession of Native Americans and the enslavement of Africans. Modern slavery required the acquiescence of scholars and the cooperation of academic institutions."[8]

The connection between Faulkner's fiction and the slaves who helped build the University of Mississippi helps us see a new narrative that is evolving about Faulkner, slavery, and the University of Mississippi. In particular, the direct link between Faulkner's Rowan Oak and a group of slaves that constructed the University of Mississippi evokes questions about how Faulkner constructed the relationship between Charles Bon and Henry Sutpen in *Absalom, Absalom!*, a relationship that has the University of Mississippi as a backdrop. Whether or not Faulkner had knowledge of the connections between the University of Mississippi and slavery, this new narrative twist makes us look at this relationship—as well as its historical context—in a new light. As noted earlier, Faulkner famously withheld information to propel his narratives. But a reading of *Absalom, Absalom!* alongside historical records from the University of Mississippi and Rowan Oak leads to the question of whether Faulkner constructed historical parallels in his narrative that we are only now able to see through new historical evidence, particularly since it has only been in the last twenty-five years that we have begun to realize that American colleges and universities were not passive beneficiaries of the institution of slavery.

A few scholars who have examined the role of slavery in the narrative of *Absalom, Absalom!* approach it in light of Sutpen's voyage to Haiti and the Haitian-born slaves whom he brings back with him to help construct Sutpen's Hundred. In the *Mississippi Quarterly* Sean Latham notes that Haiti is often viewed as an intersection between Black Africa and white America, which might be why Sutpen's Haitian slaves are constantly referred to as "wild" rather than as stereotypical docile slaves, wildness being associated with Africanness.[9] This in some ways separates the character of Sutpen from the American institution of slavery as well as from the way slavery operated in Jefferson, where he builds his plantation. Rosa Coldfield even remembers Sutpen's face as "exactly like the negro's save for the teeth (this because of his beard, doubtless)" (16). Although his face may be the same as a Black man's—and he is known to wrestle and fight with his slaves—in no way does Sutpen see himself as a part of the origins of the American South. In fact, what Faulkner is saying here is that Sutpen's power may be conflated with his skin color, which in the broader society renders him superior, but his powers and desires are more primal and mercurial. White supremacy may drive certain aspects of Sutpen's life, but there is more under the surface that makes him the man he is. Faulkner is asking the reader to see the complexities of Sutpen, because a complex character helps enliven a story.

In his 1956 interview with Jean Stein for the *Paris Review*, Faulkner, answering a question about what he felt were the secrets of a good story, responded not by focusing exclusively on character but by saying, "a story usually begins with a single idea or memory or mental picture. The writing of the story is simply a matter of working up to that moment, to explain why it happened or what it caused to follow. A writer is trying to create believable people in credible moving situations in the most moving way he can. Obviously he must use as one of his tools the environment which he knows."[10]

While Faulkner may not have traveled to Haiti or have known about the slaves used for the construction of the University of Mississippi, he knew his environment. And it is well known that he used his environment to construct his stories. Faulkner used the South and his native soil as a lens through which to view the world, which included stories that were part of local lore. With the American South being an oral culture, it is likely that he knew of the University of Mississippi's use of slaves who once lived at Rowan Oak through stories related to him by local people or even from records he found at Rowan Oak. Just as Quentin Compson passes on the story of Thomas Sutpen and his family to Shreve McCannon on that chilly evening in 1910 in Cambridge, Massachusetts, someone may have relayed to Faulkner the historical stories that are part of *Absalom, Absalom!*—a history that would have been part of the very place where he wrote the novel—that we now find in documents and records.

Sutpen's story may relate to Rowan Oak, but there is also overlap between that story and the founding of the University of Mississippi. Henry Sutpen and Charles Bon both arrive at the University of Mississippi in 1857, just nine years after its founding in 1848. When both men arrive at the University of Mississippi, according to Faulkner's timeline, fifty-five slaves were listed as the property of faculty and staff of the university.[11] Between Bon's arrival in 1857 and his trip home to Sutpen's Hundred with Henry for Christmas in 1859, university records show two payments for the use of slaves: $200 to Robert Sheegog on January 1, 1857, and $400 on May 10, 1858, to Jacob Thompson, who owned the Homeplace plantation directly across what is now called Old Taylor Road from Rowan Oak. In today's dollars, those amounts are equivalent to $5,000 and $10,000 respectively, so this was not an insignificant payment. Moreover, the question remains as to how the cost of "hiring" the slaves was calculated. At the University of Virginia, for example, the cost was calculated based on the amount it cost to feed and maintain the slaves for the contracted period.[12] University of Mississippi records, however, do not indicate how the costs were calculated.

While it may be purely coincidental that the dates of the use of slaves at the university overlap with the story Faulkner tells in *Absalom, Absalom!*, Faulkner uses a larger, better-known historical parallel that is again linked to the records of the University of Mississippi: the founding of its Civil War regiment, the University Greys. In 1861, when Charles Bon and Henry Sutpen join the University Greys to fight for the Confederacy, faculty meeting records indicate that the university only had four students "in readiness to attend lectures," and the university administration decided to proceed with classes in spite of the sparse student count.[13] Further, the chancellor states, "the continuance of the war kept most of the old students with the army, and made it very difficult for the parents of others to procure money with which to send their sons to the University."[14] By the end of the term, the University of Mississippi closed, not to reopen until after the end of the Civil War in 1865.

Today, the University of Mississippi has a visible monument to the University Greys for their service to the Confederacy in the Civil War, and in many ways the campus itself stands as a silent monument to slavery. Faulkner probably knew how entangled with slavery his home at Rowan Oak was, and in turn with the university that stands just a half mile from his home. And while those entanglements may not have been spoken of directly, they are symbolically part of the narrative. Charles Bon, with his divided sense of self, is the symbol of those entanglements.

Bon, a University of Mississippi student whose ancestors were once slaves, symbolizes the role of slavery in the founding of the university—and Faulkner's acknowledgment of that connection—in *Absalom, Absalom!* A man with the singularity of purpose that Charles Bon has would certainly know that he left his elite status behind when he left Louisiana for Mississippi, yet he chose to place himself at an institution that was built by slaves. In turn, he decides to cloak himself in whiteness, to ingratiate himself to aristocratic young men (or young men with such aspirations) like Henry Sutpen, and in time to fight for the Confederacy in defense of slavery. As Mr. Compson tells the story of Charles Bon and the sway he held over both Judith and Henry Sutpen, he speaks of Bon as being like "a few old mouth-to-mouth tales" or like "letters without salutation or signature" that "we exhume from old trunks and boxes and drawers," letters "in which men and women who once lived and breathed are now merely initials or nicknames out of some now incomprehensible affection" (80). Judith, Bon, Henry, and Sutpen are "like a chemical formula exhumed along with the letters from that forgotten chest" that "you re-read . . . again and again," trying to connect them without "miscalculation" (80).

But Charles Bon and his racial passing are that miscalculation. Bon's decision to present himself as a white man, rather than follow his legal racial classification in Mississippi, is his way of exacting revenge on the very society that would oppress him. Bon represents the sins of slavery, since miscegenation is emblematic of those sins. Rather than taking on the role of the tragic mixed-race figure, Bon seeks to become the righteous avenger, only to have his mixed-race identity lead to his death. When Bon says to Henry, "*So it's the miscegenation, not the incest, which you cant bear,*" Henry does not answer (285). By not answering, the message is that race is the prevailing issue in Bon's intended marriage to Judith Sutpen, not the fact that she is his half-sister.

In *Absalom, Absalom!* Faulkner shows the historical past and socially determined systems of events as the substance of his narrative. Although these newfound historical documents that stand in parallel with Faulkner's narrative may not have directly informed Faulkner's fiction, they serve as a metanarrative that informs a reading of the text. They tell their own story, while at the same time informing the reading of Faulkner's text.

These historical documents inform the reader of the knowledge and experience of the characters in *Absalom, Absalom!*, particularly Charles Bon and Henry Sutpen. While the narrative is largely concerned with familial tensions between the two men, readers should not lose sight of the fact that their relationship is shaped in an institution built on the economics of slavery. During their time at the University of Mississippi, the institution assessed each student $5 per semester for "servant hire"—a euphemism for slaves—thus perpetuating the institution of slavery among the sons of the landed aristocracy.[15] Students were taught Albert Taylor Bledsoe's anti-abolitionist tract *Essay on Liberty and Slavery*, which promoted the idea that "God sanctioned slavery among the Hebrews" and hence "God sanctions slavery for all men at all times" to provide the philosophical underpinnings of the economic system the university supported.[16] Both of these historical parallels reinforce Faulkner's larger idea, which he reveals through Thomas Sutpen's struggles with his sons, of how the racial lines created by the South are the region's unbridgeable social and cultural divide.

In today's society, as well as in Faulkner's time, the biggest problem we face is the rationalization of slavery in a nation built on freedom. Although slavery ended more than a hundred years ago, the rationalization of slavery remains in the form of racism. In *Absalom, Absalom!*, Faulkner constructed a novel that shows the dangers of racism and its destructive power, with Sutpen as the central object lesson. Most important, the actions of Faulkner's characters and the way they move through the world—particularly Charles Bon—reveal how race is a social and political construction.

We may never know whether Faulkner had direct knowledge of the slaves who once inhabited Rowan Oak or whether they directly affected the narrative shape of *Absalom, Absalom!* But we do know that Faulkner's novels emphasize not only the presence of the past but also the value of endurance. *Absalom, Absalom!* is a novel about how the past endures and how, when that past is not confronted constructively, it can be destructive.

In the final lines of *Absalom, Absalom!* Faulkner speaks for himself about the strange tensions of the past, and I believe of race and the legacy of slavery. "Why do you hate the South?" Shreve asks Quentin. "I dont hate it," Quentin replies. "I dont! I dont hate it! I dont hate it!" (303). History casts a pall over Quentin Compson, and we know that his suicide haunts the ending with its ghostly presence even as he is very much alive. This speaks to the reason *Absalom, Absalom!* continues to take on new meaning and significance: Faulkner's work has always had inherent in it a tension between the history of the characters and actual historic events. Historical events are seen as metaphor, while the character's history is viewed as the real thing. In these newly discovered documents relating to slavery and the University of Mississippi, we see how Faulkner blurred the lines between historical events and fictional narrative. Now we can see, both in fact and in fiction, how history creates a cycle that can be difficult to escape.

NOTES

1. William Faulkner, *Absalom, Absalom!*, rev. ed. (1936; repr., New York: Vintage International, 1990), 279. Hereafter cited parenthetically in the text.

2. Board of Trustee Reports and Minutes (MUM00524), Archives and Special Collections, John D. Williams Library, University of Mississippi.

3. Carter G. Woodson, review of *Slavery in Mississippi*, by Charles Sackett Sydnor, *Journal of Negro History* 19, no. 3 (1934): 332.

4. Charles Sackett Sydnor, *Slavery in Mississippi* (New York: Appleton-Century Company, 1933), 260.

5. Faulkner quoted in James G. Watson, *William Faulkner: Self-Preservation and Performance* (Austin: University of Texas Press, 2000), 124.

6. Papers of William Faulkner, University of Virginia Special Collections, MSS 7914.

7. Cleanth Brooks quoted in C. Vann Woodward, *The Burden of Southern History*, rev. ed. (1960; repr., Baton Rouge: Louisiana State University Press, 1993), 279.

8. Craig Stephen Wilder, *Ebony & Ivy: Race, Slavery, and the Troubled History of America's Universities* (New York: Bloomsbury Publishing, 2013), 10.

9. Sean Latham, "Jim Bond's America: Denaturalizing the Logic of Slavery in *Absalom, Absalom!*" *Mississippi Quarterly* 51, no. 3 (Summer 1998): 453–63.

10. William Faulkner, interview with Jean Stein, "The Art of Fiction," *Paris Review* 12 (Spring 1956): 43.

11. Faculty Minutes, University of Mississippi, 1857–1859, folder 3, box 1, Archives and Special Collections, John D. Williams Library, University of Mississippi.

12. Wilder, *Ebony & Ivy*, 138.

13. Faculty Minutes, University of Mississippi, September 18, 1861, Archives and Special Collections, John D. Williams Library, University of Mississippi.

14. Faculty Minutes, University of Mississippi, September 18, 1861, Archives and Special Collections, John D. Williams Library, University of Mississippi.

15. Board of Trustee Reports and Minutes (MUM00524), Archives and Special Collections, John D. Williams Library, University of Mississippi.

16. Albert Taylor Bledsoe, *Essay on Liberty and Slavery* (Philadelphia: J. B. Lippincott, 1856), 139.

# More than Running: Redefining Movement in *Go Down, Moses*

## Erin Penner

Faulkner's cartographic imagination draws scholars to his wilderness stories in *Go Down, Moses*, where he charts terrain that lies beyond well-mapped American spaces.[1] Critics interested in Faulkner's more populated areas pursue a contrasting line of inquiry: comparing Faulkner's fictional county to the map and history of Lafayette County, Mississippi. Recently, however, Joseph Urgo reinstates fiction, not the resemblance to real places, as the chief lens through which to interpret Faulkner's maps. In Faulkner's work, Urgo claims, "places are subverted by narrative."[2] Faulkner inscribes on his maps the sites of major narrative events, which jockey for space among geographical landmarks. As Urgo argues, Faulkner's map "reconceptualizes what one expects a map to tell."[3] And yet, for all that Urgo is right to reclaim Faulkner's maps for fiction, Faulkner has built his fictional county atop a real one, subject to the same rules of geography and carrying much of the same history. Underplaying that connection detracts from the maps' very real benefits to minor and disenfranchised characters. Their stories rarely emerge in full force through words, but their routes complete the stories they are not given room to tell.

Some of the most remarkable mapping of *Go Down, Moses* is done by Faulkner's Black characters, as they remap familiar places within Yoknapatawpha County. Rather than attempt to rival the dominant voices of their world, they articulate their narrative arc through the Faulknerian landscape that has been established by the dominant narratives—but not defined by them. Although Urgo rightly reasserts the priority of narrative as the engine behind Faulkner's cartography, it is precisely because Faulkner's map links Yoknapatawpha to real history and geography that his disenfranchised Black characters can map their own stories within and around those of more narratively and socially prominent characters.

Marginalized people do not exhibit simply a "defiance of place" in Faulkner's texts, as Urgo suggests,[4] but rather a manipulation of it. They maintain their ground by holding the primary storytellers to the nonfictional nature of their terrain. In doing so, the marginalized characters reassert the priority of a truth and a world outside that of the white man's word. Their mapped narratives may not be visible for many generations of readers, but their optimistic mapping anticipates the archaeological investment of future generations who seek to unearth such stories.

The scholars who are collaborating to map Faulkner's fiction for *Digital Yoknapatawpha* (*DY*) regularly confront just how much a cartographer's perspective matters. The maps that can be sketched from Faulkner's fiction reflect the storyteller's lens rather than objective reality, but the occasional nod to geography lends the teller's story a sheen of factuality. The geographical constraints on such storytellers, however, reveal the work of often-silent Black characters who move within these white-narrated worlds. By recording data that helps readers reinterpret geography through the lens of particular characters, rather than simply those who tell or dominate the main narrative, *DY* remaps the space of Yoknapatawpha through the movement of characters such as the enslaved Tomey's Turl and his twentieth-century successor Rider. Their running takes readers to parts of Yoknapatawpha that seem off the map but that demand to be counted even though such characters are often discounted as storytellers. Precisely because *DY* charts the tension between fiction and reality, it can help readers notice what the subjective narrative obscures about the paths of the Black men and women who move within such stories.

The first time I taught Faulkner's story "Was," the first in the novel *Go Down, Moses*, I was pleased my students relaxed into its humor. But their laughter died when someone referred to Tomey's Turl as a "runaway slave." I saw the horror spread as my students realized they had taken as comedy something that was now recategorized as Serious American History. Even more experienced Faulkner readers have difficulty determining an appropriate posture toward the stories in *Go Down, Moses*. The aesthetics of the chase in "Was" argue for comedy: Uncle Buck is "crouched on the big horse, his little round head and his gnarled neck thrust forward," so that he and his horse "looked exactly like a big black hawk with a sparrow riding it."[5] And yet readers are haunted by the words of the storytelling deputy in "Pantaloon in Black," who also bids for laughs by making his subject out to be an animal. In comparing the character Rider and his fellow African Americans to "a damn herd of wild buffaloes" (150), the deputy manufactures comedy by denying a Black man's grief.

Readers and critics do not want to replicate the deputy's mistake. But how do we read rightly the movements of Tomey's Turl in "Was" and Rider in "Pantaloon in Black"? Where the storyteller's tone is in conflict with social reality, Faulkner allows the running men to define their stories through the maps they create with their movement. Although both narratives are thematically structured as hunts—dogs, guns, and all—Tomey's Turl and Rider display something of Faulkner's cartographic sensibilities in plotting their runs.

In *Digital Yoknapatawpha*, each text is mapped individually, so that discrepancies between texts are evident as readers compare maps. Contributors to the project are bound by the rules of the real world: traveling time, consistency, mileage, etc.[6] But when such maps are combined into a single visual representation, as on Faulkner's 1945 hand-drawn map for the *Portable Faulkner* volume, characters and stories from different fictional times coexist, facilitating a kind of temporal permeability for readers who view the map. Stephen Railton and Christopher Rieger have analyzed Faulkner's maps on the *DY* site, where they offer a range of maps that users can compare and even overlay with one another, prompting comparisons of Faulkner's maps and the ones created for the *DY* database. Railton and Rieger articulate Faulkner's motive in capturing his fiction in a single map: "Faulkner's main ambition in the 1945 map is clearly to find a place inside Yoknapatawpha for all the selections in the *Portable Faulkner*, no matter how imperfect the fit."[7] The characters Tomey's Turl and Rider echo their author's effort, attempting to create an identity for themselves by drawing out the relations among families and stories from disparate narratives and eras. The *DY* project helps readers see where and how the textual description pulls against tidy union on a map; that tension also helps readers see how characters, caught in an unforgiving landscape carved by interests other than their own, attempt to reclaim some of Faulkner's mapping magic.

Tomey's Turl's and Rider's runs lie on either side of the Civil War, but both have reason to run: Tomey's Turl to escape slavery, and Rider to escape prison or lynching. Neither character runs, however, in order to escape. Although the deputy in "Pantaloon" expects Rider to flee north to Tennessee, Rider is discovered asleep in the yard of his own house. His eventual lynching takes place in a gap in the narrative, as the story breaks down around such a gruesome act. But Rider has ensured that his story is mapped within Yoknapatawpha County; he will not allow himself to be sent to Jackson, where injustice can occur off the map. In the earlier story, "Was," Tomey's Turl intends to return to the McCaslin plantation after winning his bride in an escapade that is framed as a fox hunt. The problem with the metaphor of the hunt is that it assumes two conflicting goals: the hunter hopes for an arc of return, but the prey hopes for a straight shot to freedom. Tomey's Turl occupies the place of the fox, but he is no prey. Not only is he hunting a bride to take home, he uses the fox role as a lure, so that the man who hunts him will be ensnared in a marriage of his own. In these two stories, Tomey's Turl and Rider upend expectation by making return the goal of their running. They become map-makers amidst a sea of storytellers. Both characters use cultural expectations to cement new identities, a tactic drawn from Frederick Douglass in the real fight against slavery in America. In his famous speech, "What to the Slave Is the Fourth of July?" Douglass draws on the very laws that threaten a Black man in order to make his case:

> Must I undertake to prove that the slave is a man? . . . The slaveholders themselves . . . acknowledge it when they punish disobedience on the part of the slave. There are seventy-two crimes in the State of Virginia, which, if committed by a black man . . . subject him to the punishment of death. . . . What is this but the acknowledgement that the slave is a moral, intellectual, and responsible being? . . . When you can point to any such laws, in reference to the beasts of the field, then I may consent to argue the manhood of the slave.[8]

Like the narrators of Faulkner's *Go Down, Moses*, Douglass employs animals in his rhetoric, but he does so in order to contrast animals with men, both Black and white:

> When the dogs in your streets, when the fowls of the air, when the cattle on your hills, when the fish of the sea, and the reptiles that crawl, shall be unable to distinguish the slave from a brute, *then* will I argue with you that the slave is a man![9]

Although both Tomey's Turl and Rider understand their running will be read as an attempt to escape punishment, they manipulate others' assumptions that desperation motivates their movement. Rider and Tomey's Turl make use of such assumptions to craft an identity that is, surprisingly, grounded in family and community ties.

## Tomey's Turl

Tomey's Turl's mapping in the story "Was" takes advantage of Sophonsiba Beauchamp's own remapping of her plantation. Does Tomey's Turl run off to the Beauchamp plantation, or does he run off to the Warwick estate? Warwick is what Sophonsiba calls the Beauchamps' plantation, in a nod to "the place in England that she said Mr Hubert was probably the true earl of" (5). Here the fabric of Faulkner's fiction gets quite thin, as he implicitly links the Oxford, Mississippi, on which Jefferson is modeled to Oxford, United Kingdom, which is only fifty miles from Warwick Castle. When scholars map the Beauchamp plantation for *Digital Yoknapatawpha*, they follow the commonsense Jefferson townsperson's proclivity for illustrative names. But Sophonsiba's renaming obscures the plantation's ownership and location and, with them, Tomey's Turl's whereabouts. In the midst of the chase, Faulkner's narrative drags its feet, pausing to unfurl the story she has wrapped around her plantation:

> [F]or a while Tomey's Turl didn't seem to be at Mr Hubert's either. . . . [T]his was what Miss Sophonsiba was still reminding people was named Warwick even when they had already known for a long time that's what she aimed to have it called, until when they wouldn't call it Warwick she wouldn't even seem to know what they were talking about and it would sound as if she and Mr Hubert owned two separate plantations covering the same area of ground, one on top of the other. (9)

Warwick is a convenient fiction not only for Sophonsiba, but also for her brother, who is in no hurry to let Uncle Buck return home to safety. It is to Sophonsiba's reimagined space that Tomey's Turl runs; in some of the few words he utters in the narrative, he declares, "I got more protection than whut Mr Hubert got even. . . . [J]ust get the womenfolks to working at it" (12–13). Warwick is a fiction that facilitates Sophonsiba's aristocratic airs (à la Countess Sophonsiba) but, because it is also a reference to a real place, it plays a key role in Tomey's Turl's plans. If the Beauchamps transform their plantation into Warwick Castle, originally built by William the Conqueror in 1068, they should abide by English laws, which, at the time of Sophonsiba's pretensions, prohibit slavery on English soil and throughout the British Empire. Here the tension between fiction and reality comes to the foreground. If, as Urgo argues, places are subverted by narrative, then it still remains to be seen precisely how much the events of the real world accompany the reference to place within the fictional narrative. Sophonsiba's appropriation only makes sense as the result of inferences drawn from the real world. But when she or the reader also remembers the Somerset Case of 1772, England's Slave Trade Act of 1807, and the Slavery Abolition Act of 1833—that last in the year of Tomey's Turl's birth—suddenly the question of whether we are on English soil or American becomes a pressing matter. Can you have your aristocratic airs and your slavery, too?

With the specter of the title of Earl of Warwick hanging in the background, "Mr Hubert said he not only wouldn't buy Tomey's Turl, he wouldn't have that damn white half-McCaslin on his place even as a free gift" (6). Given the history of the McCaslin family, which unfolds over the course of *Go Down, Moses*, one assumes that it is Tomey's Turl's white blood that disturbs Hubert Beauchamp. Given the racial history that is dredged up by the contrast between British and American positions on enslavement in the middle of the nineteenth century, however, it may well be Tomey's Turl's Black blood that unnerves Beauchamp. Faulkner's phrase is not, as one would expect, "that damn half-white McCaslin," but rather "that damn white half-McCaslin." Beauchamp insists on the man's whiteness, and only qualifies his McCaslin-ness. Tomey's Turl's being half-Black would mean that the purported Earl of Warwick was contemplating international slave trading, which was abolished by both the United States and England in 1807. If Buck and Buddy McCaslin do not fetch Tomey's Turl, Beauchamp will have to bring Tomey's Turl and Sophonsiba—and, by extension, Warwick and all of the cultural baggage that it suggests—to the McCaslins. In doing so, he would, under the fiction constructed by Sophonsiba, create an international incident. So it matters just how much Beauchamp flirts with Sophonsiba's idea that the plantation is its own little kingdom.

Thadious M. Davis calls Tomey's Turl's run a "mockery of escape,"[10] since his work to procure a wife will only tie him more firmly to plantation life. Cleanth Brooks characterizes Tomey's Turl's run as a "ritual, rather than a practical act," since it is clear that "this is no Uncle-Tom's-Cabin-style pursuit of an Eliza trying to escape over the ice."[11] Indeed, when Cass Edmonds looks out at the Beauchamp yard, "Tomey's Turl wasn't even running" (12); "It wasn't any race at all" (14). The fact that this is a non-race, with a non-runner, prompts most critics to dismiss the run as a joke. They attend, instead, to the poker game at the end of the story.[12] I would not discount the significance of that event; by asking "Who dealt these cards, Amodeus?" (28), Hubert Beauchamp acknowledges that, whatever his hand, he must still reckon with the dealer.

Critics' emphasis on the conclusion of "Was," however, obscures an important piece in Tomey's Turl's act of reclamation. Tomey's Turl risks accusations of theft in using a mule to force his observer to recognize—in the visual language of the time—a *man*, rather than runaway property. But he does not use the mule's relative speed and stamina to pass beyond the McCaslin sphere of influence, where his parentage is well known if not publicly acknowledged. Just as he uses Sophonsiba's pretensions to his advantage, he uses slaveholders' distaste for miscegenation against Hubert Beauchamp. If he travels too far, those he encounters will know nothing of his blood inheritance. Only by choosing his distance wisely, as he travels twenty-two miles to a plantation where his name has currency, does he wring some advantage from his situation. Here he carefully invokes both the real-world significance of Sophonsiba's fanciful mapping and the significance of the McCaslin name and history within his fictional region. For Tomey's Turl, connections to the McCaslin family can be mapped and exploited in service of a love story, as he seeks the woman he will eventually marry.[13] Perhaps most importantly, however, his insistent remapping helps him reclaim the very land that Ike McCaslin will relinquish. If, as Ike believes, "the earth was no man's but all men's" (4), it is still the case that, when the story begins, the white men only run in response to Tomey's Turl. One gets the sense that they will only move when they are forced to do so, which has serious implications for other forms of social progress. "Uncle Buddy never went anywhere" (6), we read, but he will visit the Beauchamps in this story because of Tomey's Turl's planning. Davis reads Tomey's Turl through game theory;[14] Richard Godden argues that his run evokes the Great Migration to the north.[15] I would, however, turn to the map Faulkner drew of Yoknapatawpha County and suggest that Tomey's Turl and Rider reclaim the land and their place on it through their manipulation of both reality and the fiction that saturates it.

## Rider

In "Pantaloon in Black," Rider tests the fictional nature of Faulkner's Yoknapatawpha in much the same way that Tomey's Turl tests Sophonsiba's "Warwick" gloss on the Beauchamp plantation. Can Faulkner's fictional county reflect the real South on which it is based, or will Faulkner swerve to a more optimistic rendering of race relations when he has an opportunity to do so? Is culture changing fast enough to uphold the laws and conventions of Faulkner's America in 1940? Or are there lingering fictions that prevent such change from taking hold? Sophonsiba is not the only one suffused with Anglophilic aspirations; Faulkner once dressed himself and his family in "imperial drag" for a hunt, and was photographed in the attire of an English lord.[16] Although Sophonsiba never succeeds in getting others to call her plantation "Warwick," Faulkner's map for the *Portable Faulkner* notes that the Native American inhabitants "had learned to call [the land] 'The Plantation' just like the white men did."[17] Sean Latham argues that this addition to the map reveals the "provisional" nature of

Faulkner's new map, as it accommodates new names and landmarks.[18] But it also indicates that a new set of guiding principles about ownership and hierarchy enters Yoknapatawpha. No later map indicates that those principles are superseded by new ones after Emancipation, and nothing about Faulkner's person, as he performs the role of an English landlord on the steps of an antebellum Mississippi home, suggests an updated set of mapping guidelines as we near the middle of the twentieth century. Although Ike McCaslin relinquishes his plantation inheritance, Faulkner remains, as he wrote on his 1936 map, "sole owner and proprietor" of Yoknapatawpha County.[19]

Although Rider does not live under slavery or even sharecropping, his concerted efforts to remap his life after his wife's death enable him to see that the habits of plantation life continue to define his world. Though he is not "mappable" through genealogical ties to Faulkner's Beauchamp and McCaslin families, he does rent land from Carothers Edmonds (133). As a result, he is interpreted by many readers in part through his relationship to the land. How can the land "mean" if not tied to the stories of those families? And can Rider get caught in those stories even if they are not his own? Rider challenges the significance of the event-saturated map Faulkner has drawn. Rider's story mocks the implicit emphasis on change that such events chart, as the map markings trace the decades since Emancipation. There, his story argues, is the "fiction" for which Faulkner will be held accountable: that change is coming, however gradually it does so. Within *Go Down, Moses* Faulkner plants a challenge to his own narrative, one that aligns him uncomfortably with Sophonsiba Beauchamp. Both insist on a grandeur, whether of the aristocracy or of human nature, that presumes eventual triumph. But, as with Tomey's Turl's, Rider's challenge finds its mark.

In "Pantaloon in Black," Rider's run is prompted by the loss of his wife. He leaves the cemetery, "stepping over the three-strand wire fence without even breaking his stride, and crosse[s] the road and enter[s] the woods" (133). His initial response anticipates the association of woods with escape in the three *Go Down, Moses* stories that follow Rider's. The woods he enters are nothing like the sprawl near Major de Spain's nineteenth-century camp in "The Bear," a forest that will be sold to a lumber company much like the one at which Rider is now employed. But Rider's turn to the woods suggests that there he will find relief. It offers a temporary reprieve from reader's eyes, as Faulkner stops short of the seemingly unmarked, unmeasured woods that Rider enters. Instead of following him, the narrative waits for him to re-emerge so as to capture what drew him back: the hope of seeing Mannie's footprints, other impressions of her on the world they shared, and her ghost in their home. Rider disregards the roads that score the map, but like Tomey's Turl, whose escapes echo the regularity of the seasons, he also reappears, knitting together the different locations of his world.

Rider's run conjures the different paths of his life over its distinct stages: childhood, bachelorhood, and the six months of his relationship with Mannie. He has no category for the narrative's present day, when he is bereaved, but his tendency to read his life in patterns, habits, and movement forces him to recognize just how easy it would be for him to return to old ways, spending his money on gambling and women. In his run, Rider finally joins all of the identities that have followed him under different names: "Spoot" from his aunt, "Rider" from the "men he worked with and the bright dark nameless women he had taken in course and forgotten" (146), and, in a suggestive ellipsis, whatever name he developed after his marriage to Mannie.

Rider's strides map an internal struggle, as he seeks evidence of his wife but also freedom from the social constrictions that remain after her death. This conflict prompts him to seek relief in the woods but will not let him rest there, so that his breathing sounds "like someone engaged without arms in prolonged single combat" (138). In a challenge to the escape that seems possible in "The Old People," "The Bear," and "Delta Autumn," Rider's prolonged combat with the landscape prepares the reader both to appreciate and to criticize the freedoms of the subsequent wilderness stories. To run to the wilderness is also to turn away from the losses that dot the landscape of one's home. In order to escape the economic and social system he is recognizing for the first time, Rider would need to leave behind any trace of his wife, a cost that proves too great.

Only now, early in his grief, does Rider recognize how much his life has been bound up in rhythms not of his own making. Faulkner draws out the web of roads and business exchanges that bind Rider to a history of confinement and exploitation he never sought or recognized. Realizing for the first time how much of his pre-Mannie life was consumed by an empty rotation of work and leisure, Rider fights to retain the impression of her influence on his world, from the freshly washed overalls he wears to the lane he walks, where he sees

> the pale, powder-light, powder-dry dust of August from which the long week's marks of hoof and wheel had been blotted by the strolling and unhurried Sunday shoes, with somewhere beneath them, vanished but not gone, fixed and held in the annealing dust, the narrow, splay-toed prints of his wife's bare feet where on Saturday afternoons she would walk to the commissary to buy their next week's supplies . . . and bank the rest of the money in Edmonds' safe and return. (133–34)

Rider has to make her legible to others, and he must do so in a world that, he realizes, thinks only in the routes of trade and work and merchants. It is not a world that will recognize the new value he began to place on money when he was married, as distinct from a bachelor life in which he "had not actually needed the money" he earned, "when a lot of what he wanted, needed perhaps, didn't cost money," so that he was ready to throw his funds at "dice and whisky" (134). When Rider sees Mannie, he says, "Ah'm thu wid all dat," and money becomes newly significant, as he returns home from payday to "ring the bright cascade of silver dollars onto the scrubbed table" (134). What he sees in the road are his wife's footprints when she would gather those silver dollars and walk to buy weekly supplies "and bank the rest."

The promise of gradual improvement, born of domestic bliss and fiscal prudence, is the map that Rider seeks, and the passages that characterize it contain some of the story's most lyrical language. But equally important to Rider's run is the sudden halt of any dreams of improvement through domesticity: "when he put his hand on the gate it seemed to him suddenly that there was nothing beyond it. The house had never been his anyway, but now even the new planks and sills and shingles, the hearth and stove and bed, were all a part of the memory of somebody else" (135). Just as Tomey's Turl makes use of the Warwick fiction mapped onto the Beauchamp plantation, Rider is torn between competing visions of the house before him. Which is the fiction? His improvements to the house are imperiled by the fragility of his claim to it—it "had never been his anyway"—and neither his labor nor his money will enable him to separate the house and its memories from the white-owned plantation. Although he is a free man, unlike Tomey's Turl, the money Rider earns is revealed as a false way of distinguishing the present from slavery past.

Rider's economic investment remains invisible, a state that threatens to render his wife's footprints and weekly investment in their future similarly unmappable. The map, as Elizabeth Duvert argues, is "spatialized time" or "Faulkner's image of reality as shaped by the history of place."[20] Sean Latham describes the 1936 map Faulkner drew for *Absalom, Absalom!* as "a visual synthesis of Faulkner's earlier fiction."[21] The map may reflect Faulkner's organizational priorities, as Duvert argues, but in placing Jefferson and its courthouse at the center of the map,[22] Faulkner highlights a mode of legal authority that is not the driving form of "justice" employed in Rider's narrative, either by him or by those who seek revenge for the murder he commits. Although Rider is lynched, the narrative elides the event; instead, the second half of the story reflects the narrating deputy sheriff's inclination to report primarily the events that take place in town at the jail, which is also where his story concludes. The deputy replicates Faulkner's own mapping priorities, in returning again and again to a courthouse square that is merely an empty promise of legal authority. That prioritization of the legal and commercial centers is not one that the editors of *Digital Yoknapatawpha* intend to replicate uncritically. As Rider's own effortful running makes clear, what is significant in his story will not be found at the jail or the commissary, and so he must wrench the story in his direction by interweaving white fictions and Black reality.

Through his movement in "Pantaloon in Black," Rider links the home he shared with his wife and the home of the aunt who raised him to the sawmill where he works, repositioning labor between the bookends of familial life. In shifting the emphasis from work or escape to family connection, Rider echoes Tomey's Turl's routes to Tennie. But Rider also draws on the mapping legacy of Tomey's Turl's grandmother, Eunice, whose insistence on death as the appropriate response to wrongdoing forces the white storytellers, Buck and Buddy McCaslin, to inscribe her intentions in the ledger that contains her name and price. Even as, like Tomey's Turl, Rider rewrites the map of his own actions to inscribe his love for a woman, he uses those same actions to prompt a rewriting or a reconsideration in the white storyteller. When Eunice's death is corrected from "*Drownd in Crick Cristmas Day 1832*" (255) to "*Drownd herself*" (256), both place and story are marked as deviations from the familiar white narrative. Sean Latham sums up the racialized expectations for characters in Faulkner's narratives when he refers to "the deluded suicide of a character like Quentin or the mute endurance of the black characters."[23] Significantly, Rider draws on Eunice's refusal of mute endurance; both he and she claim an action that is coded white, so as to ensure that Black men's and women's grief will be registered on a white map. Rider will add an additional wrinkle to Eunice's tactic, provoking the reader to recognize in his murder of Birdsong a suicidal impulse. In doing so, he reclaims from white prejudice not only Black grief but also Black criminality. Rider is out not only to rescript his own run but also to challenge the white map that makes his wife's prints so hard for others to see. In seeking reunion with Mannie in death, Rider also makes her influence visible to all who remain; his violent disruption of the white world moves his community one step closer to the good life he had known with Mannie, one without Saturday-night gambling losses.

Like Eunice's interpreters, Rider's storyteller, an unsympathetic white deputy, is driven to ask questions, prompted by the seemingly nonsensical actions of the Black man. In Eunice's case, Buck McCaslin scrawls, "*Who in hell ever heard of a niger drownding him self*" (256). The boy Ike, reading the ledgers, is prompted to ask "*But why? But why?*" Such questions drive Ike to uncover more of his family ties to the Beauchamp lineage. The deputy sheriff in Rider's story, on the other hand, uses questions to make Rider seem inhuman, as a rhetorical means of forestalling commentary from his listener. As the deputy asks at the beginning of his story, "Because why? Because they aint human" (149). However, he concludes his story with a plea for his audience's attention, "And what do you think of that?" (154). The deputy's questions acknowledge points of incoherence in his own story. They are incoherent not in terms of the Black character's actions but rather in terms of the narrative map that their white observers have drawn. Like Hubert Beauchamp's question, "Who dealt these cards, Amodeus?" (28), the deputy's questions drive characters and readers to a reconsideration of the Black man or woman who not only acts but also shapes the narrative being told. In all three cases, the stories that emerge place the Black man or woman in tension with the lingering expectations of slavery. Although Eunice's actions take place deep in slave history, they offer Rider a means of claiming deliberate action, rather than accident, as the impetus for maps both white and Black, fictional and historical.

*Digital Yoknapatawpha* records not natural landscapes but man-made ones that reflect the Faulknerian stories' emphasis on commerce and plantation life; this is the map against which Rider inscribes his own, as he runs to his aunt's house, "passing the black-and-silver yawn of the sandy ditch where he had played as a boy" (145). He finds himself "altering his course each time a lighted window came into sight" (138). In navigating field, wood, home, childhood, swamp, and mill, Rider fights for a story that is not a ready part of the *DY* framework, which reflects the significance of the Compsons and McCaslins in Faulkner's fiction. But in its adherence to real-world features and spaces beyond the domesticated ones, *DY* gives Rider room to run. Like Tomey's Turl, Rider's run from home and work enables him to inscribe in the landscape his personal agency, and his unwillingness to remain on the roads that reflect white commercial priorities.

*Digital Yoknapatawpha* does, of course, reflect Faulkner's narrative emphasis on plantations and the courthouse square. But *DY* also enables readers to trace routes that steer clear of such locations. *DY* can represent data as it is focalized through the character Rider, or it can offer maps of the story "Pantaloon in Black" that, because of their need to maintain real-world consistency, preserve the woods and fields through which Rider runs. They do so even when those fields are not mentioned by a deputy sheriff who is reluctant to venture outside the jail.

Readers may be used to gathering around the storytellers of a narrative, seeing along with them. But Faulkner's and now *Digital*

*Yoknapatawpha*'s cartography demands that readers take seriously the movements of characters as an interpretive tool. By claiming movement, not escape, to attest to their agency, Tomey's Turl and Rider undermine yet one more fiction that lurks beneath their stories: the presumption that Black men and women can be driven from the South under the pretense of liberty. In mapping courses that remain within Yoknapatawpha, Tomey's Turl and Rider make it possible to see the link between Black characters and the land as something more than the relic of forced labor.

NOTES

1. For example, see Robert W. Hamblin, "Beyond the Edge of the Map: Faulkner, Turner, and the Frontier Line," *Faulkner in the Twenty-First Century: Faulkner and Yoknapatawpha, 2000,* ed. Robert W. Hamblin and Ann J. Abadie (Jackson: University Press of Mississippi, 2003), 154–71.

2. Joseph R. Urgo, "William Faulkner's Map of the Unseen World, Yoknapatawpha County," *Literature and Belief* 24, no. 1–2 (2004): 45.

3. Urgo, "William Faulkner's Map of the Unseen World," 60.

4. Joseph R. Urgo, "The Yoknapatawpha Project: The Map of a Deeper Existence," *Mississippi Quarterly* 57, no. 4 (2004): 643.

5. William Faulkner, *Go Down, Moses,* rev. ed. (1942; repr., New York: Vintage International, 1990), 8. Hereafter cited parenthetically in the text.

6. Stephen Railton and Christopher Rieger, "Faulkner Mapping/Mapping Faulkner," *Digital Yoknapatawpha* (University of Virginia, 2017). http://faulkner.iath.virginia.edu, accessed November 18, 2018. "[W]e follow the text rather than his maps to establish locations on the maps" (Railton).

7. Railton and Rieger, "Faulkner Mapping/Mapping Faulkner."

8. Frederick Douglass, "What to the Slave Is the Fourth of July?" in *The Norton Anthology of American Literature, Shorter Eighth Edition, Beginnings to 1865,* ed. Nina Baym (New York: W. W. Norton, 2013), 1004.

9. Douglass, "What to the Slave Is the Fourth of July?," 1004.

10. Thadious M. Davis, *Games of Property: Law, Race, Gender, and Faulkner's* Go Down, Moses (Durham, NC: Duke University Press, 2003), 62.

11. Cleanth Brooks, *William Faulkner: The Yoknapatawpha Country* (1963; repr., Baton Rouge: Louisiana State University Press, 1990), 246.

12. See, in particular, David W. Robinson and Caren J. Town, "'Who Dealt These Cards?': The Excluded Narrators of *Go Down, Moses,*" *Twentieth-Century Literature* 37, no. 2 (1991): 192–206.

13. Tennie Beauchamp's entry in the McCaslin ledgers in section four of "The Bear" includes this addition: "*Marrid to Tomys Turl 1859*" (259).

14. Davis, *Games of Property,* 26.

15. Richard Godden, *William Faulkner: An Economy of Complex Words* (Princeton, NJ: Princeton University Press, 2007). As Godden notes, Tomey's Turl and Rider may be "contained within narratives of pursuit and capture," "but in every case apprehension serves a black purpose" (88). Despite the circular patterns of movement evident in the narrative, Godden insists that this is part of the larger narrative of migration.

16. Sean Latham, "An Impossible Resignation: William Faulkner's Post-Colonial Imagination," in *A Companion to William Faulkner*, ed. Richard C. Moreland (Oxford, UK: Blackwell, 2006), 267.

17. William Faulkner, "1945 Map of Yoknapatawpha," *Digital Yoknapatawpha*, http://faulkner.iath.virginia.edu/media/resources/MANUSCRIPTS/WFMAP4.html, accessed November 1, 2018.

18. Latham, "An Impossible Resignation," 266.

19. William Faulkner, "1936 Map of Yoknapatawpha," *Digital Yoknapatawpha*, http://faulkner.iath.virginia.edu/media/resources/MANUSCRIPTS/WFMAP2.html, accessed May 8, 2019.

20. Elizabeth Duvert, "Faulkner's Map of Time," *Faulkner Journal* 2 (1986): 14.

21. Latham, "An Impossible Resignation," 252.

22. For further discussion, see Duvert, "Faulkner's Map of Time," 15.

23. Latham, "An Impossible Resignation," 253.

# Playing Monopoly with William Faulkner

## Tim Armstrong

Begin with a fable. There is a dutiful burial; a young man goes on an eventful journey and returns to receive a blessing. There is a woman, later a wife, imprisoned in the hands of the "demon of lust." There is a guardian angel who claims to be a kinsman and collects some money owed. And there is a magic fish. This is the apocryphal Book of Tobit, that touching story that is the subject of so many renaissance paintings (apocryphal if you are Jewish or Protestant; it is in the Orthodox and Catholic canons). Faulkner liked to refer to Yoknapatawpha as an "apocryphal" geography—the word actually means "hidden" or "obscured"—and the fact that many readers may have thought the text summarized above was *The Reivers*, with its funeral, journey, brothel, and magic sardine, suggests a certain parallel.[1] We might, at a stretch, see Boon and Lucius Priest as a redistributed Tobias, even in their names, Corrie as Sarah, and Ned as an admittedly unlikely archangel Raphael, saving the day.

I will loop slowly back to Faulkner's last novel. But here is another image, admittedly unlikely. It is a quiet evening at Rowan Oak in the 1940s, and the Faulkners pull from the cupboard an item most of us know from childhood: a Monopoly board. They throw the dice and begin (in America at least) their clockwise circuits of Atlantic City: Mediterranean Avenue, Baltic Avenue, Reading Railroad.

I start with a journey and a square because I want to raise the issues of shape and trajectory. Canonical readings of Faulkner often work in the spirit of Jean-Paul Sartre's memorable comment on *The Sound and the Fury*: "[T]he story does not unfold; we discover it under each word, like an obscene and obstructing presence, more or less condensed."[2] Meaning is like a toad under every stone, rather than like a racehorse one might follow with one's more distant gaze. The resultant readings involve the hermeneutics of suspicion turned to the utmost screw: nod and you might miss a clue to Charles Bon's status, or Buddy's concealed desires. The justification for that critical mode is in origin Malcolm

Cowley's: that Faulkner's ideologically fractured works display clues to what is hidden, even—or perhaps particularly—from their author. I have no real dispute with that. But I also want to propose a mode of reading that looks at things in plain sight: the apocryphal *shapes* of Faulkner's texts and the cultural poetics of in-forming shapes and emblems evoked *in* his texts:[3] topology rather than topography, the mathematical study of mappable shapes (the discourse networks examined by Charles Hannon under the heading of "topology" in a recent collection are somewhat mislabeled in that respect).[4] So I will consider, with a sometimes deliberately blurred vision, how a square of land might be like a jail cell, or a postage stamp.

The topic of this collection is slavery. Given that we never see in Faulkner's work a fully developed representation of the subjectivity of a slave, what we are often dealing with are the apocryphal traces of slavery, its echoing places, whether present socially and politically in the neo-slavery of sharecropping or in the subjectivity of descendants of slaves and slaveholders. Three general issues relating to slavery will inform the argument here: first, the generalization that the slave is not only denied rights but is, in theory, *without recourse* in law;[5] second, the fact that slavery is often conceptualized in terms of debt, classically a debt to the owner who has spared the slave's life—in the American context, also a debt imposed on the ex-slave for the cost of liberation, but also, potentially, a debt owed in reparation to slaves and their descendants;[6] and third, the link between slave and land.

## The Slave and the Land

Begin with the land. The foundational act of territorial usurpation in Faulkner's corpus is Thomas Sutpen dragging his plantation out of the wilderness wrested from the Chickasaw, evoked in Quentin's opening vision in *Absalom, Absalom!*:

> Immobile, bearded and hand palm-lifted the horseman sat; behind him the wild blacks and the captive architect huddled quietly, carrying in bloodless paradox the shovels and picks and axes of peaceful conquest. Then in the long unamaze Quentin seemed to watch them overrun suddenly the hundred square miles of tranquil and astonished earth and drag house and formal gardens violently out of the soundless Nothing and clap them down like cards upon a table beneath the up-palm immobile and pontific, creating the Sutpen's Hundred, the *Be Sutpen's Hundred* like the oldentime *Be Light*.[7]

There is a topographical imagination at work here because *"the arbitrary square of earth which he had named Sutpen's Hundred"* (132), ten miles by ten miles, is the original space of slavery in Faulkner's texts. And as Scott Romine remarks, this violent "territorial mastery" involved in the planation parallels the author's own writerly appropriation of what he called his "postage stamp of native soil."[8] (We will return to the gambling motif—the "cards upon a table"—later in this essay.)

In the South, the boundaries of the estates so created were, axiomatically, also lines of power and policing. As part of what Ted Atkinson calls "the racialization of space and the spatialization of race," slaves were restricted to the farm on which they worked, crossing roads only with permission.[9] If Reconstruction notionally detaches the slave from the land, at least briefly—witness the disturbing spectacle of shuffling, starving slaves on the road in *The Unvanquished*—the post-Reconstruction period re-forges that link, its controls and mutual dependencies, in the form of vagrancy laws, prison labor, and sharecropping.[10] Faulkner typically sees slaves and their immediate descendants as attached to the land in this way, propping up the Compsons, living on as tenants. Indeed, one could see an ideological formation in Faulkner's distrust of those who wander too far, like Percival Brownlee and Butch Beauchamp in *Go Down, Moses*—though in the latter book Ike does suggest to the unnamed mother of Roth's child that she go north.

In southern ideology, the link between slavery and land was underpinned by "thermal law," binding together a climate and an agriculture said to be impossible without slave labor. To some extent, the ideology that attached slaves to land was also reflected in the actual law; as Thomas D. Morris notes, one legal tradition had intermittently attempted to see slaves as real estate rather than as chattel, a view that would make them subject to different laws in relation to inheritance or the reclaiming of debt. To be real estate is to be tied to land, and thus more closely to the patriarchal values of family and succession, and potentially, to take one implication, to be protected from sale at an owner's death. But Morris's summary is heavily qualified: "For one reason or other rules of real property law were applied to slaves in some instances in over one-third of the jurisdictions that made up the slave South." He stresses that in the nineteenth century slaves were increasingly defined as movables; courts resisted entails, for example, on the basis that they were more suited to the aristocratic succession of the Old World than the mobile capital of the New.[11]

Morris suggests, however, that there was one area in which the residual ideology associated with real estate was more commonly protected. When owners attempted to reclaim slaves, the doctrine of specific performance, more normally applied to land, could be asserted.[12] Just as you could not replace a piece of land integral to your farm with damages, so you could not replace all slaves with market value; they were adapted to the needs and feelings of your family or the farm, the argument ran, so that "damages" did not fully meet their loss. While this doctrine was limited in application and articulated exclusively in the interests of owners, it did, at the margins, acknowledge nonfungibility. Faulkner refers to something like this, commenting through Ike McCaslin on the ledgers in "The Bear," as "the specific tragedy which had not been condoned and could never be amortized."[13] But the fact that this argument often came up where slaves had previously been mortgaged suggests a legal tension between the capitalist gamble of insurance or mortgage and the paternalist ideology of close bonds.

The heading under which I want to consider this issue of the slave and real estate is the "predial," a rather archaic legal term meaning "attached to the soil," from *praedium*, farm. "Predial slaves" were those attached to a farm; the term is also used of Russian serfs and of agricultural tithes. A brief excursion into Common Law might suggest how prediality and the notion of "servitude" are linked. Predial rights in the distinctive Louisiana legal code—a mixture of Napoleonic and Common Law—are defined as attached to a piece of land rather than an owner, as in the case of easements and rights of way. The notion of "servitude" in civil law—a term that was in the first instance used to define slavery—is in fact linked to that of prediality, because if your land has a right of way, railroad, or aqueduct on it, say, you owe a "predial servitude" to someone else.[14] Prediality qualifies and distributes the right of ownership of land to different stakeholders, "dominant" and "subservient," giving a perpetual right to someone other than the ostensible landowner. It thus implies a division within the property held, rather like that which some southern jurists tried to make between the slave's labor, which could be owned, and the slave's person, which could not, but over which an owner was obliged to assert domination to extract that labor.[15]

That is to say that the metaphors involved in land use have a symmetry with the relations involved in slavery. Oliver Wendell Holmes put it this way in *The Common Law* (1881):

> The language of the law of easements was built up out of similes drawn from persons at a time when the *noxae deditio* was still familiar; and then, as often happens, language reacted upon thought, so that conclusions were drawn as to the rights themselves from the terms in which they happened to be expressed. When one estate was said to be enslaved to another . . . men's minds were not alert to see that these phrases were only so many personifying metaphors, which explained nothing unless the figure of speech was true.[16]

For Holmes, this is the echo of a primitive law in which an axe or a bull that has done damage could be sued as persons and surrendered in full recompense (*noxae deditio*)—and implicitly of an equally primitive state of affairs, slavery. As an example of this thinking, Holmes cites the thirteenth-century jurist Henry de Bracton: "The servitude by which land is subjected to [other] land, is made on the likeness of that, by which man is made the slave of man" (385, brackets in original). This, Holmes insists, is a mistaken use of metaphor: land is not a legal person. Nevertheless, the connection between enslavement and predial servitude is established: "It strikes our ear strangely to hear a right of services from an individual called a right of property as distinguished from contract. Still this will be found to have been the way in which such rights were regarded" (388).

So slaves and land can both be subservient to others in particular respects; both involve divided ownership and a relationship that is perpetual and noncontractual. Predial servitude signals an aspect of land over which others have a claim. In the UK such rights might include the right to cut turf, gather wood, or mine for lead; even customary rights to "hold horse-races or to dance on the green" were sometimes placed in this category.[17] My question then becomes: what is the consequence of the breakdown, after 1865, of what Holmes calls the "personifying metaphor" of slavery, in which servitude reverts (in theory) to being contractual? One possible answer, largely unfulfilled in practice and indeed reversed after some early occupation of land by former slaves, was land redistribution, the expression of a claim to the land on the part of the former slave.[18] If slaves and land are like each other, then that relation haunts the land. Faulkner's chiasmus in *The Unvanquished* suggests some of the inversions involved, describing those slaves "who had followed the Yankees away and then returned, to find their families and owners gone, to scatter into the hills and live in caves and hollow trees like animals I suppose, not only with no one to depend on but with no one depending on them . . ." (424).

Faulkner nowhere uses the term "predial." But Charles W. Chesnutt does, writing his sly allegories in the form of conjure tales in the harsh period after Reconstruction. Chesnutt was a court stenographer who passed the Ohio bar, so he was aware of legal categories. In "Mars Jeems's Nightmare," the frame-narrator John refers to the former slave Julius as exercising "predial" rights:

> Toward my tract of land and the things that were on it—the creeks, the swamps, the hills, the meadows, the stones, the trees—he maintained a peculiar personal attitude, that might be called predial rather than

proprietary. He had been accustomed, until long after middle life, to look upon himself as the property of another. When this relation was no longer possible, owing to the war, and to his master's death and the dispersion of the family, he had been unable to break off entirely the mental habits of a lifetime, but had attached himself to the old plantation, of which he seemed to consider himself an appurtenance.[19]

This is in fact a customary claim on the land, as Julius helps himself to grapes and other produce and finds jobs for various relatives. It is close to another common-law servitude: the right of usufruct, which derives from Latin *usus* ("use") and *fructus* ("fruits"); essentially, the right to enjoy use of another's property. In Julius's inset stories we see the haunting, pain-ridden traces of slavery, but also a poetics of resistance as his folktales become a way of asserting an intimate relation to the land.

I think we see a similar persistence of rights in the figure of Lucas Beauchamp and his tenure on the land of successive generations of the Edmonds family. Unlike his grandfather and father, he accepts his morganatic inheritance, the underpayment of an ancestral debt. In *Intruder in the Dust* his tenure is described in explicitly topological terms as a disruption of unitary ownership. Chick ascends

> a savage gash half gully and half road mounting a hill with an air solitary independent and intractable too and then he saw the house, the cabin and remembered the rest of the story, the legend: how Edmonds' father had deeded to his Negro first cousin and his heirs in perpetuity the house and the ten acres of land it sat in—an oblong of earth set forever in the middle of the two thousand-acre plantation like a postage stamp in the center of an envelope.[20]

If the plantation is imagined as a square, Lucas's 1/200th is an encumbrance that presumably limits its value. Legally speaking, his land is an enclave; it involves a predial servitude in that he has a right of access over Edmonds's land, the figure of the "savage gash" alluding to and reversing in small part the violence of the sexual access Lucius Quintus Carothers McCaslin asserted over Beauchamp's grandmother and great-grandmother.

Read literally, the passage above seems a little odd—who puts a stamp at the center of an envelope? It is as if Faulkner is conflating the nonspecific stamp with the specific address that is the mark of occupation or ownership. But it is for that reason that Lucas's tenancy represents a more general claim. A postage stamp is a state-sanctioned fee paid for a service (cruelly evoked in Toni Morrison's character Stamp Paid, who believes he has paid his dues to slavery). To be a stamp, or to be on a stamp, is to command a place. Before the Confederacy issued its own stamps, for several months local offices simply stamped "paid" on envelopes or issued the "Postmaster provisionals" prized by modern collectors, asserting Secession as an abstract square. (*Intruder in the Dust* was published, incidentally, just as the second African American appeared on a stamp, George Washington Carver. The first was Booker T. Washington in the Famous Americans series in 1940, though on the little-used ten-cent stamp.[21] He had been recommended by that avid stamp collector Franklin D. Roosevelt.)

So Lucas's tenure on the land is symbolically fixed, for all that Roth Edmonds threatens to throw him off at one point, and we are to understand that tenure as the acknowledgment of an unacknowledged debt. Richard Godden writes rather curtly that Lucas "sharecrops on Edmonds's land."[22] What "The Fire and the Hearth" in fact says is that after Lucas's marriage to Molly, "McCaslin Edmonds built a house for them and allotted Lucas a specific acreage to be farmed as he saw fit as long as he lived or remained on the place" (Faulkner, *Go Down, Moses*, 85). While Roth Edmonds goes through the motions of overseeing Lucas's farming, he is ignored. As we have seen, in *Intruder in the Dust* the formulas are even firmer: a "deeded" ten acres. We are also told in *Intruder* that Lucas comes to town annually to pay his taxes, not rent, and in *Go Down, Moses* that he has a "solid pride" in his "good tools" (33). So Lucas seems more entrenched than any sharecropper, especially in the context of the unstable situation produced by the 1933 Agricultural Adjustment Act (AAA).

The cost of that entrenchment in the middle of Roth's estate is, as Keith Clark and others have pointed out, a relative isolation from the Black community, and ultimately a kind of solipsism anchored in his sense of himself as the true McCaslin heir. Writing on *Intruder in the Dust*, Richard King describes Lucas rather severely as a "backwater Nietzschean superman, supreme in his indifference to most recognizable human emotions," insisting that his gestures "never attain the status of political action (or talk)."[23] That is in my view to underplay his symbolic role in favor of a rather odd demand; the book is not set in the 1960s. And as Faulkner makes clear, the community, white and Black, is connected to Lucas and to his wife. Alan Nadel usefully suggests that Lucas's silence and imprisonment stage a reenactment of slavery: as he sits in jail, Jefferson must confront its own past as it moves around him.[24]

The legalistic formulas describing Lucas's tenure, resembling those of a will, are interesting. Two have already been cited: "deeded" in *Intruder*; and "live or remain" in "The Fire and the Hearth." The word "remain" and cognates signifying immobility or nonreaction are keynotes of descriptions of Lucas: as Edmonds understands it in an interior monologue in "The Fire and the Hearth," *"If father had beat Lucas, he couldn't have let Lucas stay here even to forgive him. It will only be Lucas who could have stayed because Lucas is impervious to anybody"* (89). The third formula is that Lucas has been given his land by his "McCaslin forbears . . . without recourse for life" (90). Here the source of the deed is shifted from Edmonds to McCaslins (presumably Buck and Buddy), and the formula is a little ambiguous. "Without recourse" in law normally means that when a bill of exchange is transferred or an item sold, the seller assumes no liability; the buyer must live with the way it turns out. Is it that Lucas can make no further claim on his inheritance—unlikely, as he has no legal claim? Rather, it seems that the Edmonds heirs have no recourse. Roth must pay Lucas's bills at the commissary; accept the way Lucas resists modernization; accept the stolen mule; and ultimately in *Intruder in the Dust*, the whole community must accept Lucas's self-assertion and refusal of the debt of Blackness, and acknowledge that he remains.

So if the slave is without recourse, that relation is reversed in Lucas by the assertion of what amounts to predial rights. But perhaps "without recourse" also signals here that the debt he represents cannot be traced back to its origin; nor can it be relinquished or repudiated, to use the terms that Isaac uses to describe his relation to the slave past. As Erik Dussere comments, "Ike's plan to balance the books through his own repudiation of property is ultimately an empty gesture."[25]

## Land as Usufruct

So far I have been pursuing the link between Lucas and the slave's prediality, considered as the inheritance of a conceptual attachment between slave and land. His state is, of course, exceptional: he is recompensed in a minimal way for slavery, where others are not. If prediality implies a claim, it is not honored. Let us rewind to our opening image of Sutpen wresting his ten miles by ten miles from the "wilderness." This is the mathematics of topology, nature parceled and sold like the blocks of ice in Walden Pond. In *Go Down, Moses*, Ike says God "created man to be His overseer on earth and to hold suzerainty over the earth and the animals on it in His name, not to hold for himself and his descendants inviolable title forever, generation after generation, to the oblongs and squares of the earth" (190). Later we have "the untreed land warped and wrung to mathematical squares of rank cotton for the frantic old-world people to turn into shells to shoot at one another" (261).

The squared-off is opposed to that which is "dimensionless," like the stag (153), or to the "myriad" (239, 241, 244), which is the wilderness itself. The question of a share in what is wild is often raised: the swamp men in "The Bear" who turn up and assert an interest in Old Ben because he ate their livestock; Boon's ownership of the seething squirrels; the families who are said to have a share in Boon himself in *The Reivers*. In *Intruder in the Dust*, the link between the mapped square and an original violence is embodied in Vinson Gowrie's family in a way that mirrors Lucas's solitude: they have made their pine hills "into a synonym for independence and violence: an idea with physical boundaries like a quarantine for plague so that solitary unique and alone out of all the county it was known to the rest of the county by the number of its survey co-ordinate—Beat Four" (310). A square number.

But as its readers know, *Go Down, Moses* has in the Big Woods section a discourse that critiques the usurpation of land, that would deny the ownership of land by Black, white, or even Native American. It is first visible in Buck and Buddy's ideas in *The Unvanquished* "about men and land, which Father said people didn't have a name for yet" (352), and in Ike's Old Testament torrent in section 4 of "The Bear."[26] Ike believes that the land "was no man's" (Faulkner, *Go Down, Moses*, 5), a usufruct that should never be parceled up and inherited, so that even Ikkemotubbe, in the original betrayal, knew "that not even a fragment of it had been his to relinquish or sell" (188).

Ike's philosophy is sometimes traced to Rousseau's *Discourse on Inequality*.[27] But a more proximate source for the notion of land as commons, as Dale Breaden pointed out sixty years ago (without anyone really following up on that claim, I think), is the economist and campaigner Henry George.[28] Though less remembered today, George's attack on the exploitation of land ownership and his suggestion of a land tax as a remedy were hugely popular—his funeral in 1897 produced what was described as the largest crowd ever seen in New York, and his influence was still strong in the 1930s. Writing in 1883, just a few years after Reconstruction (and the year of the hunt that kills Old Ben, symbolically closing the wilderness), George links slavery to cheap land, and provides a prescient account of the shift from slavery to sharecropping:

> Chattel slavery . . . only grows up where population is sparse; it never, save by virtue of special circumstances, continues where the pressure of population gives land a high value, for in that case the ownership of land gives all the power that comes from the ownership of men, in more convenient form. . . . English ships carried negro slaves to America, and not to England or Ireland, because in America land was cheap and labor was

valuable, while in western Europe land was valuable and labor was cheap. As soon as the possibility of expansion over new land ceased, chattel slavery would have died out in our Southern States. As it is, Southern planters do not regret the abolition of slavery. They get out of the freedmen as tenants as much as they got out of them as slaves. While as for prædial slavery—the attachment of serfs to the soil—the form of chattel slavery which existed longest in Europe, it is only of use to the proprietor where there is little competition for land. Neither prædial slavery nor absolute chattel slavery could have added to the Irish landlord's virtual ownership of men— to his power to make them work for him without return.[29]

For George, land and labor are simply two aspects of ownership: slavery is needed to break the soil but can be replaced by different forms of servitude. Here is Ike in a comparable mode, on his grandfather who

tamed and ordered or believed he had tamed and ordered it for the reason that the human beings he held in bondage and in the power of life and death had removed the forest from it and in their sweat scratched the surface of it to a depth of perhaps fourteen inches in order to grow something out of it which had not been there before and which could be translated back into the money he who believed he bought it had had to pay to get it and hold it and a reasonable profit too. (188)

Just a little more of squares, with a trajectory added. The game of property we know as Monopoly was in fact first developed, as The Landlord's Game, to illustrate the theories of Henry George. It was patented by a follower of George, Elizabeth Magie, in 1904, as a lesson in the pernicious accumulation involved in land ownership and rent (see fig. 1). In the 1930s, in a deep irony, it was ruthlessly taken over and exploited by Charles Darrow, who became the first board-game millionaire.[30] So the throw of the dice in Monopoly is designed to illustrate a loaded system: it might seem that chance is operating, but whoever manages to get their hands on the land—or the game—wins. We might remember that opening vision of Sutpen clapping house and garden "down like cards upon a table." Another ironic aside here: the game was first marketed in the UK in 1913 (by a Scottish political committee boosting Lloyd George, no relation) as Brer Fox an' Brer Rabbit, as if outside America a subtext could be explicitly identified.[31] It is worth noting that a Black artist, Colin Quashie, has devised a Plantation Monopoly with plantations, a "Confederate Chest," and Underground Railroad stations.[32]

So if he were to have played the game in the 1940s, Faulkner might have recognized in it a system in which control of land is central, whether for the exploitation of labor or, more recently, for receiving handouts from the public chest via the Agricultural Adjustment Acts of 1933 and 1938. He might have also seen something reflecting the gridded topology of some of his own texts, and the way that shapes turn into circuits. We might think of Chick's vision of Miss Habersham trapped by the traffic fleeing town at the end of *Intruder*, riding clockwise like the Monopoly car token, paralleling the squared boundaries of Crossman, Mott, and Okatoba Counties: "*Jefferson's behind you, lady*," to which the reply is, "*I know. I had to detour around an arrogant insufferable old nigger who got the whole county upset trying to pretend he murdered a white man*" (427). There are other circuits, including Gavin Stevens's trajectory around the Jefferson square at the end of *Go Down, Moses*, which I like to think of as anti-clockwise, back to the past like Benjy Compson's, "from store to store and office to office about the square—merchant and clerk, proprietor and employee, doctor dentist lawyer and barber—with his set and rapid speech: 'It's to bring a dead nigger home. It's for Miss Worsham. Never mind about a paper to sign: just give me a dollar. Or half a dollar then. Or a quarter then'" (277). This is a kind of rent, a land tax if you like, another payment relating to the dead land–labor system of slavery.

## Gambling as Recourse

So far I have suggested that the square is an emblem for the linked ownership of land and slave, of an accumulative and a disciplinary system that Lucas Beauchamp both inherits and resists. I have noted that by the early 1940s Faulkner was at least willing to express a theoretical critique of landownership (a critique that recent scholars have seen in environmental terms).[33] He was doing so, as Richard Godden points out, at a time when the land–sharecropper equation was becoming less stable as the subsidies provided by the AAA reduced production and provided funds for mechanization. Sharecroppers were increasingly forced off land without reparation for historical labor.[34]

My question is: how does Faulkner represent that instability, and also the historical debt involved? I pose this question more in the spirit of narrative topology than of politics since, as Eric J. Sundquist and others have pointed out, the explicit politics of the later texts can be problematic (Gavin Stevens's meditations on "Sambo" and his momentary alignment with the Dixiecrat position, for example) and the actual politics of the South continued to offer little to the African American. Faulkner's notorious gradualism—articulated in all those words that we

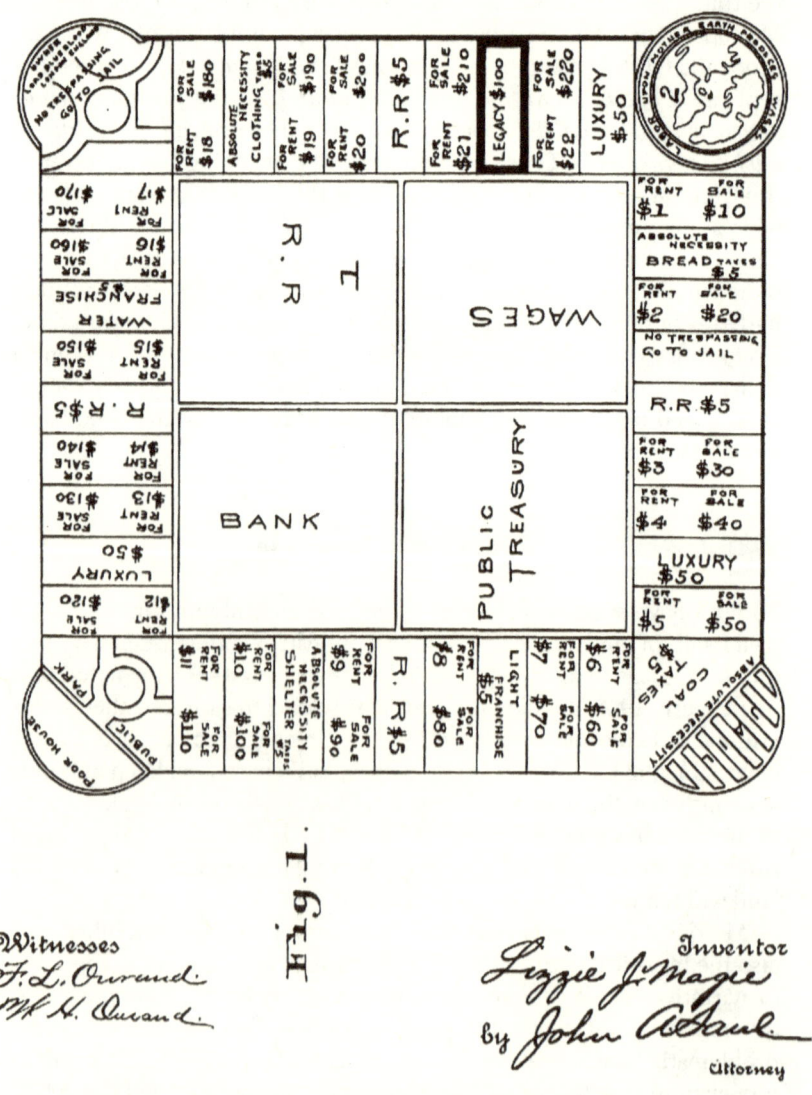

**Fig. 1:** The drawing for patent of the game board of Magie's early version of Monopoly (1904). Source: US National Archives.

know he applied to African Americans "enduring" or "outlasting" or "annealing" their pain—suggest the painfully slow process of southern accommodation, of remaining put but bracketed.[35]

My suggestion here is that Faulkner begins to imagine an almost magical redistribution not unlike those "Chance" cards in Monopoly, where money arrives from nowhere, and that for particular reasons he does so in the form of the gamble. This is an argument that intersects with Eric Dussere's suggestion that Faulkner saw the South's debt to former slaves in terms of gambling, as a debt of honor.[36] Here we typically move from the topology of squares to ellipses or ovals, from the mule to the horse, from the farm to the racetrack. There is also a change in direction: if the Monopoly board works clockwise, rents building steadily with time, racehorses (like human athletes) conventionally race anti-clockwise, against the clock. I want to deal with two elements of the argument separately—first, gambling, and then, briefly, that term *recourse* once more, in a kind of pun—before bringing them together on the race track.

We can consider gambling as a general activity.[37] Gambling was a prominent part of southern culture.[38] As a metaphor for human interaction, it is everywhere in Faulkner: in *Absalom, Absalom!*, for example, Sutpen doles out fragments of his story to Quentin's grandfather "as you might flick the joker out of a pack of fresh cards" (208), and the architect's run, like that of Tomey's Turl in *Go Down, Moses*, is a "gambit" offered in the hunt (212). Though the word *gambit* is often associated with chess, the fact that the architect has a "leg swollen" from a fall might remind us of the origins of the word in wrestling, a tripping with the leg or *gamba*, like Ab Snopes's twist of his injured limb in "Barn Burning." We might also remember the gambit of the miraculous racehorse in *A Fable*: despite its unusable leg it can outrun all competitors. A gambit, then is potentially a weakness overturned.

More specifically, gambling suggests a particular relation to capital. Land and slaves were relatively immobile forms of capital; the $3 billion or so invested in slaves in 1861 is often said to have made the southern economy inflexible and conservative. Gambling in contrast imposes speed and movement on fixed capital. In the words from a French essayist whom Walter Benjamin quotes, "Gambling cares nothing for any secured position. . . . [It] gives short shrift to the weighty past on which work bases itself."[39] The South's gamble in the war produced absolute losses. Whether in Jason's losing stock market gambles in *The Sound and the Fury* or in Rider's deliberately dangerous game in "Pantaloon in Black," gambling signals instability. In the context of the 1930s, gambling can act as a kind of allegorical marker for the uncertainties of free capital.

That instability is figured in "The Fire in the Hearth" in Lucas's obsession with buried gold. It detaches him from the land; he stakes all on his quest, even his marriage. As Molly comments to Edmonds, "when a man that old takes up money-hunting, it's like when he takes up gambling or whisky or women. He aint going to have time to quit" (Faulkner, *Go Down, Moses*, 79–80). Thus Lucas "would inform Edmonds that he had decided to quit farming, was old enough to retire, and for Edmonds to allot his land to someone else to finish the crop" (33). In doing so, he enters a risky economy. It is a capitalized "Chance and Fortune" that is invoked: George Wilkins is involved "not only to do the actual work but as a sort of justice, balance, libation to Chance and Fortune" (31). These words in combination, *fortuna et caso*, are significant—the forces unleashed in what J. G. A. Pocock famously calls the Machiavellian moment, involving a radical contingency that shakes the feudal order but also exposes the individual to the winds of fortune—which for Pocock is both secular history and, in the eighteenth century, unanchored credit. In *The Reivers* it is similarly "Fate—Rumor—gossip" (14) that kicks off the story.[40] In Pocock's formulas, individual virtue attempts to sustain itself amidst the corruption of an unstable public life.[41] Lucas, who has, so far, farmed in the ancient manner, refusing ploughs and crop dusters and capital investment, now tries to borrow the money from Roth for the metal detector (though he has $3,000 in the bank, his slave inheritance), as well as to purloin the mule. The continuity of slave-become-tenant is broken by the shake of the dice, as the South is shaken by the influx of capital in the New Deal.

There is thus an opposition between gambling—money "on which there was no sweat," as Roth Edmonds sees it (95)—and the bound labor of the fields. But that binding is itself unstable, or conceals an instability. In *Absalom, Absalom!* Sutpen's territorial ambition is presented as an alternative to the easy money of gambling:

> He was just twenty-five and a man of twenty-five does not voluntarily undertake the hardship and privation of clearing virgin land and establishing a plantation in a new country just for money . . . in Mississippi in 1833, with a river full of steamboats loaded with drunken fools covered with diamonds and bent on throwing away their cotton and slaves before the boat reached New Orleans. (13)

But that is deceptive, an index of Sutpen's desperate search for establishment: from that opening image of the cards slammed on the table to the later rumors of cotton speculation, Sutpen's story is founded on a gamble. When he returns after the Civil War, the logic is clearer:

> *His was that cold alert fury of the gambler who knows that he may lose anyway but that with a second's flagging of the fierce constant will he is sure to: and who keeps suspense from ever quite crystallising by sheer fierce manipulation of the cards or dice until the ducts and glands of luck begin to flow again.* (133)

Ultimately, this is the cast die of southern history and the slave economy itself, described in that famous Gettysburg passage of *Intruder in the Dust*, in which Gavin Stevens tells us that every southern boy can imagine a counterfactual history in which Pickett's charge might never happen.

The most significant gambles involving slaves are of course Uncle Buck and Buddy's bets over the disposition of Turl, Tennie, and Miss Sophonsiba in *Go Down, Moses*, culminating in a gamble in which, abetted by Turl himself as dealer, Buddy wins Turl a wife and frees Buck from marriage. In *Games of Property*, Thadious M. Davis sees this as part of the set of "games (such as gambling, hunting, courting) in which Blacks are positioned within the legal system of chattel slavery and its aftermath in delimiting legal codes of segregation."[42] That seems right, if a little tersely Foucauldian given the pleasures involved and the fact that the outcome suits even Hubert Beauchamp.[43] When we first meet Buck and Buddy, in *The Unvanquished*, we are told that they are the best gamblers alive and that they would bet slaves and "wagon-loads of cotton with one another on the turn of a single card" (351). This seems to signal a kind of insouciance, but one founded on a household in which slaves—leaving aside the vexed question of Percival Brownlee—are allowed to work for their freedom on the land. Their behavior is in fact oddly exceptional. Despite a few passing references to slaves as stakes in games, I have been able to find almost no documented historical cases of people gambling directly for slaves in the manner described in "Was"—though obviously slaves were at risk where debts were accumulated and plantations lost.[44] One reason slaves were unlikely wagers is obvious enough, in that gambling stakes are quantified as numbers, whereas slaves have a variable market value. But I think the residual proximity of slaves to real estate is a factor here: to gamble away slaves is close to gambling a primary productivity. So the unusual gamble in "Was" in a sense undermines that ideology, exposing the arbitrary order that underlies slavery.

For the slave or ex-slave him- or herself to gamble is normally to encounter a fixed game, as in "Pantaloon in Black." The coda of *Go Down, Moses* is Mollie's grandson Samuel Beauchamp's progress toward death in Chicago, where he is involved in "a business called numbers, that people like him make money in" (274). Losing, Samuel must be posted home to his native soil. But once again Lucas is an exception. In *Intruder in the Dust*, his encounter with Gavin Stevens in the jail is, in Chick's mind, another poker game, "no childhood's game of stakeless Five Hundred" (329) but a high-stakes game of bluff and hidden cards. Lucas plays some of those cards—when he tells Chick that Gowrie was not shot with his Colt 41—but holds others. In contrast Stevens remarks of Gowrie that "like the amateur gambler the amateur murderer believes first not in his luck but in long shots, that the long shot will win simply because it's a long shot" (458).

So in Turl and in Lucas, we see the slave and inheritor of slavery for whom the gamble *is* a recourse, in that it takes them back where they want to be, with gains in each case. The *OED* links the etymology of the word *recourse* to the classical Latin *recursus*, the action of running back to one's starting point. It also references the Italian *ricorso*, Vico's term for the cycles of history, *corsi e ricorsi*, which so fascinated James Joyce in *Finnegans Wake*. The term "without recourse" is used four times in *Go Down, Moses*, which makes it something of a feature of the text. (To take a quick sample, the word is not used at all in *Absalom, Absalom!*, *As I Lay Dying*, *The Wild Palms*, *The Mansion*, or *The Reivers*; is used once in the appendix to *The Sound and the Fury* and in the short stories; and once in *Sanctuary*.) In the passage in which Ike describes the setup with Buck and Buddy's slaves in the old house, we are told that the slaves would be paraded and locked up for the night "without question protest or recourse" (194). This is a precise joke because "recourse" is exactly what they perform, in the root sense, as they can then leave by the back door and circle the countryside as long as they return by morning. Thadious M. Davis's remarks on Turl's circuit between the McCaslin and Beauchamp plantations describe the situation: "Without using his own words to tell his story," she writes, "he nonetheless articulates a narrative by means of motion and action."[45] The motion here is a kind of game, pleasurable in itself—presumably amorous adventures are involved—and although it seems to leave the form of slavery in place, it in fact signals that the slaves are potentially free.

So gambling as recourse signals the dream of agency. And the circuits of the McCaslin slaves lead us to the ellipse in the more specific form of the horse running back to the starting line, *recursus*. (Incidentally what in America is called a "race track" is a "race*course*" in British English.) The tale of the racehorse in *A Fable*—originally the story "Notes on a Horse Thief," written either side of *Intruder*—is sometimes said to be inspired by Harry Stillwell Edwards's *Aeneas Africanus* (1920), with its nostalgic account of the pilgrimage of a loyal ex-slave with a racehorse and the family silver after the Civil War.[46] But in Faulkner's version there is no return to owner—the horse is shot rather than allowed to go to stud, breeding more profit—and there is no economic recompense. On the contrary, the three-legged thoroughbred is used in a variety of country races and wins against all comers, ending up in a small town in Missouri. My notion of an oval racetrack may admittedly be something of a conceit here, but nevertheless the horse arrives, with its attendants, as "an aggregation bizarre, mobile and amazing as a hippodrome built around a comet"—a new and distinctly ovaloid version of southern meteorology.[47] The hunt for the Black preacher, Cockney groom, and mixed-race jockey is likened to a foxhunt, as in "Was"; but the outcome is an inversion in which all escape pursuit, partly thanks to the intervention of the freemasons—a motif repeated in *The Reivers*, suggesting a secret community of effort. As the turnkey notes when the crowd seeks to free the preacher, "this thing is all wrong. It's backwards. The law spirits a nigger prisoner out of jail and out of town, to protect him from a mob that wants to take him out and burn him. All these folks want to do is set this one free" (830). History as recursus. The horse even wins "one mortgage on a ten-acre corn-patch up on the mountain" (842), a square of land mapping precisely onto Lucas's inheritance.

### *The Reivers* (1962)

So we come to the end of Faulkner's corpus with *The Reivers*, with its journey and magic fish, a final throw of the dice in Faulkner's late redistributions toward his Black subjects. Gambling is the engine of the plot. Grandfather Priest's car is itself a gambit, its purchase required to counter Colonel Sartoris's presumptuous banning of the new contraptions. The horse is traded for the car because Bobo got mixed up with a white gambler. Recourse is also part of the story, both in the sense of a final parcel of funds to a Black McCaslin and in the over-literal sense that we see a series of races run over the same track, passing GO and collecting each time. The horse, which reminds Ned of the mule he used to own, is originally called Coppermine, again suggesting a legacy of Black labor (and perhaps the convict labor often associated with postbellum mining); he is rechristened Lightning and strikes twice, a meteor running back to Ned and his fish. Bobo gets his job back.

Recursus also operates interestingly in relation to the white characters. Grandfather Priest has his car returned minus $500, which is effectively transferred to Ned. For the young Lucius, the journey is an education in the criminal and sexual ways of the world, as well as in the life of African Americans. At awkward points he imagines winding back the plot in order to undo that education:

> to be home, not just to retrace but to retract, obliterate: make Ned take the horse back to wherever and whoever and however he had got it and get Grandfather's automobile and take it back to Jefferson, in reverse if necessary, travelling backward to unwind, ravel back into No-being, Never-being, that whole course of dirt roads, mudholes, the man and the color-blind mules. (Faulkner, *The Reivers*, 866)

This is a counterfactual dream of Time's Arrow reversed, used after Faulkner by Kurt Vonnegut and Martin Amis to examine trauma; more proximately it is the last iteration of Gavin Stevens's vision—imputed to Chick—of the South's fate on the verge of Pickett's charge in *Intruder in the Dust*: "Pickett himself with his long oiled ringlets and his hat in one hand probably and his sword in the other looking up the hill waiting for Longstreet to give the word and it's all in the balance, it hasn't happened yet, it hasn't even begun yet, it not only hasn't begun yet but there is still time for it not to begin" (431). This dream is of a die never cast; Lucius's of an innocence unviolated. Lucius returns to find that the town *"hasn't even changed,"* despite all his experience (Faulkner, *The Reivers*, 967). His disappointment is expressed in economic terms: "the lying and deceiving and tricking . . . the things I had had to learn that I wasn't even ready for yet, had nowhere to store them nor even anywhere to lay them down" have to provide a return; otherwise "something had been wasted, thrown away, spent for nothing." This is again southern history as gamble, but as Lucius learns from his grandfather, we live forward and understand backwards; there is no recourse for those who have gambled and lost, and consequences of actions with which one is even indirectly associated must be accepted.

The magic fish in the biblical story cures the patriarch's sight. Faulkner's aim seems both similar and more general in some of his later works: to imagine a youth on a redemptive mission; to imagine a gamble and a payoff to those excluded from economic calculations. That this remains in the realm of the fable indicated by the biblical parallel, rather than achieving articulation in any concrete politics, is of course true. But we might also relate it to the historiography of the gamble: a disruptive intervention that loosens history; a gambit on knowledge and skill that, like Turl's, might enable one to throw those in power and imagine a different future.

In imagining contrasting shapes and movements—the square of ownership that binds slave to soil; clockwise accumulation versus the counter-clockwise race around the oval; gambling vs. fixed capital—Faulkner abstracts a potential politics in which Henry's labor-land equation, enduring harshly from slavery to sharecropping, might be undone in the controlled frenzy of the gamble. What elsewhere is attributed politically to the inheritors of slavery—the prediality of "enduring" or "outlasting" or "remaining"—is speeded up in the risky play of the card or throw of the dice. In the horserace presided over by the skilled Black subject, a fabulous recourse is offered. That may seem a dark irony, given that in modern America the dream of escaping poverty via sporting prowess or gambling seems largely a dead end, but in Faulkner's late fables the gamble enables him to figure, at least, a multiracial community of effort and a desire that history might take a different route.

## NOTES

1. Faulkner in 1945, quoted in Malcolm Cowley, *The Faulkner-Cowley File: Letters and Memories, 1944–1962* (Harmondsworth, UK: Penguin, 1966), 69.

2. Jean-Paul Sartre, "On *The Sound and the Fury*: Time in the Work of Faulkner" (1939), *Literary and Philosophical Essays* (New York: Criterion Books, 1955), 79.

3. This critical mode may seem akin to the "surface" reading advocated by Sharon Marcus, Stephen Best, Rita Felski, and others, but is more focused on implicitly allegorical values contained within everyday experience as depicted by the text.

4. Charles Hannon, "Topologies of Discourse in Faulkner," in *William Faulkner in Context*, ed. John T. Matthews (Cambridge, UK: Cambridge University Press, 2015), 91–99.

5. There were, of course, more local exceptions to the flat denial of legal standing in *Dred Scott v. Sanford*. For an overview of what is a complex issue, see Laura F. Edwards, "Law, Domestic Violence, and the Limits of Patriarchal Authority in the Antebellum South," *Journal of Southern History* 65, no. 4 (1999): 733–70; and Thomas D. Morris's concluding meditation on the legal pressures created by the humanness of the slave, in *Southern Slavery and the Law, 1619–1860* (Chapel Hill: University of North Carolina Press, 1996), 424–43.

6. On debt, see Saidiya V. Hartman, *Scenes of Subjection: Terror, Slavery, and Self-Making in Nineteenth-Century America* (New York: Oxford University Press, 1997); and Stephen M. Best, *The Fugitive's Properties: Law and the Poetics of Possession* (Chicago: University of Chicago Press, 2004).

7. William Faulkner, *Absalom, Absalom!*, in *Novels 1936–1940*, ed. Joseph Blotner and Noel Polk (New York: Library of America, 1990), 6. Hereafter cited parenthetically.

8. Scott Romine, "Designing Spaces: Sutpen, Snopes, and the Promise of the Plantation" in *Faulkner's Geographies: Faulkner and Yoknapatawpha, 2011*, ed. Jay Watson and Ann J. Abadie (Jackson: University Press of Mississippi, 2015), 21.

9. Ted Atkinson, "Long Faulkner: Charting Legacy on a Civil Rights Continuum," in *Fifty Years after Faulkner: Faulkner and Yoknapatawpha, 2012*, ed. Jay Watson and Ann J. Abadie (Jackson: University Press of Mississippi, 2016), 216.

10. William Faulkner, *The Unvanquished*, in *Novels 1936–1940*, ed. Joseph Blotner and Noel Polk (New York: Library of America, 1990). Hereafter cited parenthetically.

11. Morris, *Southern Slavery and the Law*, 64, 67–70.

12. Morris, *Southern Slavery and the Law*, 113–20.

13. William Faulkner, *Go Down, Moses*, in *Novels 1942–1954*, ed. Joseph Blotner and Noel Polk (New York: Library of America, 1994), 196. Hereafter cited parenthetically.

14. *Merriam-Webster's Dictionary of Law* (Springfield, MA: Merriam-Webster, 1996), 374, 452.

15. Morris, *Southern Slavery and the Law*, 62; Best, *The Fugitive's Properties*, 8–9.

16. Oliver Wendell Holmes Jr., *The Common Law* (Boston: Little, Brown, 1881), 382–83. Hereafter cited parenthetically.

17. Thomas Erskine Holland, *The Elements of Jurisprudence* (Oxford, UK: Clarendon, 1896), 195.

18. For one exception to the widespread stripping from slaves of lands they had occupied after the Civil War, see Sydney Nathans, *A Mind to Stay: White Plantation, Black Homeland* (Cambridge, MA: Harvard University Press, 2017). In some respects what is involved here is the contrast between John Locke and Samuel Pufendorf on the nature of property. For Pufendorf *dominium* is a result of the power of occupation of what was originally a commons, supported by human convention; for Locke property rights are related to labor and usage (though, of course, he excludes the labor of slaves and servants).

19. Charles Chesnutt, "Mars Jeems's Nightmare," in *The Conjure Woman and Other Conjure Tales*, ed. Richard H. Brodhead (Durham, NC: Duke University Press, 1993), 55.

20. William Faulkner, *Intruder in the Dust*, in *Novels 1942–1954*, ed. Joseph Blotner and Noel Polk (New York: Library of America, 1994), 289. Hereafter cited parenthetically.

21. See Smithsonian National Postal Museum articles: Patricia Kaufman, "Confederate Postmaster Provisionals," *Arago: People, Postage, and the Post*, May 9, 2006. https://arago.si.edu/category_2034846.html; and Angelo Wider and Alexander Haimann, "The Black Experience: African-Americans on Stamps," n.d. https://arago.si.edu/exhibit_461.html (both accessed April 14, 2019).

22. Richard Godden, *William Faulkner: An Economy of Complex Words* (Princeton, NJ: Princeton University Press, 2007), 64.

23. Richard King, "Lucas Beauchamp and William Faulkner: Blood Brothers," in *Critical Essays on William Faulkner: The McCaslin Family*, ed. Arthur F. Kinney (Boston: G. K. Hall, 1990), 236, 242.

24. Alan Nadel, "'We—He and Us—Should Confederate': Stylistic Inversion in *Intruder in the Dust* and Faulkner's Cold War Agenda," in *Fifty Years after Faulkner: Faulkner and Yoknapatawpha, 2012*, ed. Jay Watson and Ann J. Abadie (Jackson: University Press of Mississippi, 2015), 200–11.

25. Erik Dussere, *Balancing the Books: Faulkner, Morrison, and the Economies of Slavery* (New York: Routledge, 2003), 24.

26. See Godden, *William Faulkner*, 226, on the relation of this text to the "cross-racial activities of the Southern Tenant Farmers' Union."

27. Thadious M. Davis, *Games of Property: Law, Race, Gender, and Faulkner's Go Down, Moses* (Durham, NC: Duke University Press, 2003), 178; Michael Wainwright, *Game Theory and Minorities in American Literature* (New York: Palgrave, 2016), 138ff.

28. Dale G. Breaden, "William Faulkner and the Land," *American Quarterly* 10, no. 3 (Autumn 1958): 344–57.

29. Henry George, *Social Problems* (London: Kegan Paul, Trench, 1883), 206.

30. See Mary Pilon, *The Monopolists: Obsession, Fury, and the Scandal behind the World's Favorite Board Game* (New York: Bloomsbury, 2015).

31. For images see http://landlordsgame.info/rules/bfnbr.html (Pilon, in *The Monopolists*, mistitles the game).

32. See Quashie's website, https://quashieart.blogspot.com/2012/03/plantation-monopoly-game.html (accessed April 14, 2019).

33. See, for example, Judith Bryant Wittenberg, "*Go Down, Moses* and the Discourse of Environmentalism," in *New Essays on "Go Down, Moses,"* ed. Linda Wagner-Martin (Cambridge, UK: Cambridge University Press, 1996), 49–72; Christoph Irmscher, "Reading Faulkner Ecocritically," *Mississippi Quarterly* 52, no. 3 (1999): 511–23; and Matt Low, "'The Bear' in *Go Down, Moses* and *Big Woods*: Faulkner's (Re)Visions for a Deeper Ecology," *Mississippi Quarterly* 62, no. 1 (2009): 53–70.

34. Godden, *William Faulkner*, 73–74.

35. On Faulkner's legacy in this respect, see Sharon Monteith, "'Who Was William Faulkner to Them?' Racial Liberals and Civil Rights Workers in the Civil Rights Era," in *Fifty Years after Faulkner: Faulkner and Yoknapatawpha, 2012*, ed. Jay Watson and Ann J. Abadie (Jackson: University Press of Mississippi, 2015), 222–35.

36. Dussere, *Balancing the Books*, 67.

37. Note, however, the useful distinctions among games that Michael Wainwright makes in *Faulkner's Gambit: Chess and Literature* (New York: Palgrave Macmillan, 2011).

38. Eugene Genovese, *The Sweetness of Life: Southern Planters at Home*, ed. Douglas Ambrose (Cambridge, UK: Cambridge University Press, 2017), 246.

39. Emile Alain, quoted in Walter Benjamin, "On Some Motifs in Baudelaire," *Selected Writings*, vol. 4, *1938–1940*, ed. Howard Eiland and Michael W. Jennings, trans. Edmund Jephcott et al. (Cambridge, MA: Belknap Press, 2003), 329.

40. William Faulkner, *The Reivers*, in *Novels 1957–1962*, ed. Joseph Blotner and Noel Polk (New York: Library of America, 1999), 733. Hereafter cited parenthetically in the text.

41. J. G. A. Pocock, *The Machiavellian Moment: Florentine Political Thought and the Atlantic Republican Tradition* (Princeton, NJ: Princeton University Press, 1975).

42. Davis, *Games of Property*, 120.

43. See Helen M. Poindexter, "Faulkner, the Mississippi Gambler," *Journal of Modern Literature* 10, no. 2 (1983): 334–38.

44. The most notorious case is described by Anne C. Bailey in *The Weeping Time: Memory and the Largest Slave Auction in American History* (Cambridge, UK: Cambridge University Press, 2017).

45. Davis, *Games of Property*, 120.

46. Harry Stillwell Edwards, *Aeneas Africanus* (Macon, GA: J. W. Burke, 1920).

47. William Faulkner, *A Fable*, in *Novels 1942–1954*, ed. Joseph Blotner and Noel Polk (New York: Library of America, 1994), 841. Hereafter cited parenthetically. On meteorology and slavery, see Tim Armstrong, "Slavery in the Mind: Trauma and the Weather," *The Logic of Slavery: Debt, Technology, and Pain in American Literature* (Cambridge, UK: Cambridge University Press, 2012), 173–204.

# The Expropriated Voice: Sonority, Intertextuality, Flesh

JULIE BETH NAPOLIN

> There is no voice for the disappearance of voice.
> —Giorgio Agamben

William Faulkner's avowed artistic purpose was to "bind into a whole the world which for some reason I believe should not pass utterly out of the memory of man."[1] He was determined to capture in prose the voices and ways of talking that have since passed away, no longer audible to us except through the indices of writing. Keenly aware of the phonograph and its indexical power, Faulkner once said, "I put down the voices, and it's right."[2]

The companion of Faulkner's project may be articulated through a question once posed by Saidiya Hartman in her memoir of traveling along the old slave routes of Ghana: "What was the afterlife of slavery and when might it be eradicated?"[3] It is as if some inscription, a cut, won't dissipate with time. Faulkner's voices and sounds are to be included among the artifacts that Hartman names "afterlives," where what had once been a "horizon of hope"—first the dream of Emancipation, then the dream of Reconstruction—becomes for the present a "historical debris," not easily relinquished.[4]

I have described elsewhere how the air of Yoknapatawpha is continually imagined by Faulkner as a kind of storage and transmission system of social feeling, "like the air was worn out with carrying sounds so long," as Quentin Compson remarks in *The Sound and the Fury*.[5] Everything, even breath as the carrier of sound and voice, has already happened. Sounds, like the "the echo of a shot" that kills Charles Bon just after the Civil War in *Absalom, Absalom!*, hang in air for four and half decades, into 1909 and the novel's diegetic present. Such sounds are historical debris. Quentin reminds us in *Absalom* that a physical property of sound is to resonate outward from the sounding or vibrating body, but also from an event itself. "*Maybe nothing ever happens once and is finished*," he thinks. "*Maybe happen is never once but like ripples maybe on water after the pebble sinks, the ripples moving on, spreading, . . . that pebble's watery echo whose fall it did not even see moves across its surface too at the original ripple space, to the old ineradicable rhythm.*"[6] Faulkner's extraordinarily sensitive ear found in sounds a way to present a temporality that is nonlinear, recurrent, and above all durative: sounds in Yoknapatawpha linger long after their rightful moment has passed, Faulkner gleaning much from the sound recording technology he often claimed to resent in public and social life.[7]

Yet something of sound in Yoknapatawpha is premised in its first instance upon a delay between hearing and understanding. A voicing or a sounding requires later generations for its sense. We are quite far from the Derridean sentiment in *Speech and Phenomena* or *Of Grammatology* that sound relates to a desire for presence or life, or "hearing (understanding) oneself speak," where signifiers of the spoken word seem not to "fall into the world" but to be retained by the interiority of conception, untouched by time and space.[8] Faulkner heard and understood well the rift upon which the metaphysics of presence is premised. *Absalom*, in its approach to voicing the fact that "*happen is never once*," essentially takes a mallet to metaphysics to disclose its reverberation.

We think of the voice as a personal property, intimately ours, resonating from inwardness. But sounds and voices move across space and time in Faulkner, transgressing boundaries between moments and selves. The sexual, racial, and gendered dimension of that transgression of sound is acutely related to what I will call in this essay the *expropriated voice*, or a voice that loses its sanctified dimension of personal property. This expropriation, while first and foremost a theft of person, its usurpation and conversion into property, moves in the reverse direction: expropriation extends or stretches sounds, such that they do not and cannot be said to "belong" to any individual or a particular moment. They vibrate from a past that was not fully experienced in its first instance to carry a future that has not yet been disclosed.

Consider, for example, that when Joe Christmas is lynched by Percy Grimm in *Light in August*, the event is never explicitly seen by a focalizer. It takes place "off screen," as it were, indexed by a sound that is quickly separated from the scene in both its audibility and visibility. Faulkner does not allow the scream to linger long in the narrative space. The corporeal scream quickly ascends and bleeds into the metaphoric "scream" of a police siren. In the recitation of Joe's scream by narrative, it is displaced, hushed. The "scream" of the siren, as the hegemonic sound of law, does not simply drown out the corporeal scream, but reverses its political valence as sound. Had the scream been heard and indexed by narrative, rather than sliding metonymically into the siren, it would have implicated Grimm and the white violence in whose name he acts. The siren implicates Joe as the emergency, the outrage against the white order from which, in this moment, the narrative cannot fully separate itself.

It is not the narrative's focalizer that mutes Joe's scream, however, but rather whiteness as such: the narrative forces us to "hear" its violently muting effect. Joe's scream is indexed just before it is occluded by the narrative, Faulkner blending the sounds such that the scream cannot be eradicated by the reader's thoughts. As the chapter concludes, Joe's scream persists, cited under erasure, sounded in silencing. In the beginning of the very next chapter, it lingers in Reverend Hightower's nostalgic memory of an older Jefferson whose "fading copper light would seem almost audible, like . . . an interval of silence and waiting" out of which a sound rises.[9] To some extent, then, the narrative's mode of listening abandons the scream of Joe, which is waiting not only to be heard but to be socially and politically recognized. Afterlives involve us in sounds whose meanings are not disclosed on time, nor in their proper space—Joe's scream, though muted, resounds. We encounter a gap or interval in perception, one determined or subtended by the absence of adjudication. There is an "unbelievable crescendo" of the siren's scream, "passing out of the realm of hearing" (465).

This realm of hearing is, as Judith Butler writes in relation to the visual field, "hegemonic and forceful," race determining the field of the audible.[10] Jennifer Stoever names such a determination "the sonic color line."[11] Where Hightower has perhaps not heard the scream, he has heard the siren on the other side of the color line that organizes Joe as the outrage. In the moment of Joe's lynching, the failure of his scream to be indexed draws a direct line from the kitchen space where Joe is murdered to the hallway where Hightower stands; through sound, these spaces bleed into one. The sound and its afterlife in "the beginning of thunder not yet louder than a whisper" implicates Hightower in the refusal to listen (466). This moment of literary acoustics—positing a supersensible space—is defined by the refusal to recognize historical debris on the part of collective memory.

How are such sounds to be typologized and located in Yoknapatawpha? Joe's scream is the sound of becoming an object, an undifferentiated thing to be possessed. At the same time, the almost immediate muting of the scream from the realm of hearing mandates by Faulkner's logic a return, one whose resonance I will follow in this essay: it gives shape to Yoknapatawpha itself.

In relation to music and storytelling voices, the sound of Yoknapatawpha is defined by a wide spectrum of sounds racialized as Black ("A dog's voice carries further than a train.... And some people's. Niggers," Quentin says in *The Sound and the Fury* [114]).[12] Such sounds are not environmental per se, yet no less function as an indelible sound of place. These literary sounds, at times heard at an uncanny spatial and/or temporal distance, have the capacity to make and define Faulkner's fictional spaces. Within literary sound studies, it is increasingly common to speak of the "soundscape" in the way one would a landscape. However, the term "soundscape," as it originated in R. Murray Shaffer's *The Tuning of the World*, perpetuates imperial conceptions of space derived from ethnology and field recording, but also conceptions about the value of so-called natural sound over something like noise. "Soundscape" is a false locution when applied to spaces structured by violence. As a concept, it cannot accommodate the sounds of colonial and imperial ruination or the afterlives of slavery—these are sounds that, if attended to, attack the subject position of the auditor who wishes to organize them.[13]

Despite the air that carries all sounds in Yoknapatawpha, "acoustic ecology" also seems not the right term for the way that violence often ties sounds to each other, there being a connective tissue between them.[14] What would it mean to suggest that the scream is the sound of what Hortense J. Spillers calls "the flesh"? While the sonic color line organizes, surveils, and controls bodies, it is inseparable from the sounding "flesh" that ontologically precedes both the social and the body. For Spillers, the flesh is "that zero degree of social conceptualization" and the site of the wounding of the person of African males and females that is engendered and re-engendered transhistorically by "the calculated work of iron, whips, chains, knives, the canine patrol, and the bullet."[15] In *Habeas Viscus*, Alexander Weheliye returns to Spillers anew to argue that where the body is the site of legal personhood, the flesh is "human life cleared."[16] In other words, before the sonic color line that both ties and severs the scream of Joe and the scream of the siren in the *social* realm of hearing, there is the sounding flesh transmitted through the transhistorical sonic matrix of slavery. In sounding out, however, Joe also bears witness to what cannot be narrated, Faulkner making a space in narrative for flesh as it opens, for Weheliye, the liberatory possibility of a future not determined by the human/inhuman distinction.[17]

When it emanates from the flesh, then, sound is not characterological. Rather, flesh "is transmitted historically so as to become affixed to certain bodies,"[18] a transmission that, Weheliye suggests, exceeds the very logic that would claim to organize it as a spectrum of value. Joe's scream is the sound of the flesh, one in which a primal scene of slavery studies resounds: the scream of Frederick Douglass's Aunt Hester, whose "extreme texture of noise," Fred Moten writes after Édouard Glissant, ought to be considered the origin of a Black radical sonic tradition.[19] Among the primary objections of this tradition is to the humanist logic that deems bodies discrete, separate, and autonomous units. The scream, for Moten, radically "embodies the critique of value, of private property."[20] Such critique has bearing on Joe's sound as a matrix of radical historical transmission.

When Joe cries out in the twentieth century, physically and aurally his death ceases to be singular. Such plural resonance of the extreme texture of noise revises Roland Barthes's famous sentiment that "[t]he text is a tissue of quotations [un tissue de citations] drawn from the innumerable centers of culture."[21] Though Barthes invokes the origin of text in Latin *texere* or "to weave," one must ask what kind of tissue is at stake when Hester resounds from Douglass's *Narrative* into *Light in August*, or how Faulkner, in describing the "unbelievable crescendo" of the siren, had already used this same phrase in relation to the amplitude of the cry of another character, Benjy Compson, in *The Sound and the Fury* (320). The connective tissue of these sounds, between Aunt Hester, Benjy, and Joe, is the flesh, through which a captured flesh is torturously brought into being as subject, discrete and autonomous.

In following the transgenerational transmission of sonorous flesh in Faulkner, whose Yoknapatawpha he understood fundamentally as a single and contained landscape, we necessarily engage the problem of sexual difference in its most general sense: where one body can be said to end and another to begin. "The loss of the indigenous name/land provides a metaphor of displacement for other human and cultural relations," Spillers writes of the slave ship, "including the displacement of the genitalia, the female's and the male's desire that engenders the future."[22] Beginning with the name Yoknapatawpha itself, Faulkner meditates on the loss of indigenous name and land, and with it, the future-engendering desire. Sexual difference itself cannot be thought through outside of the Middle Passage: it begins as a violent construction, the New World being, Spillers writes, "written in blood."[23]

The castration of Joe (like Benjy) is a reinjury, a (re)instantiation of the larger and original wound to futurity. It would seem that even temporality itself in Yoknapatawpha falls under the sign of native expropriation and, on a deeper and more unconscious level, the slave body, the expropriative event of the slave trade such that everything has already happened. As we will find, however, sonic excrescences in Faulkner also register—over and against Faulkner's own master plan as author—what Weheliye posits as alternative temporalities, including in sexual difference itself. The transmission of a sonorous substance assumes different corporeal and characterological manifestations and implications across different historical moments in Faulkner, but each returns us to a "grammar" or tense premised upon the flesh. For Weheliye, the crucial dimension of Spillers's grammar—"the liberation in the future anterior of the now"—is primarily opened by Black women.[24]

The remainder of this essay takes the sonic measure of enslaved women like Clytie and her mother in *Absalom*, and Jim Crowed women like Dilsey and Nancy, but also the characters these women care for across different moments, figures like Jim Bond and Benjy, and their counterpart (on the other side of the color line) in figures like Rosa Coldfield, old enough to remember slavery, and Quentin Compson, both speaking and listening through a transhistorical memory of the flesh. While the sonic color line is differently inflected by these different instances, the fleshly substance ties and severs them into a single "ontological totality."[25] Weheliye's invocation of totality is precise: "the concentration camp, the colonial outpost, and slave plantation suggest three of many relay points in the weave of modern politics, which are neither exceptional nor comparable, but simply relational" (*Habeas Viscus*, 37). This totality requires that we move between textual moments by way of their connective tissue, transgressing both textual and personal boundaries in ways not fully circumscribed by Barthes's theory of the intertext.[26] Faulkner's tendency to return to sounds across the corpus—also a "viscus," as Weheliye might say—becomes one such imaginative site where beings relate across time and space in a tissue not simply of quotations but of corporeal sounds.

## The Possessive Grammar of Listening

In the Oxford English Dictionary, under "genitive," we find the following citation from 1955: "W. L. Westermann Slave Syst. Greek & Rom. Antiq. xiv. 92/1 The names of their owners appear in the genitive case after the slave names." The slave name is not the name of the father, but names a possession, being in the possessive case. The genitive case: "n. (in inflected languages) a case of nouns and pronouns, and of words in grammatical agreement with them, the typical function of which is to indicate that the person or thing denoted by the word is related to another as source, possessor, or the like; (also in uninflected languages) a word or word form having a similar possessive function." The genitive is thus conditioned by an ontological and biological meaning of "source" but quickly rerouted through a logic of property, the proper, and possession. The genitive rests on the possibility that things might belong to each other, that one might possess another. We say that a sound is "of" a particular object, or we can be confused as to a sound's "source"—the scream sounds out the fleshly dilemma of the genitive as the possessive case.

A comment by Faulkner is revelatory of this defining tension of the textual corpus. In his sessions at the University of Virginia, Faulkner was asked about the apparent resurrection of Nancy, a Black woman, in *Requiem for a Nun*, her death having been seemingly imminent in the earlier story, "That Evening Sun." Faulkner responded by saying that Nancy was, in both texts, "the same person, actually." He added, "These people I figure belong to me and I have the right to move them about in time when I need them."[27] When he narrates to us from the vantage point of 1915 his childhood memories of Nancy, Quentin Compson, a young white man, seems to have survived his 1910 suicide as posited by *The Sound and the Fury*. To say that the two Nancys or Quentins are the same person, as Faulkner suggests we do, we must do a bit of mental work or figuring. This work hinges *a priori* upon two conceptions: that the personhood of the character is constant, so constant that it unifies something that might be called a literary corpus; and that in this corpus, characters, across works, take on personality, but a special kind of personality that defies the absolute death sentence of mortal life. This is life that in the end so thoroughly belongs to the author as property that it can be resurrected at will.[28] Faulkner is with "right" to Nancy in time as intellectual property. But the first proposition, that Nancy is a person, a kind of life with enduring characteristics over time, is only negated by the second remark if we bypass the specter of slavery wherein it becomes possible for personhood to be expropriated, that is, to be owned by someone else.[29]

The concept of "person" relates not only to "personhood," but to "personification" and "impersonation," such that the legal and the poetic are folded into one another, the former continually requiring the latter for its sense in what Stephen Best names "the poetics of possession."[30] It is through the poetic, as the linguistic work of transformation, that the legal may turn the ephemeral or otherwise abstract into concrete things, quantifiable.[31] The phonograph made possible the storage of sound not only after death, but after the sound's own vanishing instance—the poetics of possession, in other words, is intimately tied to its acoustics. In Faulkner's moment of writing, the age of Edison, the recording of sound also turned the fugitive phenomenon of sound into a thing, making it possible to possess and exchange sounds in ways that borrowed from the poetics of slavery. Listeners to the new machine grappled not only with the metaphysical meaning of the technology but with the laws that might describe and circumscribe its use and application.[32] From the beginning, Best shows, not only the laws governing the circulation of recorded sound but the desire to control the ephemerality of sound waves in recording were shot through with the poetics of possession and the echoes of the Fugitive Slave Act.

At the same time, early respondents to sound recording found the phonograph to be co-extensive with a "feminization of person" (the violent androgyny of a horned mouth that both devours the sound for an inscribing needle and plays the sound back): the phonograph takes "me" without my consent.[33] To the extent that the phonograph is entangled with the metaphysics of property, it is entangled with the metaphysics of liberal personhood and its foundational notion of consent to be found in social contract theories. It is also entangled with the ancient remonstrance of written marks, bastard to their "legitimate brother" the voice, leaving written words without the protection of the "father" (a filial poetics that will prove central to sounding flesh in Faulkner).[34]

The poetics of possession is haunted by the specter of the slave, and with it, the distinctly modern sensibility that my *person* is something that I own like property, that is inalienable and cannot be exchanged.[35] A series of propositions follows from this notion when it comes to recording what I take to be *my* voice. Property, Hegel argues in *The Philosophy of Right*, is the expression of the self, all right beginning with the image of property or the ability to say "this is mine." In order for the marks inscribed on the phonograph record to be counted as *mine*, the inscription must be understood as an indexical sign.[36] That mark is a trace not only of my voice but of my very person; so to take a recording of my voice without my consent or to infringe upon the copyright of my recording is to dispossess me. Copyright law, in other words, must do quite a bit of figural and poetic work to find in this otherwise ephemeral and fugitive expulsion of air the concretion of thingliness that we associate with property, whose original model is land.[37] If sounds can be poetically transformed, Best writes, "from forms exchanged between persons . . . to properties circulated between things," then this circulation involves not simply forms and their genitive case (corporeal, poetic) but events and their tense.[38] A phonograph record is an event that, having once been in time, achieves new status as a thing.[39] Such phonography—the discrete phonographic form that contains previously unbound sound—bears significantly on Faulknerian literary form as a record of events. Persons are less agents than sites of mediation. That (re)articulative relation defines sonic afterlives, which both animate and dispossess Faulkner's characters such that phrases, voices, and sounds move between them in iterative ways.

The specter of slavery and the specter of the phonograph were there in Yoknapatawpha from the beginning in Faulkner's ambivalent thinking of the relation between character, body, person, voice, and authorial identity. Faulkner declares his proprietorship in print for the first time on the map in the endpapers of *Absalom*, his greatest novel of slavery. Yet at the same time, Faulkner understood that if the novel is to critique the proprietary and paternalistic logic upon which family, declension, and genealogy are founded, then novelistic form could not be linearly conceived.[40] The visualist logic not only of the map but of the flashback is shattered by the novel's approach to voices in voices, inward selves being possessed and animated by voices from the exterior. These include the penumbra of shorter texts, from "That Evening Sun" to the unpublished "Evangeline," that surround *Absalom* with variations. The body of the novel's protagonist, Quentin, is said to be "an empty hall echoing with sonorous defeated names" (7). These resonances exceed the insignia of the map to move across the Faulknerian corpus to repeat across bodies, selves, and their condition in flesh: sounds circulate within and between works in at times transatlantic and diasporic ways that also hybridize spaces and temporalities, exceeding Faulkner's claim to ownership.

The corpus, then, has two intertwined meanings: the body of works by which we recognize an author and his written belongings, and the "recalcitrant" body, as Jay Watson might say, that gives shape to actions, memories, and sentiments at the level of character and form. But there is perhaps also a third meaning: the flesh that shapes the gendered and raced distinction between captured and liberated positions, flesh being prior to both the body and the subject for Spillers. In the Faulknerian corpus/viscus, there is a transferability of sounds and voices that demands consideration of the poetics of possession and, with it, of fungible personhood. At the core of Faulkner's oeuvre is not only the generative problem of the voice, but with it a generative anxiety about the person. These issues are generative because, as Weheliye argues of the flesh, their temporality is not fully reducible to what can already be described through the human/not quite human/nonhuman distinction.

## Iterative Sonorities

We know of Faulkner's fraught relationship to technology, particularly sound technology like the jukebox, radio, and phonograph, which Faulkner allowed into his hearing space in highly circumscribed ways, particularly as technology expanded to include sound cinema.[41] The slave poetics haunts the realm of hearing—a slave acoustics—through the invasion of the right to privacy. One cannot close one's ears, making one, to some extent, not one, but rather vulnerable, open, and supine. A second problem unfolds from the first. If technology could so easily rend voice and body, what had held them together? This transformation of sound into a form of exchange between persons animates the expropriative and relational movement of sounds and voices in Faulkner, which move across works in ways that, while haunted by dispossession, also underscore a radically antiliberal philosophy. Faulkner understood that liberalism, the same thinking that gave us the individual who cannot be expropriated from himself (even when recorded), gave us the institution of slavery.

*The Sound and the Fury* is the moment in which Faulkner, turning away from "publishers' addresses," returns to a series of childhood memories to develop a newly experimental form defined by a pessimistic vision of family and family declension. It is the moment and form through which Faulkner also discovers his "voice."[42] Does not part of his pursuit of a "voice" involve an omission or repression of the slave body? Jason Compson briefly notes that his family had once owned slaves, but if the slave past is largely occluded from *The Sound and the Fury*, the slave sound is not. In interviews, Faulkner avows the image of Caddy as the origin of a novel whose title directs us to its neglected beginnings in sound. Situated at the threshold of the Compson estate, the moan of Benjy Compson, Caddy's severely mentally disabled brother, punctuates the opening of Faulkner's first great experiment in form. "Hush up that moaning," Luster tells Benjy within the first paragraph of the novel's first draft, "Twilight." Perhaps his bellow cannot be properly credited as the origin of a form because it is the expurgation of form—Benjy's cry knows no limits, no shape, no restraint, but only loss, lack, and rebuke. But it is not simply a sound of dispossession: it participates in a critical tradition. To the extent that Benjy is a displaced slave body, his cry resounds its fleshly freedom drive: in writing the cry, Faulkner bears witness to what is difficult to narrate.

It is a sound that Faulkner returned to many times across his fiction. The Compson saga closes in *Absalom* with Jim Bond, the so-called "idiot" mixed-race descendent of Thomas Sutpen, crying out at the conflagration of the Sutpen plantation house. In this moment, the reader of the Faulknerian corpus cannot help but recall how Benjy's cry "*hammered back and forth between the walls in waves . . . as though there were no place for it in silence*" (*The Sound and the Fury*, 124). Such a cry pushes out from the novel, the silent inscription, that would seem to contain it, but also from the logic of plot (the novelistic term sharing an origin with the territorial one):

> —and he, Jim Bond, the scion, the last of his race, seeing it too now and howling with human reason now since now even he could have known what he was howling about.... [Quentin] could see ... one last wild crimson reflection as the house collapsed and roared away and there was only the sound of the idiot negro left. (*Absalom, Absalom!*, 300–1)

This sound is not ephemeral; it is a remainder; it persists like a thing.[43] Here, Faulkner ends the novel, and the image of the southern plantation dynasty itself, Sutpen's Hundred, in a single sound. And yet it is plural. It is a sonorous and tenuous bond to a long, drawn-out history of barbarism, the circumambience of sound its history, propelling it in time such that it becomes possible to say that Benjy and Bond sound out an ontological totality.

This sound ends the Sutpen narrative (to the extent that it is held by the novel). Yet the sound of Quentin's voice—denying and negating—ends the text proper when he shouts or cries aloud that he does not hate the South. Faulkner crafts the 1909 (Sutpen) and 1910 (Compson) narratives to end, within a page of each other, upon human voicings. Recall, too, that within the first chapter of the novel, Rosa remembers Sutpen's slaves who spoke to the carriage's team of horses "without words ... in that tongue in which they slept in the mud ... the carriage whirling up to the church door while women and children scattered and screamed" (17). Rosa then remembers "the sound, the screaming" of Henry Sutpen before the spectacle of Sutpen wrestling with slaves, a spectator conjecturing "'It's a horse' then 'It's a woman' then 'My God, it's a child'" (21). In some precise sense, we confront in these soundings the limits of grammatical "voice" as the subject of the verb's mode of action. It moves to and fro along a spectrum of humanity. While Quentin's shout mounts toward a cry, it is one that still clings to this side of color line and language itself. Nevertheless, Faulkner had already written its conclusion in *The Sound and the Fury* and Quentin's act of suicide; Quentin would perhaps rather die than scream.

When Bond cries out at the conflagration, the narrator repeats the word "now," bringing the grammatical tense of the sentence to its knees. The present, Weheliye might say, is "in brackets."[44] It is quite literally so, for Faulkner frequently places the name "Quentin" in parenthesis such that the subject of certain sentences, their grammatical "voice," is unclear. The "now," Weheliye writes, "transmutes" the simple present such that what is heard is what "will have [been] actualized."[45] But the "now" also names the transmutation of the first-person voice that guarantees it grammatically: if the "now" is what is imagined but not yet described, then it is not localized in any actualized subject. Bond sounds out from the infrarational dimension of the present. Confronting that sound of the flesh and with it the limits of liberal reason, Quentin can only put the period on the long sentence that is the novel and end his life. In death, he preserves himself for liberal logic upon sensing the extent to which he, too, might be flesh. The map that ends *Absalom* as a printed artifact doubles down on this effect, plunging us back into the silence of cartography. To the extent that the other side of the image of the map is unprintable, an extreme texture of noise, we must leave the frame of the single work to realize its texture.

There is a genealogy that leads, compositionally, from Benjy's moaning in 1929 to Jim Bond's howling in 1936, the latter explicitly traceable to slavery and the flesh. There is also a genealogy that, in the history of Yoknapatawpha itself, leads from Bond (1909) to Benjy (1928), thus inscribing Benjy's already Hester-like sounds in the lineage of slavery. The task is not simply to rightfully instate Benjy's cry as the origin of Yoknapatawpha, but rather to confront what in this sound is difficult to transcribe and localize. When Faulkner introduced this cry from an ostensibly white body circa 1929, it would have been radically decentering for readers accustomed to the screams of slaves in American literary fiction to encounter such a sound from a white body. But Benjy is only ostensibly white: if he has been castrated, his name has been taken from him, and he is spatially confined to the Compson "estate," then there is something of his body that is already on loan to the poetics of the slave and the flesh.

By what means can we link these sounds between Benjy and Bond? Who cries first, and what does it mean to say that the sound is shared by their bodies? The fact that Faulkner thought it possible to write and rewrite these bodies and selves, but also to assign them a fleshly sonority, means that he thought it possible to defy the grammar of the simple past (Faulkner's language continually invokes non-grammaticalities). The fleshly sonority moves between Benjy and Bond, but also between Dilsey and Nancy—Benjy is the only white term in that movement, and perhaps Quentin, to the extent that his closing shout in *Absalom* mounts toward a cry. Quentin thus does not stay dead long; risen from the dead in "That Evening Sun," he remembers the cry of his caregiver, Nancy:

> One night we waked up, hearing the sound. It was not singing and it was not crying, coming up the dark stairs. . . . Our toes curled away from [the floor] while we listened to the sound. It was like singing and it wasn't like singing, like the sounds that Negroes make.[46]

In this story, Quentin begins his recitation of the past from the vantage point of adulthood, an age that (if we are to believe he is the same person who commits suicide in *The Sound and the Fury*) he could not possibly have reached. Remembering Nancy, the narrative voice falls away from the linguistic mastery of the adult and into that of a child. The voice no longer correctly conjugates its memories ("we waked up"). In some precise sense, the voice no longer recites; the narrative ceases to be a *récit*, which depends upon the simple fact that something has happened. Such ungrammaticalities are the only way to put into language what is neither past nor present. This conjugation—in the face of Nancy's moan—makes a space in narrative for what Christina Sharpe would call "being in the wake," a protracted mourning that attenuates Black being.[47] The toes curl away because the sound is of what precedes the body: the flesh. Something more than mere racism coming into itself frames Quentin's young listening. Nancy does not make a racially differentiated sound (a "Negro" sound), but rather the sound registers something like the violent differentiation upon which race, but also grammar itself, is premised. That is to say, the sound of Nancy's cry is racialized in Quentin's memory, but only tenuously. It is "like" the sounds that Negroes make; it is "like" singing and therefore also like crying. It is in the midst of transmutation, neither substantive nor essentially identical to itself. It is the sound of transposition itself, such that it becomes difficult to say what its rightful place is.

Benjy Compson does not appear in this story; he is either missing or not yet conceived by Faulkner.[48] If Blackness is supposedly "absent" in Benjy's cry, it is "present" in Nancy's. But if we follow the sounds, Blackness is no longer defensible as a mythos of blood but is instead an aural grammar of race: Blackness is produced by the sound; the sound is not produced by Blackness. At the level of compositional history, there is a sonic movement—we are in the presence not of a metonymic connection but of a physical and sonorous bond between bodies, a bond that subtends the individuation of the body itself. The sound resounds between them: Benjy and Nancy, Benjy and Bond, Nancy and Bond.

Compositionally, the short stories appear as negated possibilities of events that are, as it were, "fleshed out" in *Absalom* to become more comprehensive and encompassing in their scope. As evidenced by the shifting fates of recurring characters, these events were not, however, necessarily anticipated by Faulkner as having taken place in a single way, since characters share experiences, trading destinies. In one of the earliest drafts of *Absalom*, "Evangeline," Henry Sutpen returns to Sutpen's Hundred, then simply named the "dark house," to die. The house burns down in a fire set by Raby (later renamed Clytie). In this version, however, the unnamed narrator, who strikes us as an early register or preformation of Quentin, is there to witness this event principally through hearing "farcarrying negro voices":[49]

> The negroes came up, the three generations of them, their eyeballs white, their open mouths pinkly cavernous. . . . I could hear the negroes. They were making a long, concerted, wild, measured wailing, in harmonic pitch from the treble of the children to the soprano of the oldest woman, the daughter of the woman in the burning house; they might have rehearsed it for years, waiting for this irrevocable moment out of all time. . . . I think I said that the sound had now passed beyond the outraged and surfeited ear.[50]

Such rehearsal extends to or "farcarries" from the beginnings of slavery. The ear of the narrator attunes itself to a violence that determines the possibility of listening, but also of the American family itself. In this matrilineal sound (from oldest woman to daughter), what the narrator hears is the flesh. The legal condition of enslavement travels matrilineally (according to the Roman-law principle of *partus sequitur ventrem*, the status of the child follows from the mother; it is the mother who renders her child enslaved). For Spillers, enfleshment precedes such a legal frame: both paternal and maternal rights are nullified within the American grammar book of slavery. As the daughter in the burning house, Raby/Clytie both is and is not Henry's "sister," because she is and is not Sutpen's "daughter." As the sound of this alienation, what the narrator hears is thus not diminished by transmission across generations but chorally compounded by it.

It becomes impossible to say who or what is acting and with what force to hand down such sounds, but also to hand them across within a tissue of citations. In *Light in August*, Faulkner uses nearly the same language that will recount Jim Bond's howl five years later when he writes of Hightower, "[i]t seems to him that he can see, feel . . . the presence of fecund [Black] women . . . and the big house again, noisy, loud with the treble shouts of the generations" (*Light in August*, 407). Recall that Hightower's aural consciousness will, not long after this passage, prove to repress Joe's scream; here he revives the slave past rather than confront the Jim Crowed present. The reader registers what the character cannot. If the realm of hearing out of which Joe's scream passes is, as we have found, determined by the sonic color line, then the "outraged and surfeited ear" of "Evangeline" is also fully within that realm and it is attached to Raby/Clytie: with historical insight, the young daughter of a slave hears and relays in her turn an "irrevocable moment out of all time." It is just on the verge of adopting such an ear that Quentin decides he can hear no more.

Does Faulkner merely repeat himself from "Evangeline" to *Absalom*, from "That Evening Sun" to *The Sound and the Fury*, and back again—or does the sound of flesh mix and hybridize characters and events such that it is no longer possible to say, with any certainty, who is descended from whom, which text from which, as the logic of property and social status would require? "Property is individual," Best writes, "i.e. indivisible (Latin, sixth century, *individuus*, from Greek *atmos*, not cuttable, not divisible)—'not divisible,' incapable of possession by any other than that 'one' who bears 'title.' Property is in this instance the ground of autonomy."[51] If Faulkner were to subvert this ground, then he could no longer put faith in the voice as a kind of property. In fact, the moment the voice exceeds its status as property, it becomes "sound," moveable and transposable. In the movement of sounds across the works, and across bodies, Faulkner incites anxieties of dispossession, yet at the same time the sound of the flesh opens autonomy's tight embrace.[52]

In the Compson saga, Quentin is continually subject to the chastising voices of fathers that enter his ears unbidden, a direct route to his inner life. Yet to the extent that listening renders him vulnerable, his autonomy gives way. In that giving way, sound becomes a site not only of subjectification but of its excess. In listening, one can become flesh, and in becoming flesh, one becomes more than one. Thus as Quentin listens to Shreve tell the story and Shreve to Quentin, they are said to become their forebears, two half (not) brothers, one white and the other Black, Henry and Bon, each of them two and so together four. In listening, they exceed *"the irrevocable repudiation of the old heredity"* (277). Similarly, the monovoice of *Absalom* seems to pick up on the language of characters and to overhear them, to absorb them into its system such that they cannot be absolutely differentiated from each other. But if "these people belong to me," what were the limits of Faulkner's critique of personhood and ownership? As if in answer to this question, Rosa announces *"the citadel of the central I-Am's private own"* (112) to declare that it is *"the touch of flesh with flesh"* that *"cuts"* the private own, defiles the sanctity and containment of the person in both love and enmity (111). The sound, lyric sensibility, and hypnotic action of Rosa's voice—her sonority—renounce the understanding of flesh that she articulates. Through the act of speaking, she continually lives out fantasies of touching across race. She did not "spy" upon Judith and Bon, Rosa says, but rather became a part of

> 'that slow and mutual rhythm wherein the heart, the mind, does not need to watch the docile (ay, the willing) feet'; [I] would think 'What suspiration

*of the twinning souls have the murmurous myriad ears of this secluded vine or shrub listened to? what vow, what promise, what rapt biding fire has the lilac rain of this wistaria, this heavy rose's dissolution, crowned?'* (119)

Rosa's lyric voice exceeds grammar—which insists upon the separation between things, between past and present—to open a series of alternative potentials, *"a might-have-been which is more true than truth"* (115). If by Western logic, the voice is internal to me cannot be taken from me, and is intimately defined as my inmost self, Rosa defies this logic in practice during her soliloquy in chapter 5. Her sonority, though not a howl, is within the howl's sonic realm and cuts across fleshly boundaries and privacies. Joined with or twinned by Clytie, who grasps her white arm, Rosa remembers, *"I had instinctively cried . . . perhaps not aloud, not with words"* (112). Such effects underscore chapter 5 as among the most enigmatic voices in the history of literature. Situated between Rosa and Quentin who listens to her, its voice exists somewhere *between* entities: a "twinned" yet also fundamentally expropriated voice resonating between two people who have been deindividuated. The voice belongs to both of them and neither of them. The result is text that literally vibrates on the page.⁵³ It is not so much verbal as sonic, an event of speech, no longer bound to the image of property, as Quentin is affectively receiving it from Rosa.

In Rosa's sonority, but also her act of listening to the echo of the shot that reverberates the event of Bon's death, Faulkner seeks another and temporalizing logic for the voice beyond property, beyond the object that is supposed to guarantee identity and unity in time. Against this background is the emergence of Clytie, the slave daughter, as the remainder and (un)rightful residue of the voice of the father. Clytie speaks in perhaps the most authoritative voice in *Absalom*—a voice *"quiet"* and *"still"* (111)—when she grasps the arm of Rosa and calls her by her first name. Touching flesh with flesh, Clytie says (in one of her few moments of speech), *"Dont you go up there, Rosa."* The voice is also authorial, but what does it author? The plantation had been torn "violently out of the soundless Nothing" by Sutpen's fiat (4), "the *Be Sutpen's Hundred* like the oldtime *Be Light*." Though Clytie to some extent identifies with the father when she grasps Rosa, a father she will ultimately protect with her final act of conflagration, the grammar of the command, like the language of genesis, is not meant for her: it is a radical usurpation of paternal speech.

To amplify this subtle radicality, we might consider the various speech situations that define narrative transmission in *Absalom* as well as its margin. There are forms of address, for instance, that shape not only the

Sutpen clan, determining who may and may not have a rightful place in the family, but also the Compson men, for whom the story of Sutpen acts as a patrimony, sounds handed from father to son like a name (in a reverse corollary, Shreve postulates that the sound of Bond haunts Quentin). In a different listening situation from those of the sons, Rosa is without right to speak because everything she knows she learned by listening at closed doors. When Rosa does speak, that is, she does so thanks to fugitive sounds, sounds capable of escaping closed doors. Clytie's command, however, is fleshly and emanates from a different situation, that of the slave mother. Not only is Clytie more profoundly without right than Rosa, but her imperative utterance, though it has the trappings of normative grammar, is absolutely outside the realm of such grammar: it is as if the silence beneath all voice suddenly could speak. In Spillers's terms, Clytie is mama's baby, but mama herself was a maybe, a slave and quasi-person. It is from this maternal line that she inherits her silence, her radical nonright to speak.

This slave mother—whose name we never learn—was without the sanctity of the body. Thus the story of her arrival in town, the story of Clytie's birth, is actually not a story at all. It is at the limits of the novel's modes of recitation, which convert event into narrative. It is somewhere between recitation and silence when Mr. Compson says to Quentin, "Miss Rosa didn't tell you that two of the niggers in the wagon that day were women?" (48). Clytie's mama could be one of two unspeaking women. Isn't the unnamed slave woman, the zero degree of the expropriated voice, the origin of the novel's claim to discourse? To some extent, it is she who determines the beginning of the story (its voicing) and the dynasty, because she gives their end in Clytie.

There is a distinction, then, between the voices that Faulkner does not allow us to hear, voices that, like Joe's, are alluded to and unrecorded, and the voices that we are allowed to hear, like Benjy's, Nancy's, Dilsey's, Rosa's, and even Clytie's. But beneath these two possibilities, the recorded and the unrecorded, is a third, what Giorgio Agamben, in the epigraph to this essay, calls "the disappearance of voice" for which "there is no voice." Faulkner understood that he must write toward that voice, an asymptote that could not be heard or transcribed.

NOTES

1. William Faulkner quoted in Joseph Blotner, "William Faulkner's Essay on the Composition of *Sartoris*," *Yale University Library Gazette* 47, no. 3 (January 1973): 124.

2. William Faulkner quoted in Malcolm Cowley, *The Faulkner-Cowley File: Letters and Memories, 1944–1962* (New York: Viking Press, 1966), 114.

3. Saidiya Hartman, *Lose Your Mother: A Journey along the Atlantic Slave Route* (New York: Farrar, Straus, and Giroux, 2007), 45.

4. Hartman, *Lose Your Mother*, 39.

5. William Faulkner, *The Sound and the Fury*, rev. ed. (1929; repr., New York: Vintage International, 1990), 114. Hereafter cited parenthetically.

6. William Faulkner, *Absalom, Absalom!*, rev. ed. (1936; repr., New York: Vintage International, 1990), 210. Hereafter cited parenthetically.

7. For a discussion of air as a recording medium in Faulkner, see Julie Beth Napolin, "The Fact of Resonance: An Acoustics of Determination in Faulkner and Benjamin," *Symploke* 24, no. 1 (2016): 171–86. For a related discussion of sound recording as an absent presence in Faulkner, see Sarah Gleeson-White, "Auditory Exposures: Faulkner, Eisenstein, and Film Sound," *PMLA* 128 (2013): 87–100. Also see Julian Murphet, *Faulkner's Media Romance* (New York: Oxford University Press, 2017).

8. Jacques Derrida, *Of Grammatology*, trans. Gayatri Chakravorty Spivak, rev. ed. (1967; repr., Baltimore: Johns Hopkins University Press, 1997), 166.

9. William Faulkner, *Light in August*, rev. ed. (1932; repr., New York: Vintage International, 1991), 466. Hereafter cited parenthetically.

10. See Judith Butler, "Endangered/Endangering: Schematic Racism and White Paranoia," in *Reading Rodney King/Reading Urban Uprising*, ed. Robert Gooding-Williams (New York: Routledge, 1993), 17.

11. See Jennifer Lynn Stoever, *The Sonic Color Line: Race and the Cultural Politics of Listening* (New York: New York University Press, 2016). For Stoever, this color line, while traceable to slavery and its modes of listening, continues to control and surveil Black bodies in the present.

12. Several scholars have shown Yoknapatawpha to be populated by Black musical forms in racially amalgamating ways. See Thadious Davis, "Lingering in the Black: Faulkner's Illegible Modernist Sound Melding," in *Faulkner and the Black Literatures of the Americas: Faulkner and Yoknapatawpha, 2013*, ed. Jay Watson and James G. Thomas, Jr. (Jackson: University Press of Mississippi, 2016), 36–58. Also see Erich Nunn, *Sounding the Color Line: Music and Race in the Southern Imagination* (Athens: University of Georgia Press, 2015), 154–72; and Charles A. Peek, "'That Evening Sun(g)': Blues Inscribing Black Space in White Stories," *Southern Quarterly* 42, no. 3 (Spring 2004): 130–50.

13. I discuss this issue at length in my book, *The Fact of Resonance: Modernist Acoustics and Narrative Form* (New York: Fordham University Press, 2020).

14. The phrase "acoustic ecology" was coined by composer Francisco Lopez as a critique of Shafer's tendency to value some sounds above others.

15. Spillers quoted in Alexander G. Weheliye, *Habeas Viscus: Racializing Assemblages, Biopolitics, and Black Feminist Theories of the Human* (Durham, NC: Duke University Press, 2014), 39.

16. Weheliye, *Habeas Viscus*, 39.

17. Also see Kaja Silverman, *Flesh of My Flesh* (Stanford, CA: Stanford University Press, 2009). Silverman argues for an alternative Western lineage descended not from Descartes's insistence on the individual but from Ovid's notion "that everything derives from the same flesh," promoting transformation and equality rather than stasis and hierarchy (2).

18. Silverman, *Flesh of My Flesh*, 38.

19. Fred Moten, *In the Break: The Aesthetics of the Black Radical Tradition* (Minneapolis: University of Minnesota Press, 2003), 7.

20. Moten, *In the Break*, 12.

21. Roland Barthes, "The Death of the Author," in *Image, Music, Text*, trans. Stephen Heath (New York: Hill and Wang, 1977), 146.

22. Hortense J. Spillers, "Mama's Baby, Papa's Maybe: An American Grammar Book," *Diacritics* 17.2 (Summer, 1987): 73.

23. Spillers, "Mama's Baby, Papa's Maybe," 67.

24. Weheliye, *Habeas Viscus*, 39.

25. Weheliye underscores how "specific instances of the relations that compose political violence realize articulations of an ontological totality" (13).

26. The flesh for Weheliye serves as a site for new ways of being and thinking that cannot be reduced to humanism and its comparative template of human/not quite human/nonhuman.

27. Frederick Landis Gwynn and Joseph Leo Blotner, eds., *Faulkner in the University* (Charlottesville: University of Virginia Press, 1959), 49.

28. Daina Ramey Berry has shown how enslavement persists beyond death, enslavers receiving value from slave mortality through a variety of legal and financial instruments, including speculation and insurance. See Berry, "'Broad is de Road dat Leads ter Death': Human Capital and Enslaved Mortality," in *Slavery's Capitalism: A New History of American Economic Development*, ed. Sven Beckert and Seth Rockman (Philadelphia: University of Pennsylvania Press, 2016), 146–62. In that analogy between authorial proprietorship and slaveholding, the author too derives value, if not from mortality, then from the claim to own characters as a kind of fungible "life."

29. Stephen Best, *The Fugitive's Properties: Law and the Poetics of Possession* (Chicago: University of Chicago Press, 2004), 53.

30. Best, *The Fugitive's Properties*. Best also describes how nonhuman entities such as corporations are personified by law.

31. For Best, the *sine qua non* of this transformation is to be found in the paradox of the recorded voice. In "The Phonograph and Its Future," for example, Thomas Edison remarks on "the almost universal application of the foundation principle [of the phonograph], namely, the gathering up and retaining of sounds hitherto fugitive, and their reproduction at will." See Thomas A. Edison, "The Phonograph and Its Future," *North American Review* 126, no. 262 (1878): 527.

32. In this way, Best shows, both copyright law and the constitutional right to privacy act to delimit how sounds can move in public space; where property, law, and the person intertwine, we immediately confront the specter of the slave.

33. For a discussion of feminization in relation to early European responses to phonography, see Charles Grivel, "The Phonograph's Horned Mouth," in *Wireless Imagination: Sound, Radio, and the Avant-Garde*, ed. Douglas Kahn and Gregory Whitehead (Cambridge, MA: MIT Press, 1992), 31–62. In this same vein, Michael Taussig shows how phonography was quickly adopted to imperial forms of capturing the curious life of the primitive other, life thought to be elastic, more susceptible to mimesis—in other words, without propriety. See Michael Taussig, *Mimesis and Alterity: A Particular History of the Senses* (New York: Routledge, 1993), 230–31.

34. Plato, *Phaedrus*, trans. Alexander Nehamas and Paul Woodruff (Indianapolis, IN: Hackett Publishing, 1995), 81 (lines 275e–276a). This section of the *Phaedrus* is at the core of Derrida's critique of Plato's metaphysics of voice in *Dissemination*.

35. Best, *The Fugitive's Properties*, 60–62.

36. Best, *The Fugitive's Properties*, 62.

37. To some extent, Faulkner repeats such a gesture in deeming Yoknapatawpha "my own little postage stamp of native soil," a metaphor haunted by the gesture of primitive accumulation that erects its most famous plantation, Sutpen's Hundred. See James B. Meriwether and Michael Millgate, eds., *Lion in the Garden: Interviews with William Faulkner 1926–1962* (1968; repr., Lincoln: University of Nebraska Press, 1980), 255.

38. Best, *The Fugitive's Properties*, 56.

39. That sonic events may be circulated and exchanged as things is one condition of the nineteenth century's spectacular acts of violence and crimes against the flesh. For a related discussion of the staged recording of the 1893 lynching of Henry Smith in Paris, Texas, that made the rounds at festivals, see Gustavus Stadler, "'Never Heard Such a Thing': Lynching and Phonographic Modernity," *Social Text* 28, no. 1 (March 2010): 87–105.

40. Similarly, Weheliye describes his theoretical project in *Habeas Viscus* as a task for the formal possibilities of writing. Also see Christina Sharpe, *In the Wake: On Blackness and Being* (Durham, NC: Duke University Press, 2016). Sharpe describes her project, after the work of Maurice Blanchot, as a "writing of the disaster." The Middle Passage is *the* disaster on which modernity pivots, yielding an alternative approach to the book form.

41. With cinema, the imaginative problem became one of "synching" voice and body. See, for example, Jay Watson, "The Unsynchable William Faulkner: Faulknerian Voice and Early Sound Film," in *William Faulkner in the Media Ecology*, ed. Julian Murphet and Stefan Solomon (Baton Rouge: Louisiana State University Press, 2015), 93–114.

42. See Philip M. Weinstein, "Crisis and Childhood," in *Becoming Faulkner: The Art and Life of William Faulkner* (New York: Oxford University Press, 2010), 11–65.

43. Also see Barbara Ladd, "'The Direction of the Howling': Nationalism and the Color Line in *Absalom, Absalom!*," *American Literature* 66, no. 3 (1994): 525–51.

44. Weheliye, *Habeas Viscus*, 138.

45. Weheliye, *Habeas Viscus*, 138.

46. William Faulkner, "That Evening Sun," *Collected Stories of William Faulkner* (1950; repr., New York: Vintage, 1995), 296.

47. See Sharpe, *In the Wake*. Such being includes the work of living within the aftermath of what the slave ship's passage leaves behind.

48. While the handwriting of the first draft of "That Evening Sun" is similar to that of "Twilight," the Benjy section of the manuscript of *The Sound and the Fury*, the paper is similar to that used for the revised opening of Quentin's chapter. See Gail M. Morrison, "The Composition of *The Sound and the Fury*," in *William Faulkner's* The Sound and the Fury, ed. Harold Bloom (New York: Bloom's Literary Criticism, 2008), 13.

49. William Faulkner, "Evangeline," in Joseph Blotner, ed., *Uncollected Stories of William Faulkner* (1979; repr., New York: Vintage International, 1997), 606.

50. Faulkner, "Evangeline," 607.

51. Best, *The Fugitive's Properties*, 326n91.

52. Weheliye similarly describes the flesh in relation to an "expansive spatiality of the chorus" (*Habeas Viscus*, 138).

53. Chapter 5 is the only chapter of the novel printed completely, but for a few lines over its final two pages, in italics. I understand the technique to be a graphicization of vibration, a kind of phonographic imprint of the sound waves of Rosa's voice reaching Quentin's ear.

# Jason Compson, Belated Slave Master

## JULIA STERN

Among Faulkner's greatest novels, *The Sound and the Fury* would seem to unfold at a long distance from the lived reality of African American slavery. Black matriarch Dilsey Gibson slots into "the monumental Mammy role," Miriam Petty's term for Hattie McDaniel's tour de force character in *Gone with the Wind*.[1] Petty argues that the impulse to memorialize African American maternal figures is a Janus-faced endeavor: on first glance, it would seem to suggest the celebration of cross-racial family feeling in the southern white imaginary. Petty shows, in fact, how mammies were ossified in the de-historicizing amber of such idealization and forgetfulness. Mammy phantasmagoria has had a long, post-Emancipation afterlife, well into the 1950s with McDaniel's own work as *Beulah*, originally on radio and then early television. Despite being the first African American to win an Academy Award, the great actress faced blistering backlash for playing a devoted slave.[2] McDaniel's rejection by activist sectors of the Black community foreshadowed the way that monumental mammies would never be mistaken for figures of African American independence and achievement.

When it comes to considering Faulkner and slavery, *Absalom, Absalom!* offers the obvious proof-text: a liveried Black butler turns young Thomas Sutpen away from the front door of a great plantation house. That slave's rebuke produces an immediate, metaphysical injury, propelling Sutpen into the creation of his Design. Faulkner's protagonist re-routes his scheme after it runs dangerously aground in Haiti. Still believing the damaged plan remediable, he relaunches it in the antebellum American South. There, Clytie is born to him and a never-named Haitian slave woman. She is daughter and chattel, a liminal figure, both Black and white, neither slave nor free. Race and gender make Clytie ineligible to take the baton of Sutpen's patriarchal whiteness. Still, she constitutes his most loyal offspring. It is she who preserves his visionary legacy by immolating herself and her dying half-brother Henry in suttee-sacrifice to the Design when she sets the house ablaze at novel's end.

Enigmatic Clytie works as major-domo of a domestic world she rarely leaves, silently engaging with her white half-sister and her multiracial nephew and grandnephew. Until the final moments of her life, and as if to echo her incommunicativeness, Faulkner affords the reader access to Clytie only through dramatic tableau in chapter 5 and reported speech in chapter 9. She features in a crucial facing scene in each. On the great house stairs, Clytie succeeds in blocking Rosa's ascent just after Charles Bon's murder. She is protecting her half-siblings, one living, the other newly dead. Rosa dwells outside of the family circle, where the reality of Lee's surrender itself doesn't prevent fratricide at the gates of Sutpen's Hundred.

In an uncanny reenactment and revision of this scene forty-five years later, Clytie fails to stop her aunt manque when Rosa summons Quentin to investigate who is in the house. Their confrontation and Rosa's violence toward Clytie lead to Quentin's discovery of the dying Henry Sutpen, face yellowed with illness and age. The Design's prodigal son has become an abject shell of his once-legitimate self. Nearly fifty years of exile have sullied his whiteness.

As the sole offspring of Sutpen and one of only two imported Haitian slave women, Clytie is also not kin to and remains aloof from the American-born bondspeople who fill out Sutpen's quarters. Her community, such as it is, is exclusively white and Sutpen. Faulkner provides few traces of Sutpen's eldest daughter's extended Haitian family. He gestures toward them only obliquely through the Black slave combatants in the pseudo-Hegelian wrestling scenes that close chapter 1.

It is in these agons that Faulkner reveals Sutpen's one-of-a-kind conception of slaveholding:

> "It seems that on certain occasions, perhaps at the end of the evening, the spectacle, as a grand finale or perhaps as a matter of sheer deadly forethought toward the retention of supremacy, domination, he would enter the ring with one of the negroes himself. Yes. That is what Ellen saw: her husband and the father of her children standing there naked and panting and bloody to the waist and the negro just fallen evidently, lying at his feet and bloody too save that on the negro it merely looked like grease or sweat."[3]

Having toiled along with Sutpen himself during the erection of the great house, and having fought him during his blood-sport matches, these Haitian immigrant slaves have lived in idiosyncratic relation to their master. Faulkner never elaborates, but the reader cannot disregard the possibility of coercion or menace, explicit or implicit, in considering Sutpen's perfect winning record in such brawls.

The master's unheard-of labor and leisure practices violate ancient plantocratic norms of white supremacy. Sutpen's transgressions of the color line provoke the white community to imagine that the unique dynamic with his Haitian bondsmen is some sort of special exception to the infinite reversibility of Hegelian master and slave. But human bondage is human bondage, regardless of special exceptions. Despite the bespoke Haitian slaves' seniority on Sutpen's Hundred, when the war comes they prove that they are far from their owner's most faithful "people." And in fact, Sutpen's Haitian-born chattel are the first of all his property to decamp to the Yankees in 1861.

Against *Absalom*'s invention of a decidedly non-normative slaveholder, *The Sound and the Fury* imagines Jason Compson as the archetypal white master born a century too late. Material vestiges of the peculiar institution remain in the novel. Dilsey, Frony, and Luster live in their own cottage on the Compson property. Its proximity to the white family's kitchen suggests that Dilsey's abode may once have been part of the Compson quarters. Given her references to prior Compson generations, Black and white, it is hard to imagine Dilsey's people having been owned by any other white family. But in *The Sound and the Fury*, nearly sixty-five years have passed since Emancipation. Large portions of Jason's narrative, as well as the fourth section of the novel, are set in 1928. Legally speaking, slaves no longer exist.

Orlando Patterson's work on the sociology of slavery informs my arguments about Jason's anachronistic incarnation of a plantation master. Most illuminating are Patterson's concepts of slavery as social death, fictive kinship, natal alienation, human parasitism, and ideological reversal. Patterson defines social death as a state of non-being vis-à-vis the legal system: slaves are denied surnames and are known by their masters' appellations; slaves cannot testify in court; slave fathers have no paternal rights; and it is a crime for a slave to learn to read and write.[4] Natal alienation entails a slave being ripped away from mother, father, family, kin.[5] Fictive kinship is a strategy to reinsert a slave into the white plantation family as "Uncle Tom" or "Aunt Chloe," mystifying the reality of being wrenched from African or African American origins. In human parasitism, the master complains that he is being eaten out of house and home by his slaves, when in fact, it is the bondsperson's grueling labor that allows the master to expropriate and devour what the slave has created. Ideological reversal is the mechanism by which the idea of who produces and who consumes gets flipped on its head and misattributed: masters claim elaborate credit for production; and slaves are identified as the rapacious consumers of foodstuffs and material goods.

For seventeen years, Jason's treatment of Miss Quentin, Caddy's castoff daughter, has involved a sustained dehumanizing of his niece. He sees her as a white-trash version of the slave "Jezebel." From the baby girl brought into his once-genteel southern family, Jason constructs an abject, alienated, sexually promiscuous pariah. He compares her to a "nigger wench."[6] His self-appointed mandate to destroy his niece is not impulsive or whimsical, but systematic and premeditated. When Mr. Compson returns from Memphis with Caddy's rejected infant, Jason notes, "Well, they brought my job home tonight" (198). This is a bitter reference to the long-promised bank position Caddy's ex-husband will no longer provide for Jason. It also marks his immediate determination to monetize the baby's value through extorting Caddy and, soon after, stealing the child support money she sends for her daughter.

As his section unfolds, Jason engages his forsaken niece in a series of Hegelian encounters: his struggle for mastery and her attempt at resistance reprise the dynamics that the great German philosopher outlined in *The Phenomenology of Spirit*.[7] There, Hegel details the way in which the master-slave relationship depends on a dynamic of mutual recognition. The master cannot maintain his preeminence without possessing a slave or slaves. In the absence of such bondpersons to confirm his status, he no longer is a master. Conversely, a slave must not have access to the awareness that the products of his creation could be thought to be his own. A slave must cede such consciousness, according to Hegel, in order to serve as a bondsperson. When the slave realizes his potential to claim agency over his own labor, such insight marks the beginning of what may become the end of the master's totalizing hold.

In a family in which pathological attachments are the norm, Miss Quentin offers triumphant evidence of the power of her uncle's attentions. Her precocious sexuality and indifference to school have been inculcated, after all, by a man who remains "the nearest thing to a father you ever had," according to her grandmother (259). Miss Quentin knows better: "It's his fault. . . . He makes me do it." And to Jason: "Whatever I do, it's your fault. . . . If I'm bad, *it's because I had to be. You made me*" (260, emphasis added). Raised in a hothouse of paternal abuse and grandmotherly neglect, it is remarkable that Miss Quentin has survived for as long as seventeen years. In Jason's mind, she is far inferior to Lorraine, his prostitute companion in Memphis. This bleak vista of natal alienation links Miss Quentin to the great rejected offspring of Anglo-American literature, particularly Mary Shelley's Monster in *Frankenstein*. In the face of Mr. Compson's alcoholic, fatalistic pronouncements about hereditary doom, Jason embodies Faulkner's insight that human misery is less an organic than a man-made phenomenon.

Jason is one of Faulkner's most effective social engineers. I also think here of Doc Hines, the psychotic villain of *Light in August*, who inscribes Joe Christmas's putative "Negro" identity on his soul by training his orphan peers to call Joe the n-word. Instruction in soul-breaking is a Faulknerian motif. Consider Jason's parasitic relation to his niece, featuring the carefully choreographed embezzlement of Caddy's child support checks. Jason's criminal program includes sourcing superannuated bank drafts and orchestrating an elaborate monthly ritual. Every four weeks, the loathsomely narcissistic matriarch Caroline Compson makes a spectacle of incinerating what she fleetingly wonders may or may not be fully kosher financial documents. "But she just sat there, holding the check. 'This one is on a different bank,' she says. 'They have been on an Indianapolis bank'" (219). Jason has a pat response, of course: women can put their money in more than one bank, after all. So Mrs. Compson strikes her match.

Playing with fire, in fact, would seem to be Jason's métier: the most sadistic scene in the novel involves his spectacular burning of complimentary show tickets in the face of Luster's horror and Dilsey's disgust. From the novel's opening pages, Luster has been obsessing about finding a quarter that would garner him entrance to a traveling musical show. As fellow victims of Jason's heartlessness, Dilsey and Luster should be Miss Quentin's natural allies. But life under her uncle's influence has rendered Caddy's daughter oblivious to other people's suffering. And marinated in her grandmother's highly cultivated race- and class-based snobbery, Miss Quentin would never imagine such a cross-color alliance.

But the passive-aggressive Mrs. Compson's non-recognition and verbal abuse of her Black employees is nothing in comparison to Jason's pathological treatment of Dilsey, Luster, and Job. The latter, Jason's colleague at the hardware store, is on the receiving end of much of Jason's rage, expressed through constant, baneful remarks. He chronically attributes his own parasitic behavior to these African American subordinates. He also practices a textbook version of Patterson's ideological reversal. Beginning with Dilsey, he thinks, "She was so old she couldn't do any more than move hardly. But that's all right: we need somebody in the kitchen to eat up the grub the young ones cant tote off" (185). In Jason's imagination, Dilsey and her daughter and grandson exist as no more than personified mouths and hands, sucking up his resources. Enraged that Luster, tasked with caring for Ben all day, has failed to replace Jason's car tire, he rants, "Yes. . . . I feed a whole dam kitchen full of niggers to follow around after him, but if I want an automobile tire changed, I have to do it myself" (186).

In his fantasies about the ongoing parasitism of the Compsons' Black employees, Jason fixates on Dilsey's biscuits and particularly, the ever-diminishing supply of white flour he must constantly replenish. An essential staple on the menus of elite planters, biscuits were produced by Black bondspeople to satisfy white appetites.[8] If at all, they were available only to those slaves (and their kin) who labored in the mistresses' kitchens. Cornbread was the fundamental foodstuff of slave diets in the quarters. In his perseverative rage about white flour and biscuits, Jason telegraphs that Dilsey's family, several of whom are toiling without wages (or so is my guess about thirteen-year-old Luster's responsibility for Ben), is dining above their station, a belief that makes him apoplectic.

Jason's low-level wrath over the itinerary of Dilsey's biscuits foreshadows a rage he will not be able to metabolize when the stakes are high. Miss Quentin absconds with Jason's stolen money, funds that are rightfully hers, setting in motion the final Hegelian reversal of the novel. Before this cataclysm, her uncle has been palliating her with small sums, giving her $10 at time when her mother intended her to have $50. In 2018 dollars, 1928's $50 would be equivalent to $712—enough money for a train ticket far out of Jefferson and money to live on for some time. Miss Quentin is fully aware that for seventeen years, her uncle has robbed her blind. She wails to Jason that she knows he is deceiving her about the extent of her mother's support, yet she remains minimally compliant in order to guarantee a monthly pittance from his shakedown of his sister and mother. Jason is garnishing Miss Quentin's "wages" as did former slaveholders during Jim Crow; these men charged exorbitant prices at the plantation store so as to keep Black sharecropping families in perpetual debt over basic necessities. But because she is a white victim of Jason's sadistic master, Miss Quentin has viable options. She has been tutored in criminality by the very man who has accused her of "badness" for years.

It is unclear how much money Miss Quentin has reaccessioned from her uncle's stash before absconding from the Compson place. Presented with a classic Faulknerian math problem, we might compute that Jason has purloined as much as $45,000 ($648,000 in today's money), the sum total of Caddy's checks for over a decade and a half. Jason's narrative includes a scene of unsuccessful speculation on the cotton market at the telegraph office; he also describes his other life with the prostitute in Memphis. These activities require cash, but whether the bulk of his stolen money is in Miss Quentin's hands as she decamps is anyone's guess. Given that American banks were struggling and many would fail a year after Faulkner published his novel, we may hypothesize that Jason kept tens of thousands of dollars hidden in the locked box under his closet floorboards, in which case, Miss Quentin may have reclaimed her birthright. Or, over nearly twenty years, he might have squandered it all on trifles.

So habituated is Jason to lying—to Miss Quentin, to his mother, to Earl, his boss—that even his report to the sheriff centers on a falsehood about the missing money. He complains that he's been robbed of $4,000, knowing that a greater amount would raise red flags about how a hardware store clerk could have accrued a fortune. So it is that Miss Quentin, Jason Compson's white-trash wench, reverses the master-slave dynamic of exploitation and nonrecognition through which he nearly destroyed her. Her revenge is aimed at the intersection of Jason's psychological and economic vulnerabilities: his rage against Caddy and his conviction that her daughter's money rightfully belongs to him.

Jason's other victims may have less mobility than Miss Quentin, who has been venturing off campus, so to speak, since attaining sexual maturity. Luster notes on Easter morning that for months, he and Ben have witnessed Miss Quentin shimmying down the pear tree at night (287). Luster, Frony's son, is a Black subaltern whom Jason seems to believe exists to do his bidding. The young man's relative youth may have much to do with Jason's perception that he has a proprietary claim on Luster's time. But in Luster, Faulkner gives the reader one of the few Black characters in his great tragic novels who questions the old ways of the plantation still permeating the Compson ménage.

Luster's ambitions differ from those of Faulkner's other Black characters. He does not share vocational plans with his father, a Pullman porter whom Faulkner never represents. The Pullman workforce created the first African American labor union in the United States. While their toil was grueling, with long hours of domestic service, Pullman porters enjoyed unlimited travel and, after unionization, middle-class wages. Faulkner reveals a brilliant sociological imagination in creating this unnamed and absent character and giving him this career. Pullman porters became representative men in the cultural imaginary of African American uplift.

But Luster's desire is not to accrue money. His interests are aesthetic. Obsessed with going to the "show," he longs to hear what I infer is a traveling white Dixieland band covering ragtime and early swing, both African American musical forms. Such a performance would be a late 1920s version of what Eric Lott calls love and theft. It is possible that Faulkner understands Luster's zeal as something negative, some sort of shiftlessness or distraction from (unremunerated) labor on the Compson place. Certainly that is Jason's view, inspiring the aforementioned incineration of his free show passes before a frantic, ticketless Luster.

The name that Faulkner gives this character who resists southern white social conventions for Black employees in 1928 is telling: *Luster* refers to the glow of reflected light, specifically a sheen, and to a glow of light from within; luminosity, an inner beauty, radiance. I understand all of these associations as speaking to something extraordinary about the young man whom Jason Compson cannot see. Accordingly, there is another way to read the show and Luster's fascination with a featured musical saw, whose sounds he tries to recreate in the kitchen cellar on Easter morning. Luster's passion for the performance marks his resistance to Jason's attempt to keep everyone on the Compson place, Black and white, under his authoritarian thumb. A generation earlier, Luster's mother Frony took possession of a jar of lightning bugs that her brother T. P. had assembled. They became the aesthetic magnet that kept the young Quentin, Caddy, Benjy, and Jason occupied on the night of Damuddy's funeral, a magical distraction from a darkening world.

Luster, of course, is far from a redemptive figure: his ill-conceived plan to show off before his Black friends results in the disastrous surrey ride around the left side of the Confederate monument at novel's end. Routine shattered, Ben unravels, wailing until Jason pummels Luster's head, throws him out of the vehicle, grabs the reins, reverses direction, and restores order. Inflicting brutality on his chattel within a split-second of the infraction, Jason dominates through violence up to the last page of the novel.

Still, in *The Sound and The Fury* the superannuated slave master has overstayed his welcome. Faulkner reveals Jason's anachronistic status by creating him as a proud car owner pathologically allergic to gasoline. He is a man who cannot cope with the tools that make modernity run. Meanwhile, Jason's African American foils, descendants of slaves, remain the only characters in the novel with hopes for a better life: Dilsey's eyes remain on heaven, while Frony and Luster are firmly grounded in this world. Between *The Sound and the Fury*'s spiritually focused grandmother and her flesh-oriented grandson, the novel's Black characters are the only figures within sight of redemption, whether their faith rests in Jesus Christ or in the power of art.

NOTES

1. Miriam Petty, *Stealing the Show: African American Performers and Audiences in 1930s Hollywood* (Berkeley: University of California Press, 2016).
2. See Jill Watts, *Hattie: Black Ambition, White Hollywood* (New York: Amistad, 2005).
3. William Faulkner, *Absalom, Absalom!*, rev. ed. (1936; repr., New York: Vintage International, 1990), 21.
4. Orlando Patterson, *Slavery and Social Death: A Comparative Study* (Cambridge, MA: Harvard University Press, 1982), 38–39.
5. Patterson, *Slavery and Social Death*, 7–8.

6. William Faulkner, *The Sound and the Fury*, rev. ed. (1929; repr. New York: Vintage International, 1990), 189. Hereafter cited parenthetically.

7. G. W. F. Hegel, *Phenomenology of Spirit*, trans. A. V. Miller (Oxford, UK: Oxford University Press, 1977), 111–12.

8. See for instance Harriet Jacobs, *Incidents in the Life of a Slave Girl, Written by Herself*, ed. Jean Fagan Yellin (1861; repr., Cambridge, MA: Harvard University Press, 1986), 12.

# A Literary Genealogy of "Slavery's Capitalism" in Chesnutt and Faulkner

Stephanie Rountree

Over the last thirty years or so, a growing number of scholars have suggested William Faulkner's literary indebtedness to Charles Chesnutt, specifically for his depictions of characters from ambiguous racial backgrounds.[1] This essay takes seriously the suggestion that Faulkner's 1932 novel *Light in August* does indeed owe a kind of "debt"[2] to Chesnutt's literary work, though not only in the manners that scholars have previously suggested. Rather than exploring Faulkner's stylistic or symbolic inheritance of Chesnutt's legacy, I consider their works as trans-generational contributions to an American literary genealogy of socioeconomic recovery work—a body of literature that recovers US liberal democracy's inaugural and indelible dependence upon Black enslavement both materially and structurally. Examining Faulkner's *Light in August* through what I argue is one of its literary, historical, and economic antecedents—Chesnutt's 1900 short story "Lonesome Ben"—I demonstrate that US authors have intuited for over a century what US historians are just now beginning to study in earnest under the discipline recently entitled "Slavery's Capitalism."[3] As Sven Beckert and Seth Rockman assert, "American slavery is necessarily imprinted on the DNA of American capitalism";[4] my literary research evidences how authors have discerned and depicted slavery's genetic "imprint" as it organizes mechanisms of US corporeal governance beyond Emancipation, coordinating all facets of human life in support of the economic "health," and therefore the national sovereignty, of the US nation-state.

American authors like Faulkner and, before him, Chesnutt have long intuited a continuity of enslaving logics as manifest in post-Emancipation (neo)liberal governance, and these authors have crafted a literary genealogy tracing that influence at least since the nineteenth century. I term this literary genealogy *American anteliberalism*, indicating the triangulation of capitalism, citizenship, and corporeality in post-Emancipation US governance as it is organized by enslaving logics and rendered visible in national literature. Ultimately, the concept of anteliberalism reasserts Audre Lorde's declaration that "it is through poetry that we give name to those ideas which are—until the poem—nameless and formless, about to be birthed, but already felt."[5] The authors who, like Chesnutt and Faulkner, intuit those truths "already felt" by the American body politic have been composing for more than a hundred years a nascent language that animates with humane urgency the consequences of an enslaving logic manifested in public policies that subordinate human life to capitalism's abstracting violence. What follows, then, is an exploration of how *Light in August*, when historicized through its literary and socio-economic antecedents in Chesnutt's short fiction, can bring into relief American enslavement's lasting legacy in US liberal democracy.

*Light in August* traces the corporeal contours of capitalism's violence as early as its opening scene. Faulkner illustrates Lena Grove's hometown of Doane's Mill, an Alabama pine mill at the peak of what the Alabama Forestry Commission calls the "cut-out and get-out"[6] method of logging during the early twentieth century, as follows:

> All the men in the village worked in the mill or for it. It was cutting pine. It had been there seven years and in seven years more it would destroy all the timber within its reach. Then some of the machinery and most of the men who ran it and existed because of and for it would be loaded onto freight cars and moved away. But some of the machinery would be left . . . gaunt, staring, motionless wheels rising from mounds of brick rubble . . . a stumppocked scene of profound and peaceful desolation, unplowed, untilled, gutting slowly into red and choked ravines. . . . Then the hamlet . . . would not now even be remembered by the hookwormridden heirs at large who pulled the buildings down and burned them in cookstoves and winter grates.[7]

Faulkner's phrase "hookwormridden heirs at large" has formed the centerpiece of a handful of economic inquiries into the novel.[8] I intervene in this scholarship to ask in both literal and figurative terms: what does the hookworm parasite have to do with the capitalist enterprise of pine logging? Moreover, what does it mean to think about citizenship in Doane's Mill as it relates to the pine mill? And further still, what is at stake for the bodies and lives of those people who "existed because of and for" that mill? Through this depiction of Doane's Mill in the wake of industrial exploitation, we can trace the interconnected workings of anteliberalism's three technologies: capitalism, citizenship, and corporeality.

Of the three, Faulkner's critique of capitalism is surely the most conspicuous. Over its fourteen-year run, the mill would "destroy all the timber within its reach," producing "profound and peaceful desolation." Here, the author underscores the logic of capitalism as one of violent colonization: extracting resources to feed a foreign system, leaving behind nothing but the discarded tools of that extraction ("gaunt staring, motionless wheels rising from mounds of brick rubble"). Following the logic of capitalism, the laborers who produce the commodity are not the benefactors of the capital it generates, as they are abandoned in poverty to scavenge, "pull[ing] the buildings down and burn[ing] them in cookstoves and winter grates." Emphasizing the inherent irony of such a system, Faulkner declares those left behind as the mill's "heirs at large," that is, the rightful benefactors of an estate upon a forefather's death. In this case, though, their "rightful" inheritance is refuse, scraps discarded after capital is extracted. The mill's industry enacts a kind of corporeal blood violence against the earth, too, as it "gut[s] slowly into red and choked ravines." This portrait renders the "cut-out and get-out" capitalism of Doane's Mill in both its corporeal and its ecological violence.

Further, the material production of Doane's Mill as an incorporated town and the ontological production of its citizens first depends upon the arrival of this capitalist enterprise. It stands to reason that the spatial incorporation of the geography of Doane's Mill as *town* at all is inaugurated by the enterprise's arrival in the space. The very name itself indicates both private ownership in the possessive (belonging to one named "Doane") and an operation defined as a structure or location "where a specified industrial or manufacturing process is carried out."[9] At the same time as the mill inaugurates the codified space, it likewise inaugurates citizenship status of the locals. But, Faulkner pushes this status further. Not only is their belonging to the mill established, even their very *being* is existentially dependent upon the mill; the workers not only "ran" the mill but also "existed because of and for it." Their existence is manifested via their employment relationship to the mill as laborer-citizens of Doane's Mill.

The pine-logging enterprise's power to constitute both the incorporated town and its citizens evokes the historical shift in political philosophy in Europe and its colonies from the sixteenth century to the nineteenth century, moving away from feudal monarchy, through mercantilism, and ultimately to the birth of liberal democracy in the United States. Michel Foucault explains in his 1978–79 lecture series *The Birth of Biopolitics* that a fundamental defining shift in political logic that ushered in the era of liberal democracy was an emphasis on state sovereignty and legitimacy as measured no longer by the divine right of a monarch but by the nation's economic wealth.[10] Indeed, even as holistic governmental control of the economy in mercantilism fell out of vogue with the rise of liberal economic ideals, the measurement of state sovereignty via economic health remained the same, and indeed, remains so to this day. As Wendy Brown underscores in *Undoing the Demos: Neoliberalism's Stealth Revolution* (2015), "economic growth has become both the end and legitimation of government."[11] Therefore, that both Doane's Mill as a municipality and the existential citizenship of its inhabitants are produced through their relationship to a profiteering enterprise naturally proceeds from the logic of US liberal democracy. That Faulkner narrates how "most of the men who ran" the mill ultimately "moved away" once the area's timber has been exhausted clearly underscores the workers' fealty to the enterprise, not to the cultural or socio-geographical entity of the hamlet called Doane's Mill. Capitalist enterprise inaugurates both municipal incorporation of place and constructs of citizenship in Doane's Mill.

Third, and perhaps most significantly, Faulkner concludes this portrait with the embodied consequences of the mill, focusing on the individual's corporeal experience: "Then the hamlet . . . would not now even be remembered by the hookwormridden heirs at large who pulled the buildings down and burned them in cookstoves and winter grates." He leaves us with a lasting image of diseased scavengers, humans scraping at the dregs of the pine mill's industrial excrement. Hookworm is, indeed, an appropriate talisman for the human experience of abject poverty in the rural South. For the cycle of anteliberalism's abstracting inequities churns with a rotation of resource consumption, exploitation, production, disposal, and contagion: it is an outward-moving, self-replicating technology that produces a diaspora regenerated from the shit of capitalist consumption. This cycle mirrors closely the pathology of the hookworm parasite, which is typically contracted by barefoot exposure to human feces. As Wayne Flint describes:

> The hookworm usually entered its victim's body through the skin between the toes. . . . The bloodstream carried the parasite to the lungs, where it entered the alveoli. From there it continued its journey up the bronchial passage into the throat, where it was swallowed into the gastrointestinal tract. Fastened onto the lining of the small intestine, it feasted on the host's blood. The female could lay as many as ten thousand eggs a day, most of which exited the body with the victim's feces to begin the cycle again.[12]

More than a passing stereotype connoting abject poverty in the rural South, the hookworm pathogen underscores the very literal bodily consequences wrought by an anteliberal system that coordinates human life and health to capitalist gain. The citizens of Doane's Mill live solely at the mercy—or more accurately, the neglect—of the mill owners, in abject filth, ostensibly unable to afford sufficient footwear, let alone hygienic sewage management, to prevent the contraction and spread of the disease. The consequences of this enterprise physically cost the laborer-citizens their blood as it is "feasted upon" by the parasitic worm. And this process is more than symbolic. Historically, hookworm has plagued poor communities in the region because it presents a perfect intersection of geography, climate, economic neglect, and sociopolitical exploitation. Government failure to invest in public health infrastructure like sewage and water management leaves impoverished and especially rural communities to live in waste. Meanwhile, the warm climate incubates the parasite, making it a ready hitchhiker to the nearest bare foot. This cycle was true in the 1930s of Faulkner's *Light in August*,[13] and it remains true today: in 2017 a study at Baylor College of Medicine found continued evidence of hookworm infection in Lowndes County, Alabama,[14] demonstrating that for the poorest, and often Blackest, most remote communities in the US South, hookworm remains a very real threat.

What is particularly chilling about hookworm is its long-term impact both on the conditions of citizenship via socioeconomic class and on the opportunity for the kind of upward mobility promised by ideals of US liberal democracy. People infected with the parasite suffer from chronic lethargy due to iron deficiency caused by the worm's blood leaching, and the iron deficiency of hookworm further turns the skin a sallow or yellowed color.[15] This "poor" disease has often compelled the infected to geophagia or clay eating—another practice that has fueled national stereotypes framing poor southerners as lowly, abject, even animalistic.[16] Children infected by hookworm also experience moderate to severe delays in cognitive development,[17] further compromising their ability to contribute to a productive laboring population. These symptoms—lethargy, yellowed skin, clay eating, and cognitive disability—together with the epidemic levels of infection across the US South historically, have fueled the longstanding "stereotype" of "poor whites in terms closely related to the symptoms of the disease: yellow skinned, shiftless, and lazy,"[18] hardly the ideal productive American citizen. Moreover, those who contract the disease might have children of their own, and the cycle begins again. Researchers have long documented this generational foreclosure of economic mobility. For example, one 2013 Pew study reported: "43 percent of Americans raised at the bottom of the income ladder remain stuck there as adults, and 70 percent never even make it to the middle."[19] This transgenerational economic replication of socioeconomic agency is animated in the hookworm pathology of the Doane's Mill bankrupt inheritance as the "heirs at large": birth determinism (via abject poverty), resource consumption (scavenging among unhealthy environments), exploitation (ravaging the pine and extracting surplus labor), production (generating lumber), disposal ("mounds of brick rubble"). Faulkner's figurative choice of hookworm—rather than pellagra or malaria, which both also ravaged impoverished southern communities in the 1930s[20]—proves an evocative talisman for the farce of economic ascendance promised by the "American Dream" of liberal democracy.

In this light, the *ante-* of anteliberalism asserts that, because the inherent structure of US (neo)liberalism replicates a sociopolitical system of birth determinism—where one's political subjectivity is, in many ways, ontologically predetermined before one is born—the invention of US liberal democracy was *not* as new in the annals of civilization as many like to imagine. For all the innovative technologies developed at the rise of US capitalism that revolutionized calculations of wealth exchange and accumulation,[21] the lived human experience under this abstracting economic revolution largely recalls systems that are antecedent to the emergence of liberal democracy. The feudal logics inherent in US liberal democracy manifest most clearly in arguments about the foundational role of Black enslavement to the establishment of American capitalism.

To establish this genealogy of power and exploitation and to render slavery's inaugural role in it visible, one must begin by comparing the feudal relationship between lord and serf with the capitalist relationship between employer ("capitalist") and employee ("worker"). Ellen Meiksins Wood demonstrates in *Empire of Capital* (2003) how both relationships are organized by a logic of "capital accumulation [that] could not take place without a net transfer of surplus labor from workers to capitalists."[22] Where the serf is legally bound to the land and thereby obliged to pay rent, taxes, and/or tributes in addition to working that land, the worker-employee is not legally bound, yet without capital of his own, he is nevertheless compelled extralegally to forfeit his surplus labor: "Capitalists—unlike, say, feudal lords—generally need no direct control of coercive military or political force to exploit their workers, because workers are propertyless, with no direct access to the means of production, and must sell their labor-power in exchange for a wage in order to work and to live."[23] Indeed, as Wood asserts in her earlier work *Democracy against Capitalism*, the freedom achieved in the evolution from feudalism to mercantilism and, ultimately, to capitalism was *not* a universal freedom for all men under a liberal economic system but, instead, a liberation for the propertied class from their political accountability for managing society.[24] This shift to economic liberation explains why, in an eighteenth-century American moment dominated by Lockean philosophy, capitalism appeared so "compatible with ideologies of civic freedom and equality in a way that non-capitalist class systems never were."[25]

Nevertheless, it was precisely this "new" economic liberalism that inaugurated the demand for a new form of codified, subordinate, unpaid, unfree labor via Black enslavement: "the growth of Britain's capitalist economy gave a new impetus to this old form of exploitation, in the southern American colonies as well as in the Caribbean. For a time, capitalism even increased the demand for slave labor, as it expanded markets for plantation commodities, at a time when capitalist social property relations made other forms of dependent labor unavailable and a mass free proletariat did not yet exist."[26] Wood's argument echoes W. E. B. Du Bois's sixty-eight years earlier in *Black Reconstruction in America*: "the black workers of America bent at the bottom of a growing pyramid of commerce and industry; and they not only could not be spared, if this new economic organization was to expand, but rather they became the cause of new political demands and alignments, of new dreams of power and visions of empire."[27] More than merely subsidizing overzealous aims of early American entrepreneurs, the very presence of enslaved Black laborers fostered growth in both economic and imperial ambition. For this reason, a growing body of archival histories identify "slavery as a constitutive element of American capitalism."[28] What remained in the transition from feudalism to capitalism was an economic logic that leveraged citizenship (including the denial thereof) as a political mechanism to replicate an old hierarchy of power and agency that ontologically produced a person's political subjectivity—subjugation even—before birth.

Fundamental in the survival of such an anti-democratic system as slavery within US liberal democracy was the creation of elaborate legal and ideological mechanisms to underwrite racism as an exception to democratic ideals. A long, robust history of scholarship on race and slavery has explored these enslaving ideologies, including Orlando Patterson's foundational *Slavery and Social Death* (1982). This body of scholarship demonstrates how property laws of "unconditional"[29] and disposable[30] ownership of enslaved people qua chattel required a justifying ideology: "slaves had to be placed outside the normal universe of natural freedom and equality to justify their permanent subordination. This was accomplished by the construction of more rigid racial categories than had ever existed before—in the form of pseudo-scientific conceptions of race or patriarchal ideologies in which African slaves were perennial children,"[31] including quite infamously Thomas Jefferson's denigrating "Query XIV" in *Notes on the State of Virginia* (1781).[32] Importantly, such ideology was tied both to enslaved persons' relationship to national citizenship as "non-humans" and therefore non-citizens, and to US slavery's legal designation as a hereditary condition manifested via the body and passed down according to the "condition of the mother."[33] This corporeal structure of citizenship in support of a burgeoning liberal, or rather *ante*liberal, democracy inherently replicated the logic of birth-determinism intrinsic to feudalism.

Rather than eradicating the last vestiges of feudal logic, however, Emancipation dramatically reshaped the relationship between citizenship and laborer, and antiliberal governance evolved in turn, marking (of course) *not* a net decrease in governance over the corporeality of Black Americans but rather a broadening of that same governing logic to implicate a more and more diverse population of US subjects according to varying forms of embodiment: race, gender, sexuality, disability, and so on. This broadening logic is evident in *Light in August*, but to understand Faulkner's recovered history, and to contextualize his contribution to an antiliberal literary genealogy, we must first understand Joe Christmas's literary forebear: lonesome Ben in Chesnutt's 1900 short story of the same name.

Chesnutt's story opens on a Reconstruction-era plantation in North Carolina as purchased by white northerners John and Annie. "[L]ocal capitalists" have "approached" John about the possibility of constructing a "cotton mill on Beaver Creek."[34] They offer John an opportunity to buy into the enterprise by establishing a brick mill on his clay-rich property: if John's bricks can be used to build the cotton mill, then they will accept the materials as part of John's capital investment. John and Annie solicit a buggy ride to inspect the clay banks of their property, and they are chauffeured by the central protagonist of all Chesnutt's conjure stories, Uncle Julius, a formerly enslaved Black man who in each story recalls tales about enslaved life before Emancipation. At the clay bank, the trio encounters several neighbors whose skin appears "a rather sickly hue" (51). John narrates, "I had observed a greater sallowness among both the colored people and the poor whites thereabouts than the hygienic conditions of the neighborhood seemed to justify." Shortly after John's observation, the group witnesses a woman on the side of the bank gathering clay to eat. Disgusted, Annie recoils, and the encounter prompts Julius to share a tale of "lonesome Ben" from before Emancipation (52).

Ben was an enslaved man who was "black ez coal" (52) and "a good wukker" (53), but his one vice was an affinity for drinking. One day, the overseer caught Ben drinking whiskey and promised to whip him, so Ben ran away and survived by eating clay from the same bank that John and Annie later inspect with Julius. Eventually, he tried to return to his wife, but she rejected him, claiming "I never seed yer befo' in my life" (55).

Ben was so dejected that his wife did not recognize him that he could not eat his daily clay portion. Later, he discovered his son Pete walking along the road, but when Ben approached him, Pete ran away. Later, Ben's friend Primus came along, and he, too, did not recognize Ben: "Youer de mos' mis'able lookin' merlatter I eber seed. . . . [Y]o' better take yo' yaller hide 'way f'um yer" (56). Having grown more lonely and desperate, Ben made one final attempt to reunite with his former life upon encountering his enslaver-owner Marrabo along the road. But Marrabo similarly failed to recognize him, calling Ben a "yaller rascal" for claiming to be his runaway slave and exclaiming that "Ben wuz black ez a coal an' straight ez an' arrer. Youer yaller ez dat clay-bank, an' crooked ez a bair'l-hoop" (57). Utterly devastated, Ben returned to his clay bank and looked in the water only to discover that, just as his wife, son, friend, and enslaver-owner had suggested, his dark skin had lightened to a yellow color, rendering him completely unrecognizable to the people he loved most. So lonely, so bereft by his loss of identity and a sense of belonging to those he loved, "hit 'uz all he could do ter crawl up on de bank an' lay down in de sun . . . 'til he died" (58).

What follows Ben's death is perhaps the most curious event of all. Julius explains, "de sun beat down on 'im" until finally Ben's corpse grew "ha'd as a brick" (59). Then a tree "fell on 'im an' smashed 'im all ter pieces," and at last, the rain "washed 'im in de crick," turning the water yellow, water and clay destined to be consumed by the next generation of clay-eaters. Julius concludes his tale about lonesome Ben, "dat's de reason w'y I knows dat clay'll make brick an' w'y I doan nebber lak ter see no black folks eat'n it" (59). Chesnutt ends his story with John admonishing the poor Black and poor white clay-eaters for being lazy; he then declares his reasons for declining the brickmaking enterprise.

Several elements of Chesnutt's story clearly anticipate *Light in August* thirty years later. Most evidently, the depiction of abject poverty, particularly as it manifests symptoms of hookworm, underscores the disease as a widespread, longstanding public health crisis in the rural US South, as the poor white and poor Black people living along John and Annie's creek exhibit sickly appearances, yellow skin, and clay eating, all symptoms of hookworm. Furthermore, Ben's ambiguous racial presentation contributes to literary traditions of both the "tragic mulatto" and "passing" narratives with which Faulkner's Joe Christmas similarly engages; but more specifically evocative of the evolving public perception of Joe's racial identity, lonesome Ben likewise moves through changing "shades" of public perception, first as a Black man who is as dark as coal and later as a lightened, mulatto-looking man with yellow-tinged skin. Both protagonists like their alcohol, as Ben first discovers trouble in a drink of "[w]hiskey" (53) and Joe "get[s] rich" bootlegging "whiskey" (Faulkner, *Light in August*, 43). Further, where John rejects the local capitalists' offer to buy into a cotton mill enterprise—yet another industry of capital extraction infamous for its corporeal, economic, and environmental violence—the portrait of Doane's Mill offers an eerie postmortem to the industry John might have ushered into the community, as the prospect of brickmaking in Chesnutt resurfaces in Faulkner's portrait of the "mounds of brick rubble" at Doane's Mill. Something about this anteliberal genealogy constructed by Chesnutt and Faulkner—about the coordination of corporeality, race, digestion, capitalism, and even bricks—sounds familiar.

In his 1901 autobiography *Up from Slavery*, Booker T. Washington famously animated his capitalist pedagogy for racial uplift through the skill of brickmaking. Advocating the importance of teaching Black Americans industrial trades in order for them to ascend from their economic despair, Washington recalls that "the matter of brickmaking" provided an opportunity to consolidate three line items in the school's budget: student instruction, facility management, and fundraising.[35] Washington's capitalist approach to racial uplift was widely celebrated by white leaders in his time, and his pedagogy was in many ways coopted into an oppressive culture of white paternalism that Faulkner himself participated in, as best evidenced in his lectures at the University of Virginia.[36] What is lesser studied, however, is that Washington's capitalist pedagogy via brickmaking was only one of *two* key goals for his work at Tuskegee. He also emphasized practical training in hygiene, diet, and housekeeping:

> The students had come from homes where they had had no opportunities for lessons which would teach them how to care for their bodies. [. . .] We wanted to teach the students how to bathe; how to care for their teeth and clothing. We wanted to teach them what to eat, and how to eat it properly, and how to care for their rooms. Aside from this, we wanted to give them such a practical knowledge of some one industry, together with a spirit of industry, thrift, and economy, that they would be sure of knowing how to make a living after they had left us. (*Up from Slavery*, 60)

Washington's approach to preparing African American students for productive citizenship in the United States follows a nineteenth-century history of "reform movements" that sought to establish "the ideal citizen" through "quotidian practices of correct consumption, self-care, and sexual hygiene."[37] As Kyla Wazana Tompkins observes in *Racial Indigestion*, rigorous bodily conditioning in terms of diet, hygiene, manners, and other modes of being in one's own body was ubiquitous in the 1800s, especially regarding the raced body. Such standards of respectability followed white ideals of national citizenship. It stands to reason that, if Washington's aim was to elevate the conditions of Black Americans above the impoverished, subcitizen status that was slavery's inheritance, then he needed to render his students both economically productive *and* corporeally respectable.

Notwithstanding the acclaim Washington garnered from white America, he sustained much criticism from African American activists.[38] One such critic was Charles Chesnutt. He and Washington shared a sincere friendship that balanced fierce respect with passionate debate.[39] Indeed, Washington and Chesnutt maintained frequent personal communication throughout their lives and found occasions to publish both with one another[40] and about one another.[41] Given the extensive, ongoing debate between Washington and Chesnutt both in critical publications and in private letters, and especially considering Chesnutt's own experience as principal of State Colored Normal School in North Carolina, I argue that we can read "Lonesome Ben" as a literary rebuttal continuing their epistolary debate—an allegorical critique of Washington's brickmaking pedagogy.[42]

Consider the plot elements of "Lonesome Ben" vis-à-vis Washington's pedagogy. An enslaved Black man escapes the system of slavery and believes he can survive by eating the dirt from the margins of a white enslaver-capitalist's plantation. Rather than saving him, though, the clay lightens (*whitens* even) his skin until his Blackness is compromised, rendering him unrecognizable to the people he loves the most—a detail that suggests social conditioning according to ideals of "white citizenship." Distraught and isolated, with no place to survive, let alone thrive, as a Black man beyond the rigid construct of noncitizen property-laborer created for him under US liberal democracy, he dies. Hardly lifting Ben "up from slavery," such conditions literalize his objectification, rendering his corporeality a commodity[43]—a brick that, in the context of John's prospective cotton mill enterprise, would help build a new structure of white capitalist exploitation. Ben's victimization is corporeal, based on capitalist ideals, and ensured through legal denial of his citizenship. And as his commodified body returns to the plantation's ecosystem as dust to the river, Chesnutt's allegory suggests that the clay-eaters of John's Reconstruction-era plantation exist "downstream" from another, older regime of capitalist exploitation that has long dominated the region. They are the "hookwormridden heirs at large" of slavery's capitalism. Chesnutt seems to say that if Black Americans follow Washington's approach to racial uplift through brickmaking and bodywork, then they only ensure self-destruction and complicity in a system designed to benefit not *all* Americans but white capitalists.

Taking Chesnutt's allegory to its fullest extent, the anteliberal triangulation of corporeality, capitalism, and citizenship is regenerated through a transgenerational process of consumption when both poor Black people *and* poor white people consume the clay comprising Ben's decomposed corpse. Prefiguring Faulkner's reference to hookworm, Chesnutt's Ben performs literary recovery work that demonstrates the foundational role slavery played in establishing US capitalism, its parasitic violence against the body for capital extraction, and its pernicious regeneration and expansion beyond Emancipation to encumber both Black and non-Black subjects according to this anteliberal logic. Chesnutt's transhistorical setting, too, underscores the presence of this logic both before and after slavery, and John's white paternalism in the end—blaming the poverty of the clay-eating poor on their own laziness—replicates the enduring stereotyping of impoverished southerners that obscures the systemic legacy of Black enslavement intrinsic to modern US capitalism. Still further, Chesnutt illustrates the systemic relationship between poor Black and poor white abjection under US capitalism. Compared to Faulkner's portrait of Doane's Mill, Chesnutt's allegorical critique of Washington more clearly identifies the origin of anteliberal logic in Black enslavement and traces how that logic broadens to encumber more and more diverse groups who may not have been subjected directly to histories of enslavement but who nevertheless experience forms of subjugation first developed on enslaved Black Americans.

What does this have to do with Faulkner's *Light in August*? Notwithstanding the author's moderate, paternalistic belief in Black uplift through respectability pedagogies like Washington's, we can read Joe Christmas as a victim of such anteliberal controls, specifically through his digestive encounters with women as they seek to define his citizenship status via the racial hierarchy of the 1930s Jim Crow South. At the orphanage as a child, where the dietitian is responsible for teaching the children lessons in nutrition and hygiene (à la Washington), Joe's formative experience consists in overconsuming the dietitian's toothpaste, unwittingly witnessing her attempted rape by the intern, and vomiting himself into discovery (121–22). This encounter ends with the dietitian calling him a "nigger bastard" (122), possibly for the first time in his life, underscoring both racialized citizenship ("nigger" in Jim Crow South) and fatherless disinheritance ("bastard" as a legal status). Joe's conditioning in this formative moment is reinforced when the dietitian later tries to buy his silence with a dollar (125). This foundational moment in Joe's character development, then, is organized by the three elements of anteliberal governance: capitalism (buying his silence off with the dollar), corporeality (pedagogy in diet and dental hygiene, vomiting the toothpaste), and citizenship (legal citizenship categories as both "nigger" and "bastard").

Additionally, Joe Christmas's early childhood experience in the orphanage is clearly shaped by Washington's pedagogy for racial uplift. Notably, five-year-old Joe misuses the toothpaste, swallowing it rather than brushing with it; such behavior clearly fails the curricular objectives Washington outlines in *Up from Slavery* in 1901: "care for their teeth . . . what to eat, and how to eat it properly" (60). Joe's "uncivilized" consumption leads to his discovery and, by the respectability standard, warrants his denigration as a "nigger bastard," the antithesis of a respectable Black boy reared in the Tuskegee tradition. Furthermore, Joe's age during the encounter coincides precisely with *Up from Slavery*'s 1901 publication. Faulkner began *Light in August* as "Dark House" in 1931, and the text clearly indicates that Joe Christmas is thirty-five years old at his death.[44] Thus, Joe's five-year-old experience with the dietitian occurred the same year Washington's pedagogy was widely disseminated on a national scale. Ultimately, reading Joe's experience through "Lonesome Ben" reveals that the same anteliberal logic that enslaved Ben endures beyond Emancipation to organize Joe's experience. Joe's struggle for self-actualized subjectivity via liberal democratic ideals is foreclosed. His political and subjective agency is predestined at both his racially ambiguous birth and his racist rebirth in the dietitian's closet. Throughout the course of the novel, Joe's digestively and sadistically violent, lifelong journey replicates the isolation and foreclosed sense of belonging that Ben experiences when the clay eating alters his racial appearance.

Indeed, all of Joe's experiences with women are marked by digestion and organized by anteliberalism's triangulated controls, ever mirroring his literary ancestor Ben. Joe's relationship with Bobbie, the waitress-prostitute who makes a living ministering to corporeal needs, is inaugurated by Joe's bumbled capitalist transaction over a cup of coffee (177–81) and concludes with her departure as two men beat him to see *"if his blood is black"* (219), thus relegating him to non- or second-class citizenship in the Jim Crow United States. Similarly, Joe's relationship with Joanna Burden begins at the dinner table (229–30), progresses as she tries to "uplift" him by involving him in her "business affairs" (268), and ends with her death, which renders Joe the "black rapist"[45] of southern white supremacist mythology.[46] Even his lynching-castration by Percy Grimm manifests these elements, as Grimm's sadistic zealotry for the "State national guard" (449–50) ultimately stems from his failure to function as a productive citizen in school or employment (451), disappointing his capitalist "father, a hardware merchant" (450). Compensating for his failure as a capitalist laborer-citizen, Grimm lynches Joe with a butcher knife in Hightower's kitchen—another space associated with the corporeality of digestion, here compounded by violent bodily death (464)—ultimately asserting Joe's racialized citizenship under Jim Crow by denying him due process in favor of mob violence. In these ways, Christmas's character arc continues a literary genealogy of anteliberalism inherited from his literary ancestor, Chesnutt's Ben.

In closing, I want to underscore how Joe's and Ben's experiences illuminate the same corporeal consequences of anteliberalism evoked by Faulkner's hookworm imagery. Noting that digestion deeply informs both Ben's and Joe's narratives, we can go on to read bodily consumption in their life stories as analogous to capitalist consumption. Indeed, the two characters' capitalist life-cycles reprise the basic elements of hookworm pathology: birth determinism (via hereditary enslavement in Ben's case and racial ambiguity in Joe's); resource consumption (Ben's clay eating and Joe's digestion-marked relationships with women); economic exploitation (Ben's forced labor and Joe's "negro's" work at the planing mill [36]); production (Ben's "production" as a brick and Joe's of bootleg whiskey); disposal (Ben's abandonment on the creek bank and Joe's lynching); and contagion (Ben's smashed body returned to clay that will be consumed by others and Joe's story that lives on in the community's memory).[47] Ben's and Joe's sufferings across a seventy-year chasm before and after Emancipation demonstrate the ongoing parasitic logic of anteliberalism, as it triangulates technologies of capitalism, corporeality, and citizenship based upon logics established in Black enslavement. Moreover, the abject experience of hookworm among the poor Black and poor white neighbors on John and Annie's Reconstruction-era plantation, interpreted together with Doane's Mill's 1931 "hookwormridden heirs," evidences the continuity of anteliberalism's enslaving logic as it broadened after Emancipation and into the twentieth century.

To be clear, the conditions and severity of anteliberal controls differ across varying forms of embodiment; I do not equate poor white abjection with the systemic racial violence, exploitation, and abjection that has terrorized African Americans throughout US history. Rather, tracing the workings of this parasitic system through the lived experiences of hookworm victims renders visible how the exploitation illustrated in Faulkner's whitewashed Doane's Mill shares an economic and political ancestry with the racialized exploitation of Black people during enslavement and beyond. Indeed, though Faulkner never narrates his protagonist so much as passing through Doane's Mill, Joe Christmas's racialized journey remains deeply tied to the system perpetuated in Lena Grove's hometown, so much so that the author saw fit to establish the opening scene of Joe Christmas's tale in a setting he would never see.

When read through Chesnutt's story, Faulkner's introductory portrait renders visible how, as disparate as they may seem, both Joe Christmas and the hookwormridden heirs of Doane's Mill exist "downstream" from Ben's inheritance in slavery. Ultimately, if Beckert and Rockman are right that "American slavery is necessarily imprinted on the DNA of American capitalism," then in order to dismantle the neoliberal violences of modern-day America, we must trace slavery's capitalism back to its archetype in the lived Black experience under America's enslaving empire. One of the most productive archives to investigate in this effort is the literary genealogy of anteliberalism bequeathed to us over the last century by US authors like Chesnutt and Faulkner.

## NOTES

1. For example, Robert M. Slabey, "Faulkner's Nancy as 'Tragic Mulatto,'" *Studies in Short Fiction* 27, no. 3 (1990): 409–13; Charles L. Crow, "Under the Upas Tree: Charles Chesnutt's Gothic," in *Critical Essays on Charles Chesnutt*, ed. Joseph R. McElrath Jr. (New York: G. K. Hale, 1999), 261–70; Jay Watson, introduction to *Faulkner and the Black Literatures of the Americas: Faulkner and Yoknapatawpha, 2013*, ed. Jay Watson and James G. Thomas, Jr. (Jackson: University Press of Mississippi, 2013), vii–xxiv (hereafter cited parenthetically); and Peter Schmidt, "'Truth so mazed': Faulkner and US Plantation Fiction," in *Faulkner in Context*, ed. John T. Matthews (New York: Cambridge University Press, 2015), 169–84.

2. Watson, introduction, *Faulkner and the Black Literatures of the Americas*, x.

3. The term "Slavery's Capitalism" was coined in 2016 by Sven Beckert and Seth Rockman in their coedited collection *Slavery's Capitalism: A New History of American Economic Development* (Philadelphia: University of Pennsylvania Press, 2016). Scholarship exploring US capitalism's emergence through African enslavement was first posited in 1935 by W. E. B. Du Bois in *Black Reconstruction in America* (1935; Oxford, UK: Oxford University Press, 2007) and was further explored in context of the British Empire by Eric Williams in *Capitalism and Slavery* (1944; repr., Chapel Hill: University of North Carolina Press, 1994). See also Walter Johnson, Edward Baptist, and Diana Ramey Berry, along with individual work by Sven Beckert and Seth Rockman. All texts referenced here will be hereafter cited parenthetically.

4. Beckert and Rockman, introduction to *Slavery's Capitalism*, 3.

5. Audre Lorde, "Poetry Is Not a Luxury," *Sister Outsider* (1977; Berkeley, CA: Crossing Press, 2007), 36.

6. "National Tree Farm Program," *Alabama Forestry Commission*, 2001, www.forestry.alabama.gov/tree_farm.aspx (accessed August 1, 2019).

7. William Faulkner, *Light in August*, rev. ed. (1932; repr., New York: Vintage International, 1990), 4–5. Hereafter cited parenthetically.

8. For examples, see Gregory Meyerson and Jim Nelson, "Pulp Fiction: The Aesthetics of Anti-Radicalism in William Faulkner's *Light in August*," *Science and Society* 71, no. 1 (2008): 11–42; and Caroline Miles and David Anshen, "Introduction: Rebels, Failures, and Curious Folk," *Mississippi Quarterly* 61, no. 3 (2008): 309–24.

9. "Mill, n.1," *OED Online*, Oxford University Press (March 2002), www.oed.com (accessed December 7, 2019).

10. Michel Foucault, *The Birth of Biopolitics: Lectures at the Collège de France, 1978–1979*, ed. Michel Senellart, trans. Graham Burchell (New York: Palgrave Macmillan, 2004), 5–17. Hereafter cited parenthetically. See pages 13–14 specifically for Foucault's account of how the birth of "political economy" as a governing technology in the mid-eighteenth century enabled European and American transitions from feudal monarchies to modern states through the primary "objective of the state's enrichment" (14).

11. Wendy Brown, *Undoing the Demos: Neoliberalism's Stealth Revolution* (New York: Zone Books, 2015), 25. Hereafter cited parenthetically.

12. Wayne Flynt, *Poor but Proud: Alabama's Poor Whites* (Tuscaloosa: University of Alabama Press, 1989), 177. Hereafter cited parenthetically.

13. See Flynt, *Poor but Proud*, 178–79.

14. Megan L. McKenna et al., "Human Intestinal Parasite Burden and Poor Sanitation in Rural Alabama," *American Journal of Tropical Medicine and Hygiene* 91, no. 5 (2017): 1623–28. Hereafter cited internally.

15. Flynt notes that "the disease often caused a slow gait, sallow complexion, and lack of energy" (*Poor but Proud*, 177).

16. See Michael A. Flannery, "Poverty, Effects of," *Science and Medicine: The New Encyclopedia of Southern Culture* vol. 22, ed. James G. Thomas, Jr. and Charles Reagan Wilson (Chapel Hill: University of North Carolina Press, 2012), 130–33. Hereafter cited internally. Flannery reports: "the vitamin deficiencies incident with hookworm can prompt its victims to geophagia (soil eating). It may be that the often derisive reference to southern 'clay eaters' is actually a manifestation of disease common to the region" (132).

17. McKenna et al., 1623. See also Jeffrey Bethony et al., "Soil-transmitted Helminth Infections: Ascariasis, Trichuriasis, and Hookworm," *The Lancet* 367, no. 9521 (2006): 1521–32.

18. Flynt, *Poor but Proud*, 177; according to Flannery, symptoms of hookworm (among other diseases) largely contributed to denigrating caricatures of the poor rural South: "The notion of the so-called lazy southerner was largely a product of these three diseases [pellagra, hookworm, and malaria] intrinsic to the poverty commonplace in the South" ("Poverty, Effects of," 132).

19. Pew Charitable Trusts, "Moving On Up: Why Do Some Americans Leave the Bottom Ladder, but Not Others?" *Pew* (2013), accessed December 2018, https://www.pewtrusts.org/~/media/assets/2013/11/01/movingonuppdf.pdf.

20. See Flannery, "Poverty, Effects of," 132.

21. See Foucault, *The Birth of Biopolitics*, 15–16.

22. Ellen Meiksins Wood, *Empire of Capital* (London: Verso, 2003), 2. Hereafter cited internally.

23. Wood, *Empire of Capital*, 10.

24. Wood, *Democracy against Capitalism: Renewing Historical Materialism* (1995; London: Verso, 2016), 204–5. Hereafter cited internally.

25. Wood, *Empire of Capital*, 100.

26. Wood, *Empire of Capital*, 104–5.

27. Du Bois, *Black Reconstruction*, 2.

28. Beckert and Rockman, introduction, 5.

29. Wood, *Empire of Capital*, 106.

30. "Chattel, n.," *OED Online*, 1st ed., Oxford University Press (1889), accessed December 2018, http://www.oed.com/view/Entry/30963?redirectedFrom=chattel. The distinguishing difference between the feudal serf and the capitalist slave is the movability and disposability of a slave as "personal property" rather than fixed "real property." The *OED* defines "chattel" as "a movable possession; any possession or piece of property other than real estate or a freehold." Where serfs were legally committed to the land (and,

therefore, not sellable between lords), enslaved Black people under American capitalism were movable, sellable, disposable.

31. Wood, *Empire of Capital*, 106.

32. Thomas Jefferson, *Notes on the State of Virginia*, ed. William Peden (1781; Chapel Hill: University of North Carolina Press, 1982).

33. See Jennifer L. Morgan, "Partus sequitur ventrem: Law, Race, and Reproduction in Colonial Slavery," *Small Axe* 22, no. 1 (2018): 1–17.

34. Charles Chesnutt, "Lonesome Ben," in *The Conjure Stories*, ed. Robert B. Stepto and Jennifer Rae Greeson, rev. ed. (1900; repr., New York: W. W. Norton, 2012), 50. Hereafter cited parenthetically.

35. Booker T. Washington, *Up from Slavery*, ed. William L. Andrews, rev. ed. (1901; repr., New York: W. W. Norton, 1996), 70. Hereafter cited parenthetically.

36. See Faulkner's address of February 20, 1958, as documented in *Faulkner in the University: Class Conferences at the University of Virginia 1957–1958*, ed. Frederick L. Gwynn and Joseph L. Blotner (Charlottesville: University Press of Virginia, 1959), 211. Speaking of how to solve the "race problem," Faulkner paternalistically explains that only white, elite southerners are equipped to elevate the Black man because he must learn "to act not even as just any white man, but to act as well as the best of white men."

37. Kyla Wazana Tompkins, *Racial Indigestion: Eating Bodies in the 19th Century* (New York: New York University Press, 2012), 5–6. Hereafter cited parenthetically.

38. The most famous example is W. E. B. Du Bois, "Of Mr. Booker T. Washington and Others," in *The Souls of Black Folk*, ed. Brent Hayes Edwards (1903; repr., Oxford, UK: Oxford University Press, 2007), 33–44.

39. See Helen M. Chesnutt, *Charles Waddell Chesnutt: Pioneer of the Color Line* (Chapel Hill: University of North Carolina Press, 1952), 191–92. Hereafter cited parenthetically.

40. For example, in 1903, James Pott and Company of New York published *The Negro Problem*, a collection of essays that included such illustrious contributors as Washington, Chesnutt, Du Bois ("The Talented Tenth" was first published here), and Paul Laurence Dunbar, among others (H. Chesnutt, *Charles Waddell Chesnutt*, 196). Addressing their mutual contribution to the collection, Chesnutt wrote personally to Washington on August 11, 1903: "I have taken occasion, in the article which I have written for James Pott and Company, in the volume in which you are also a contributor, to express my disagreement with you upon a matter of the suffrage. I have done so without heat and with what I meant to make ample recognition of your valuable services to the country. But I believe in manhood suffrage, especially now and for the Negro; and I do not believe in a tame or even a patient submission to many other forms of injustice" (C. Chesnutt qtd. in H. Chesnutt, *Charles Waddell Chesnutt*, 195).

41. For example, in 1900 Chesnutt published two reviews of Washington's *The Future of the American Negro* (1899), one in the *Saturday Evening Post* and one in the *Critic*.

42. Henry B. Wonham, "Charles Waddell Chesnutt," in *Oxford Bibliographies* (Oxford: Oxford University Press, January 2018), www.oxfordbibliographies.com/view/document/obo-9780199827251/obo-9780199827251-0090.xml (accessed June 2019). North Carolina's State Colored Normal School is now called Fayetteville State University.

43. See Diana Ramey Berry's groundbreaking work in *The Price for a Pound of Their Flesh: The Value of the Enslaved, from Womb to Grave, in the Building of a Nation* (Boston: Beacon Press, 2017), especially her work in chapter 6 on "Postmortem: Death and Ghost Values."

44. See Faulkner, *Light in August*, 226, 265. Joe Christmas is "thirtythree years old" when he arrives at Jefferson (226). His affair with Joanna Burden lasts an additional "two years" before he kills her, thus inaugurating the manhunt and lynching (265). I am indebted to Jay Watson for bringing this timeline to my attention.

45. See Angela Davis, *Women, Race, and Class* (New York: Vintage, 1983), especially chapter 11 on "Rape, Racism, and the Myth of the Black Rapist"; see also W. J. Cash's account of the "Southern rape complex," a phrase he coined, in *The Mind of the South* (1941; repr., New York: Vintage, 1991), 114–17.

46. "Among them the casual Yankees and the poor whites and even the southerners who had lived for a while in the north, who believed aloud that it was an anonymous negro crime committed not by a negro but by Negro and who knew, believed, and hoped that she had been ravished too: at least once before her throat was cut and at least once afterward" (Faulkner, *Light in August*, 288).

47. ". . . forever and ever. They are not to lose it. . . . It will be there, musing, quiet, steadfast, not fading and not particularly threatful, but of itself alone serene, of itself alone triumphant" (Faulkner, *Light in August*, 465).

# Melodrama, Turbulence, Titillation: Silhouetting Slavery in the Works of William Faulkner and Kara Walker

RANDALL WILHELM

A recent exhibition at the National Portrait Gallery in Washington, DC, speaks directly to the issue of silhouetting and slavery in the works of William Faulkner and Kara Walker.[1] *Black Out: Silhouettes Then and Now* offers a glimpse into America's past by featuring one of the most popular art forms of the eighteenth and early nineteenth centuries: the paper portrait cutout. During the "silhouette rage" in America, from around 1790 to 1850, artists worked quickly, creating what were called "profiles" or "shades" at the time, most often by cutting the shape of a person's profile or full-length body from lightweight black cardboard and mounting the image on a pale (usually white) background.

Before the introduction of photography and the daguerreotype in 1839, silhouettes were the most popular and affordable type of portraiture for a young nation "struggling to reconcile contradictory views on such pressing issues as colonial independence, slavery, and national identity," writes Asma Naeem, the National Portrait Gallery's curator of prints, drawings, and media arts.[2] Among the exhibition's highlights were a 1796 outline of an enslaved nineteen-year-old named Flora found beside her original bill of sale in Connecticut, and a double-portrait framed by braided human hair entwined at the bottom into the shape of a heart, perhaps the earliest depiction of a same-sex couple in America.[3] Museum director Kim Sajet says *Black Out* visualizes "social underpinnings, drawing attention to those who have been previously blacked out from history, such as the enslaved, working women, same-sex couples, and those with disabilities."[4]

Certainly part of the exhibition's power resided in its range of images and its argument that the quick, inexpensive process provided the means for democratizing portraiture in America, including everyone from presidents to the enslaved.[5] Perhaps the exhibition's overarching question is best expressed by Naeem, who asks, "how did an art form that rendered everyone *pitch black* flourish, particularly at a time when the concept of 'blackness' was being contested as an alleged marker of inferiority or property far and wide—on ships, across oceans, on plantations, and at public lecterns?"[6] This was the chief irony of the show, expressed succinctly in a review by Roger Catlin: "In a nation seemingly consumed in race, silhouettes erased that distinction, rendering everyone in the same black outline."[7] In the supposedly race-free space of the silhouette, everyone is equal when rendered in "the same black outline," so a paper cutout of Pres. John Quincy Adams supposedly stands on equal ground with the nineteen-year-old Flora whose image accompanied the selling of her body into slavery.[8] This fantasy of a race-blind America, of "self-evident" truths that all men are "endowed by the Creator with certain unalienable rights," of "equality" between powerful white actors and (relatively) powerless others rendered through the popular form of the cut paper silhouette is just that: a fantasy dressed in black that speaks white.

Silhouettes, fantasy, and mystery often go hand in hand because of the medium's material surface, which creates a space where visual details *cannot* be seen within a shape that *can* be seen. While silhouettes were easily readable to family and relatives of the sitter, silhouettes also served as sites of mystery and contradiction inasmuch as the form's oppositional structures visualize a host of paradoxical indices such as mobility and fixity, black and white, "severing and totality, flatness and embodiment, opaqueness and transparency, void and likeness."[9] Unlike the hidden or out of sight, silhouettes can be seen as physical shapes set in a specific space for visual consumption. One reads a silhouette by tracking its contour for visual clues and by seeing the shape's relation to the white space in which it performs, and yet the interior refuses to reveal any visual information beyond its outline and as such remains stubbornly "unknowable," a void of undecipherable blackness. In racialized terms, the whiteness of the outline can never know the Blackness within. In aesthetic terms, this is the truth put to the lies of physiognomy and racial profiling.[10]

What Faulkner knew about silhouettes and when he used them would make a monograph in itself. Faulkner's visual aesthetics have been examined through historical, experiential, and cultural lenses directed toward his early drawings for Oxford and University of Mississippi publications, his handmade illustrated and calligraphic booklets, his work in Hollywood as a screenwriter, and his fiction, where the silhouette often performs as a dramatic figural strategy for narrative envisioning. There are far too many examples to address in an essay, but consider for example how Faulkner consistently manipulates silhouette effects to evoke the mysteries of many racialized and sexualized characters. Perhaps the most well-known Faulkner silhouette is a cutout shape, not from paper but from tin: the figure of Ab Snopes in "Barn Burning," whom Sarty sees "against the stars but without face or depth—a shape black, flat, and bloodless as though cut from tin."[11] These cutout or "stamped" figures appear as markers of radical difference, as in Horace Benbow's visual encounter with *Sanctuary*'s "little black man" Popeye, who seethes with a menacing racial sexuality: "His face had a queer, bloodless color. . . . [A]gainst the sunny silence, in his slanted straw hat and his slightly akimbo arms, he had that vicious depthless quality of stamped tin."[12]

Generally, Faulkner uses five types of silhouette structures. The earliest silhouettes are visual-visual ones, physically hand-drawn images that appear in Faulkner's illustrations and book decorations. The most prominent strategies in the fiction are the verbal-visual cue, where the word "silhouette" or a phrase such as "cut from tin" or "stamped" signals a distinct mental image, and the verbal-visual lighting effect, where the term is not mentioned but a silhouette is created through manipulation of light and dark. Two other strategies exhibit Faulkner's ingenuity in expanding the form: verbal-visual passages of baroque density and synesthesia that mimic the unreadability of the silhouette, and verbal-visual assemblages, wherein a silhouette shape subsumes textual shadows often triggered by touch or the merging of bodies in a literal, symbolic, or metaphoric manner.

Among the scholars who have examined Faulkner's aesthetics of light and dark figuration, Philip Weinstein sees silhouetted or projected shadow scenes as shapes implicating the "clottiness" of Black-white relations; Candace Waid reads Faulkner's silhouetting as a space of masking and alterity; but most importantly for opening a dialogue between Faulkner and Kara Walker, John N. Duvall, in "Faulkner's Black Sexuality," sees the silhouette as a site of metamorphic racialized sexualities.[13] In the space of this essay I must, admittedly, strategically present selected images and scenes that offer potential for deeper comparative discussion of these two artists. The racing of silhouettes, sexuality, and physiognomic profiling is so deeply ingrained in southern and American cultural histories that any comparative essay on Faulkner and Walker risks a scholar's drowning. While each artist constructs his or her own world culled from both literary and visual sources, troubling questions arise when placing African American works in conversation with white-authored texts, where the former may be framed as corrective and revisionary and the latter may be granted status as master text.

Instead, I would like to argue that Walker's art shoots the intertextual authority gap in many ways, but mainly because of her strategies of ambiguity and hyperaffectivity, which have disturbed, titillated, and angered audiences—Black and white alike—to such a degree that Sander L. Gilman refers to Walker's image-making as "work that people love to hate and hate to love."[14] Yes, the echo of Quentin Compson's tortured response to Shreve regarding Quentin's feelings about the South at the end of *Absalom, Absalom!*—"I dont hate it! I dont hate it!"[15]—is clear, even if unintended. It is a thin link between artists, a touch, a bit of wordplay by an art critic, and yet the more one looks at the work of William Faulkner and Kara Walker the more one begins to see common ground, or as Wai Chee Dimock has recently argued, a "weak" or "low bar network."

Dimock's argument proceeds from Eve Kosofky Sedgwick's theory of "paranoid" or "reparative reading," which sees "the world not as an impregnable mask but as a torn web with gaping holes" in need of repair through accretive "layers of mediation."[16] By adding the metaphor of the network to Sedgwick's theory, Dimock's reparative reading flickers between two interpretive methodologies: "ongoing contextualization versus terminal verdict," where the latter "cuts through the evidence and delivers a clean, finalized, individualized sentence," and the former "thickens the plot and prolongs the mediating process, thanks to a multiplayer and multivariable input network."[17] As Michael P. Bibler has argued, despite "the ways that Walker's work might shock and even horrify, she is merely adding to a long tradition in which sex and sexuality are central to representations of the southern plantation."[18] Walker's art, like Faulkner's narratives of antebellum and postbellum plantations, offers a productive contextualization of such concerns, as both seek to critique, reveal, and destabilize the material and psychological realities of the "peculiar institution" that continue to affect and infect our contemporary moment.

Like Walker, Faulkner was able to draw his own silhouettes for his visual art, especially in his 1920 dream play, *The Marionettes*.[19] These illustrations are among Faulkner's finest and most sophisticated visual compositions. Here we see Faulkner's use of the visual-visual silhouette, a technique that figures prominently in several important illustrations. Duvall argues that Faulkner's illustrations of the doubled characters Pierrot and Shade of Pierrot in *The Marionettes* perform "a whiteface minstrelsy that implicitly racializes white male sexuality."[20] Pierrot is pictured in typical *commedia dell'arte* attire, with his baggy white costume and white powdered mask, but he remains asleep through this dream play of subversive sexual coding, with his oddly crossed hands seemingly impotent as well (see fig. 1). Indeed, Pierrot is unable to act except

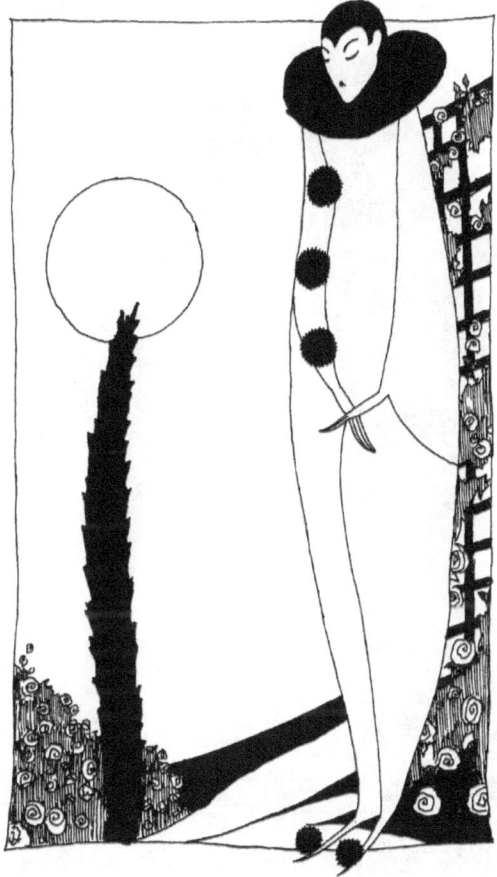

**Fig. 1:** "Pierrot Standing." From William Faulkner, *The Marionettes*. 1920. © Copyright 2019. Faulkner Literary Rights, LLC. All rights reserved. Used with permission, the William Faulkner Literary Estate, Lee Caplin, executor.

through the doubled "shade" projected from his unconscious, as we see in figures 2 and 3, when the black picture portrait cuts away from the white body and materializes with immense figural power on the page in scenes of sexual seduction. In figure 2, referred to by many Faulkner scholars as "The Kiss," Shade of Pierrot's silhouette registers as a Black male, perhaps a fantasy of both the sleeping Pierrot and Marietta as well; it is clear, though, that Marietta is entranced with this potent figure, her leaning body and upturned lips coyly asking for a kiss. The negative white space between the blackened figures forces the shape into a large

**Fig. 2:** "The Kiss." From William Faulkner, *The Marionettes*. 1920. © Copyright 2019. Faulkner Literary Rights, LLC. All rights reserved. Used with permission, the William Faulkner Literary Estate, Lee Caplin, executor.

but seemingly vacant white phallus, which is visible only because of the pressure of the black silhouettes bending toward one another. Duvall's reading uncovers the black-white racialized dynamics of the silhouette and in the process rescues Faulkner's finest work of visual art from a derivative symbolist dream play, elevating it into a sexually and racially coded meditation on performing Blackness in disguise.

Figure 3, dubbed "Marietta at the Fountain" by critics, is perhaps Faulkner's most sophisticated illustration, a graphic balancing act merging black and white shapes with a patterned flower terrace and

**Fig. 3:** "Marietta at the Fountain." From William Faulkner, *The Marionettes*. 1920. © Copyright 2019. Faulkner Literary Rights, LLC. All rights reserved. Used with permission, the William Faulkner Literary Estate, Lee Caplin, executor.

incorporating black and white silhouettes in a scene of Black-white sexual seduction. Faulkner as Pierrot is literally "a little black man," and Marietta rises to expose her breasts to his singing. What is particularly interesting is the small figure in the fountain whose shape reads female but whose heart-shaped spray suggests male orgasm. The suggestiveness of the spray within the context of the giant, slightly bending tree reads as a powerful, even overwhelming Black phallus that will ultimately lead to Marietta's death in the final illustration as the whiteface Pierrot looks on in bewilderment.

Faulkner's illustrations and silhouette games in *The Marionettes* are highly stylized, with his trademark razor-thin line work studded with black design elements and cross-hatching curly cues that create a patterned environment in which the characters live and dream. The style is refined, decorative if not always decorous, and "coolly professional," as Joseph Blotner has written.[21] There is elegance in the figural poses of Kara Walker's paper cutouts as well, appropriated as they are from genteel Victorian silhouettes of formal propriety and tasteful manners. But it takes only a glance to see that in Walker's hands, paper cutouts become entry points for murder and mayhem, power and cruelty, sexual depravity and pleasure, melodrama and turbulence, titillation and ambiguity.

These strategies serve up a vortex of meanings that play out on the museum walls within and between figures but also in the minds of viewers as they confront their own racial histories and imaginations. As Gwendolyn Dubois Shaw has argued, Walker's trenchant visual wit and fondness for allegorical obfuscation allow her to create "fantastically horrific narrative[s] out of racial stereotypes, nostalgic themes, and historical mythologies."[22] Like Faulkner, Walker's work is enormous, overwhelming in its scope and production, packing a battery of affective dissonance and interpretive play. Her 1994 masterpiece, a visual rereading and re-seeing of Harriet Beecher Stowe's *Uncle Tom's Cabin*, is retitled and recast as *The End of Uncle Tom and the Grand Allegorical Tableau of Eva in Heaven* (see figure 4). Prurience is one of the names in Walker's game, a titillating effect employed in service of challenging her viewers' imaginations as much as her own. Employing elegance, beauty, violence, and hardcore sexual content in what amounts to a visual feast of signifying codes, Walker's cutout silhouettes attack the clichés, stereotypes, and irreality of plantation life that have become so ingrained in the popular American imagination, but she does so—to many critics' dismay—with a disturbing sense of ambiguity.[23]

Faulknerian concerns of time and space necessitate a brief but focused examination of Walker's large-scale gothic panorama, which Janet Neary has called "a contemporary slave narrative."[24] The composition features four figure groupings that read as silhouette assemblages in their ambiguous merging of bodies, objects, and elements of the natural world and built environment. Reading from left to right, viewers first see a group of three women under the slave system nurturing each other in a symbolic act of community (see fig. 5). Yasmil Raymond sees the women as trying to breastfeed one another, a bizarre image wherein the maternal act of lactation is rendered as oral transfusion of ancestral lineage and as a defiant gesture undermining the slave system's white male ownership of the Black female body.[25]

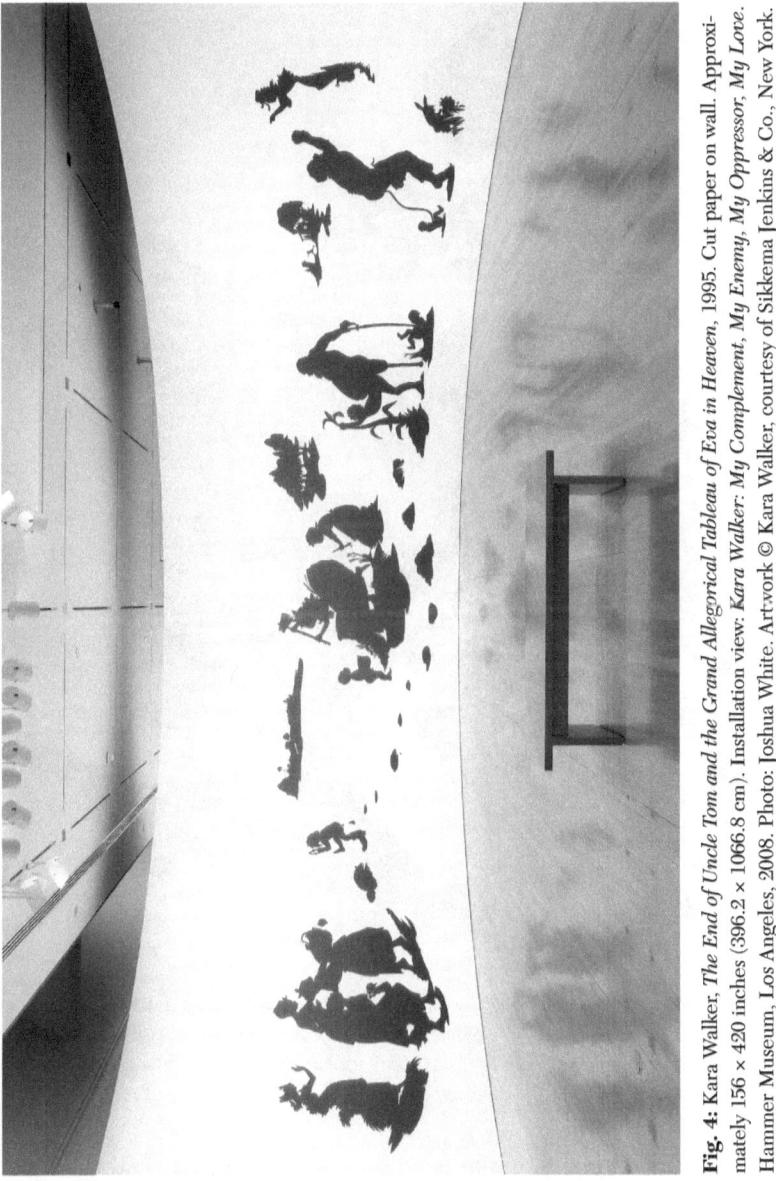

**Fig. 4:** Kara Walker, *The End of Uncle Tom and the Grand Allegorical Tableau of Eva in Heaven*, 1995. Cut paper on wall. Approximately 156 × 420 inches (396.2 × 1066.8 cm). Installation view: *Kara Walker: My Complement, My Enemy, My Oppressor, My Love.* Hammer Museum, Los Angeles, 2008. Photo: Joshua White. Artwork © Kara Walker, courtesy of Sikkema Jenkins & Co., New York.

**Fig. 5:** Kara Walker, detail from *The End of Uncle Tom and the Grand Allegorical Tableau of Eva in Heaven*, 1995. Cut paper on wall. Approximately 156 × 420 inches (396.2 × 1066.8 cm). Installation view: Wooster Gardens, New York, 1995. Photo: Erma Estwick. Artwork © Kara Walker, courtesy of Sikkema Jenkins & Co., New York.

The second figural group is trickier, for we see the body of a defecating child playing a tambourine, then follow her waste-stained footprints backwards to the central figural group featuring Little Eva, whose wild-haired silhouetted shape balloons in a monstrous shadow of impenetrable Blackness. Eva's contour is punctuated by her backward tilted axe, an instrument of power and torture that she ostensibly aims at

**Fig. 6:** Kara Walker, detail from *The End of Uncle Tom and the Grand Allegorical Tableau of Eva in Heaven*, 1995. Cut paper on wall. Approximately 156 × 420 inches (396.2 × 1066.8 cm). Installation view: Wooster Gardens, New York, 1995. Photo: Erma Estwick. Artwork © Kara Walker, courtesy of Sikkema Jenkins & Co., New York.

the young Black child holding a basket in front of her. The ironic inversion is a cue toward white affective pathologies: Eva seems to be striking herself in a frozen moment of self-loathing for her role in the economy of human domination and suffering (see fig. 6). In a 2011 interview, Walker describes "the unexpected situation of kind of wanting to be the heroine and yet wanting to kill the heroine, at the same time. And that kind of dilemma, that push and pull, is sort of the basis, the underlying turbulence that I bring to each of the pieces that I make, including the specifics: the mammy characters and the pickaninnies and the weird sorts of descriptions."[26]

We can see this turbulence in the third silhouette grouping, which is the most graphically sexual and perverse assemblage in the entire composition (see fig. 7). With its merging of bodies in a clearly outlined sexual episode, the scene titillates with affective disturbance, frustration, and, for some viewers, outrage at the seeming pleasure the Black female takes in pleasuring her master—old, obese, and amputated as he is. Walker's self-conscious role-playing as the "Negress" in her work provides another interpretive link to Faulkner, who also famously self-fashioned various roles and disguises such as wounded aviator, country gentleman, hardscrabble farmer, and the "little black man" that Duvall has so convincingly revealed. Walker's construction of a "Negress self"

**Fig. 7:** Kara Walker, detail from *The End of Uncle Tom and the Grand Allegorical Tableau of Eva in Heaven*, 1995. Cut paper on wall. Approximately 156 × 420 inches (396.2 × 1066.8 cm). Installation view: Wooster Gardens, New York, 1995. Photo: Erma Estwick. Artwork © Kara Walker, courtesy of Sikkema Jenkins & Co., New York.

is central to her strategy of hypersexuality and affective turmoil as seen in this coupling of sexual pleasure and casual infanticide. What offends most viewers is the backward gaze of the young Negress, who simultaneously pulls on the phallic corn stalk in front of her while seemingly seeking approval from the slovenly obese master who is defiling her. Walker has talked about this effect as

> a kind of turbulence that drives most of the work, and it's a turbulence that's not unlike melodrama, or the kind of dredging up of every feeling one could possibly have about a situation that is all about feeling. And it's difficult not to laugh off that behavior—that sense of being overloaded, out of control, unable to contain even the horror of being able to think

Fig. 8: Kara Walker, detail from *The End of Uncle Tom and the Grand Allegorical Tableau of Eva in Heaven*, 1995. Cut paper on wall. Approximately 156 × 420 inches (396.2 × 1066.8 cm). Installation view: Wooster Gardens, New York, 1995. Photo: Erma Estwick. Artwork © Kara Walker, courtesy of Sikkema Jenkins & Co., New York.

about something that you know you shouldn't be thinking about, or that you know isn't going to resolve itself just by thinking about it.[27]

The fourth silhouette grouping (see fig. 8) dredges up another graphic horror by picturing "the end of Uncle Tom" as a feminized male slave birthing a child from his anus, connected delicately by a fantastical umbilical cord that doubles as a tail of an animal or demon. The body comprises two distinct and seemingly opposite modes of being and consciousness that burst with affective dissonance: part squatting in an act of impossible birthing defecation and part stretching upward in an attitude of prayer, supplication, and appeal to the spiritual realm. The man's pain may be a result of the plight of the Black female who is seemingly ripped apart, a reference many critics read as the Black body's brutal disintegration under slavery.

Walker's hyper-affective work is not revisionary in the manner of many contemporary literary or visual artists because it is not "corrective" in a way that clears the stage for more accurate representations of African American history and consciousness. Her images read as emotionally accurate within the highly pitched register of melodrama, an affective space whose structures of feeling such as attraction/repulsion are mercilessly inseparable and stubbornly inescapable in Walker's work. Even advocates such as Shaw have struggled with the dizzying experience of viewing a sprawling Walker installation "that spread across the [white] gallery walls like a shadow drama being played out by actors behind a scrim of white fabric."[28] Shaw recalls being "confounded by the uncanny drama in which these . . . cut-paper figures required me to participate. I was both bewildered and elated by the exciting, yet largely incomprehensible narrative of graphic violence and sexual depravity that spread before me in a great gothic panorama."[29]

For Walker, this relentless push and pull of chaotic titillation, which is central to her deconstruction of historical narratives and racial mythologies, is made possible through an art form that seeks to hide as much, or more, than it shows. As Walker has stated, the

> silhouette lends itself to avoidance of the subject—of not being able to look at it directly—yet there it is, all the time, staring you in the face. . . . It's designed to avoid the confluence of disgust and desire and voluptuousness that are all wrapped up in this bizarre construct of racism. You know, what black stands for in white America and what white stands for in white America are all loaded with our deepest psychological perversions and fears and longings. And it's a dangerous way of doing things, but it's just human, weirdly human.[30]

Although the silhouette was designed to avoid the interiority of its subject, Walker's strategy of conflating singular bodies into taut figural assemblages ratchets up the tension until they become unavoidable, with the points of entry—a hand touch, a hip thrust, a pair of linked arms—providing elements of narrative to the blacked-out combinatory image. These contact zones transmit variegated affective energies to viewers depending on the sites of touch, the body language of the figures, and the tantalizing points of near contact between black shapes and white space.

Let's return briefly to the figure of Miss Eva at the center of *The End of Uncle Tom and the Grand Historical Tradition* (fig. 6), wielding her axe backward with flowing wild hair, her shape melding with a tree stump and small vegetation, and sprouting an ominous black shadow underneath her ballooned hoop skirt. The boy with the basket stands just outside the shape of Eva's skirt, but his stance positions him well within the axe's threatening arc, while the young Negress brandishing a stick is blocked from touching Eva by a thin reversed white shape that mirrors the axe Eva holds aloft. Walker's art creates a highly structured network of figures that interact with other figures and with the space around them, a delicate circuitry that works through oppositional structures such as mirroring and reversal as well as through constitutive methods such as conflation and assemblage. If viewers cannot see inside the blackness of Walker's silhouettes, they certainly cannot *unsee* the titillating and scandalous combinations of figures that writhe and shimmer on the museum walls before them with disturbing complexity.

As Faulkner's visual-visual silhouettes in *The Marionettes* attest, he was highly aware of the suggestive potential of the form, especially when addressing issues of race, gender, and sexuality. Turning to the fiction, consider the many scenes initiated or represented through silhouetting strategies, such the panoply of figures backlit in doorways or windows in *Light in August*, the cued verbal silhouettes in *Sanctuary* and *Go Down, Moses*, and the silhouette assemblages formed when characters touch in *Absalom, Absalom!* Jaime Harker has argued for a "lesbian sexuality" in Faulkner's plantation novel, pointing to Rosa Coldfield's titillating realization of Judith's interracial, incestuous relationship with Clytie.[31] Their separate bodies perform as a conflated silhouette: "*We just stood there—I motionless in the action of running, she rigid in that furious immobility, the two of us joined by that hand and arm which held us, like a fierce rigid umbilical cord, twin sistered to the fell darkness which had produced her.*"[32] Elizabeth Steeby has argued that "Judith's Hundred" is actually a "queer contact zone" that "disrupts the repressive surface of language—of both sexuality and race."[33] These zones spatialize sexuality and race and, like Walker's combinatory figure groupings, rupture conventional narratives and images by revealing the repressed. Looking at similar connective zones in Faulkner's plantation fiction offers opportunities to re-see scenes that have been overlooked, unseen, blacked out, or "bleached white," as Shreve McCannon or Nathaniel Burden might say.

Reading strategic scenes in *The Unvanquished*, for instance, offers subversive ways of reassessing what many critics have claimed as Faulkner's most retrograde novel in terms of race consciousness and Lost Cause valor. Sarah Mahurin has argued that "many of the most memorable moments in *The Unvanquished* center around . . . misunderstandings, during which one character is uncertain—often comically so—of another character's meaning."[34] Mahurin's concept of "underskirtedness" is presented through the fantastical scene of Bayard and Ringo hiding under Granny Millard's hoop skirt from the Union soldiers they have just fired upon in the opening story, "Ambuscade." The passage has most often been read as comic, but what happens if we read more closely while imagining figures in a Kara Walker silhouette, particularly the assemblage of Little Eva and her giant ballooned skirt charged with sexual violence? Bayard tells us that "Ringo and I were squatting with our chins under our knees, on either side of her against her legs, with the hard points of the chair rockers jammed into our backs and her skirts spread over us like a tent, and the heavy feet coming in and . . . the Yankee sergeant shaking the musket at Granny."[35] Seeing this figural composition as a silhouette assemblage that echoes Walker's work suffuses the scene with an erotic dimension that is both *hidden under* and *visible inside* the hoop-skirted southern matron protecting her "boys."

In many ways "Ambuscade" is a shadow game, for despite the story's material grounding in the natural and built environments, Bayard's narration has a stubbornly dreamy quality about it, as T. Austin Graham has argued, calling *The Unvanquished* a "vividly elusive" novel that "actively invites contentious reading."[36] The coconut cake scene, for instance, may be a moment of levity about homefront deprivation in this disjointed tale but, as Charles Hannon has pointed out, when Ringo participates on equal terms with whites in the imaginative life of the Sartoris family, his presence becomes a subversive element that attempts "to redraw the color lines that . . . determined experience in the plantation South."[37] On the surface this episode adds little to the narrative progression and seemingly presents Black subjectivity as an uncomfortably playful void; on closer scrutiny, though, Ringo's compulsive attraction to—and deferment of— pleasure regarding his having eaten a "cokynut cake" (19) or not teems with a titillating ambiguity. Faulkner's revisions to the original version published in the *Saturday Evening Post* in 1934—additions made *after* his dismantling of the plantocracy in *Absalom, Absalom!*—warrant a closer look. Why extend the coconut cake scene into an entirely new paragraph? Why raise a question that cannot, or refuses to, be answered? Divergent interpretations have arisen from this scene, but one element is clear: while the central event is spoken (whether Ringo had eaten coconut cake or not), the mystery is strangely prolonged through a series of negations, which the text stubbornly refuses to explain in any satisfactory manner.

Unless, that is, we read the passage "contentiously" as Graham suggests. Faulkner's revisions total fourteen lines of new text in *The Unvanquished*, with the first line raising the strange dilemma completely absent from the original version: "He said coconut cake every time because we never had been able to decide whether Ringo had ever tasted coconut cake or not" (19). Bayard then places the event as potentially occurring "in the kitchen," the blackened domestic space of plantation servitude. Bayard stresses four times that Ringo could not remember, but the last two seem particularly odd: "Now and then I used to try to help him decide, *get him to tell me* how it tasted and what it looked like and sometimes he would almost decide *to risk it* before he would change his mind" (19; emphasis added). What's the "risk," really? To remember or not to remember if he had literally tasted cake? And, if so, why the commanding tone in the second clause over such a trivial event? Speaking for Ringo, Bayard complicates matters further in the last sentence of the revised passage: "Because [Ringo] said that *he would rather just maybe* have tasted coconut cake without remembering it than *to know for certain* he had not; that if he *were to describe the wrong kind of cake*, he would never taste coconut cake *as long as he lived*" (19–20; emphasis added).

The system of repetitions and negations suggests an unspeakable panic throbbing behind the surface of the words, initiating a Walker-like aesthetic that focuses on the "tantalizing points of contact" between the said and unsaid, sign and signifier, language and experience. Ringo's words here should give us pause, for his halting speech may be a performance of uncertainty—"he would rather just maybe have"—or a strategic obfuscation of acts or thoughts unspeakable in a plantation logic that dictates decorum, refinement, and racial and sexual purity. The "risk" revolves around the euphemism of the coconut cake that must never be tasted by the racial other, and the mortal danger of describing the "wrong kind of cake" that could result in a "long" life cut short. Bibler has revealed the network of same-sex relations on the southern plantation in *Absalom, Absalom!*, but just as Judith and Clytie sleep together on the pallet or in the bed, so do Bayard and Ringo. In fact, Black and white bodies merge in many ways in *The Unvanquished*, often with typical Faulknerian paradox, as when Louvinia "would have to be white a little while longer" when looking for her son Loosh (21), or when Bayard tells of Ringo's birth in the same month as his own, and that they "had both fed at the same breast and had slept together and eaten together for so long that Ringo called Granny 'Granny' just like I did" (7).

But the plantation logic of this paternalistic system only goes so far, for the lines of race and sexuality must be strictly enforced, often through violent, or even deadly, means. While Walker's silhouettes make this sexuality and violence graphically visible, Faulkner's text is subtler and works through euphemism, metaphor, and suggestion. However, if we read the domestic "cokynut" cake scene as "intimately connected" with or "touching" the melodramatic episode of Bayard and Ringo hiding under Granny Millard's hoop skirt—and with Walker's silhouettes in mind—the text virtually explodes with racially and sexually charged erotic power. Hiding under Granny's skirts, Bayard utters the strange line: "We couldn't see, we just squatted in a kind of faint gray light and that *smell* of Granny that her clothes and *bed* and *room* all had and Ringo's eyes looking like two plates of *chocolate pudding*" (28; emphasis added).

These lines are also in the original version, but with the addition of the coconut cake episode in the preceding section, Ringo's eyes in this scene may signal secret taboo sexual desires or relations on the Sartoris plantation. They are described as objects ("door knobs" [25]), suggestive experiences ("white and quiet like last night" [20]) and the edible "chocolate pudding" that connects to the previously unremembered tasting of coconut cake. Combined with the smell of Granny's bed and room, the "underskirtedness" beneath Granny Millard becomes a forbidden contact zone between Ringo's wide-eyed sexual "appetite" and white female sexuality, a space of illicit thoughts and transgressive imaginings, even if never physically consummated. In Walker's hands, this scene could become monstrous and horrifying in its revelation of such nonnormative desire and sexuality, but Faulkner's text lives in a different time, cultural moment, and medium, and all remains suggestively uncertain, as Mahurin has argued.

But with the inclusion of a sexual element in this iconic scene, one that has been largely overlooked and underexamined, Faulkner infuses the text with an affective turbulence that can grow with deeper analysis and reflection. After all, in the 1933 short story "There Was a Queen," Faulkner suggests that John Sartoris had his own secret sex life on the plantation, fathering at least one of his slaves and possibly more. Elnora, pictured as a Black woman, is revealed to be a Sartoris as well, although an illegitimate daughter whose lineage must remain unspoken, unseen, erased, or silenced: "she remembered how ten years ago at this hour Old Bayard, who was her half-brother (though possibly but not probably neither of them knew it, including Bayard's father)."[38] If, as Graham has argued, part of *The Unvanquished*'s "enduring value surely lies in its ability to so completely overturn itself,"[39] then I frame this essay's conclusion with a call for excavating a novel too often seen as an "apologist" series of stories seemingly at odds with *Absalom, Absalom!*'s trenchant dismantling of the same perverse slave system that still haunts America today.

NOTES

1. *Black Out: Silhouettes Then and Now* opened at the National Portrait Gallery in Washington, DC, on May 11, 2018, and closed on March 10, 2019.

2. Asma Naeem, "Black Out: Silhouettes Then and Now," in *Black Out: Silhouettes Then and Now*, ed. Asma Naeem (Princeton, NJ: Princeton University Press, 2018), 4.

3. This framed double portrait, complete with embroidery and text, is included in Roger Catlin's online review of the exhibition. See Catlin, "Rarely Seen 19th-Century Silhouette of a Same-Sex Couple Living Together Goes on View," *Smithsonian* (May 25, 2018), www.smithsonianmag.com/smithsonian-institution/rarely-seen-19th-century-silhouette-same-sex-couple-living-together-goes-view-180969156/ (accessed June 2, 2018).

4. Sajet quoted in Catlin, "Rarely Seen 19th-Century Silhouette," paragraph 2.

5. In Europe, silhouettes had been the province of the royal and wealthy for generations, but the art form was still considered minor in comparison with the status of oil-painted portraits. In America such Eurocentrism was manifest, of course, but the cheap process of making silhouettes—an artist could create one in minutes for the price of a few pennies—allowed many people to have an intimate likeness of themselves or a loved one to place on the walls of their home for the first time.

6. Naeem, introduction to in *Black Out: Silhouettes Then and Now*, vii.

7. Catlin, "Rarely Seen 19th-Century Silhouette," paragraph 16.

8. It should be noted that *Black Out* was a historically linear exhibition, in which the silhouette renderings of the populace of the new nation seemed to echo a call for national unity, but the form was always coded in ways to differentiate the powerful from the powerless. An important part of the exhibition featured contemporary artists deconstructing traditional uses of the silhouette form, among whom Kara Walker was perhaps the most prominent inclusion. See Naeem, "Black Out: Silhouettes Then and Now," 3–33, and Anne Verplank and Asma Naeem, "Catalogue Entries," in *Black Out: Silhouettes Then and Now*, 138–43.

9. Naeem, "Black Out," 3.

10. It did not take long for the "democratization of portraiture in America" to become overtly racialized through the pseudoscience of physiognomy espoused by Swiss pastor Johann Kasper Lavater (1741–1801). His theories gained increasing popularity in the nineteenth century as fears of miscegenation spread throughout the young nation. Reading a person's "character" through facial features, of course, led to twentieth-century racial profiling, which has seen a type of rebirth in twenty-first-century facial recognition technologies.

11. William Faulkner, "Barn Burning," in *Collected Stories of William Faulkner* (1950; repr., New York: Vintage International, 1995), 8.

12. William Faulkner, *Sanctuary*, rev. ed. (1931; repr., New York: Vintage International, 1993), 4.

13. Weinstein refers to Joanna Burden's "shadow passage" in *Light in August* at the conclusion of her thirteen-page digression into her family history, as she shows Joe Christmas the ruins of the Burden family graveyard. This shadow passage, however, performs very much like one of Walker's silhouette assemblages: "I seemed to see them [African Americans] for the first time not as people, but as a thing, a shadow in which I lived, we lived, all white people, all other people. I thought of all the children coming forever and ever into the world, white, with the black shadow already falling upon them." See Philip M. Weinstein, *What Else But Love? The Ordeal of Race in Faulkner and Morrison* (New York: Columbia University Press, 1996), 253. Examining Faulkner's frontispiece for *The Marionettes*, Waid sees a "silhouetted and sculpted Africanist female" who, in contrast to Marietta's turn away from Pierrot, struts confidently toward him, "exposing what is depicted as Marietta's racialized and clearly ready sexuality"; Candace Waid, *The Signifying Eye: Seeing Faulkner's Art* (Athens: University of Georgia Press, 2014), 7. For more on silhouettes in *The Marionettes*, see Waid, *The Signifying Eye*, 1–22.

14. Sander L. Gilman, "Missus Kara E. Walker: Emancipated, and on Tour," *Art Bulletin* (December 2008): 640.

15. William Faulkner, *Absalom, Absalom!*, rev. ed. (1936; repr., New York: Vintage International, 1990), 303.

16. Wai Chee Dimock, "Weak Network: Faulkner's Transpacific Reparations," *Modernism/modernity* 25.3 (September 2018): 587, 588.

17. Dimock, "Weak Network: Faulkner's Transpacific Reparations," 588.

18. Michael P. Bibler, *Cotton's Queer Relations: Same-Sex Intimacy and the Literature of the Southern Plantation, 1936–1968* (Charlottesville: University of Virginia Press, 2009), 1.

19. To view all of the illustrations, see William Faulkner, *The Marionettes*, ed. Noel Polk (Charlottesville: University of Virginia Press, 1977).

20. John N. Duvall, "Faulkner's Black Sexuality," in *Faulkner's Sexualities: Faulkner and Yoknapatawpha, 2007*, ed. Annette Trefzer and Ann J. Abadie (Jackson: University Press of Mississippi, 2010), 135.

21. Joseph Blotner, *Faulkner: A Biography*, vol. 1 (New York: Random House, 1974), 273.

22. Gwendolyn Dubois Shaw, *Seeing the Unspeakable: The Art of Kara Walker* (Durham, NC: Duke University Press, 2004), 5.

23. Many of Walker's biggest detractors—Betye Saar, Faith Ringgold, Howardena Pindel, and Juliette Bowles—were established artists and commentators who saw Walker's work in the last decade of the twentieth century as derogatory and dangerous in its negative stereotyping of the Black female body. Later critics such as Rebecca Peabody, Yasmil Raymond, Gwendolyn Dubois Shaw, and many more have championed Walker's work precisely because of its affective energy to disturb audiences with confrontational and ambiguous racist iconography. Arlene R. Keizer, for instance, champions Walker for creating "the first widely disseminated body of visual artwork by an African American woman practitioner that engages questions of race deeply and avoids prescriptive or proscriptive answers" (Arlene R. Keizer, "Gone Astray in the Flesh: Kara Walker, Black Women Writers, and African American Postmemory," *PMLA* 123, no. 5 [October 2008]: 1671).

24. Janet Neary, *Fugitive Testimony: On the Visual Logic of Slave Narratives* (New York: Fordham University Press, 2017), 3.

25. Yasmil Raymond, "Maladies of Power: A Kara Walker Lexicon," in *Kara Walker: My Complement, My Enemy, My Oppressor, My Love*, ed. Philippe Vergue (Minneapolis, MN: Walker Art Center, 2007), 366.

26. Kara Walker, "The Melodrama of *Gone with the Wind*," Art21.org, November 2011, paragraph 10. https://art21.org/read/kara-walker-the-melodrama-of-gone-with-the-wind/, accessed May 20, 2018.

27. Walker, "The Melodrama of *Gone with the Wind*," paragraph 24.

28. Shaw, *Seeing the Unspeakable*, 1.

29. Shaw, *Seeing the Unspeakable*, 4.

30. Walker, "The Melodrama of *Gone with the Wind*," paragraph 7.

31. Jaime Harker, "'And You Too, Sister, Sister?': Lesbian Sexuality, *Absalom, Absalom!*, and the Reconstruction of the Southern Family," in *Faulkner's Sexualities: Faulkner and Yoknapatawpha, 2007*, ed. Annette Trefzer and Ann J. Abadie (Jackson: University Press of Mississippi, 2010), 38.

32. Faulkner, *Absalom, Absalom!*, 112.

33. Elizabeth Steeby, "Almost Feminine, Almost Brother, Almost Southern: The Transnational Queer Figure of Charles Bon in *Absalom, Absalom!*," in *Global Faulkner: Faulkner and Yoknapatawpha, 2006*, ed. Annette Trefzer and Ann J. Abadie (Jackson: University Press of Mississippi, 2009), 157.

34. Sarah Mahurin, "*Unvanquished* Uncertainty," in *Faulkner and Mystery: Faulkner and Yoknapatawpha, 2009*, ed. Annette Trefzer and Ann J. Abadie (Jackson: University Press of Mississippi, 2014), 178.

35. William Faulkner, *The Unvanquished*, rev. ed. (1938; repr., New York: Vintage International, 1991), 28. Hereafter cited parenthetically in text.

36. T. Austin Graham, "Reconstructions: Faulkner and Du Bois on the Civil War," in *Faulkner and the Black Literatures of the Americas: Faulkner and Yoknapatawpha, 2013*, ed. Jay Watson and James G. Thomas, Jr. (Jackson: University Press of Mississippi, 2016), 120.

37. Charles Hannon, *Faulkner and the Discourses of Culture* (Baton Rouge: Louisiana State University Press, 2005), 36.

38. William Faulkner, "There Was A Queen," *Collected Stories of William Faulkner* (1950; repr., New York: Vintage International, 1995), 727.

39. Graham, "Reconstructions," 130.

# Emancipating Faulkner: Reading *Go Down, Moses* and Jesmyn Ward's *Sing, Unburied, Sing*

SHERITA L. JOHNSON

"I hear it. Sometimes. When the sun. Sets. When the sun. Rises. The song. In snatches. The stars. A record. The sky. A great record. The lives. Of the living. Of those beyond. See it in flashes. The sound. Beyond the waters."[1]

Richie, the ghost boy in Jesmyn Ward's *Sing, Unburied, Sing* (2017), yearns for a release from his past life—his soul still imprisoned by time spent dying at Parchman Farm. With their present lives tethered to a slavery past, the Black and white McCaslins in William Faulkner's *Go Down, Moses* (1942) also want to be free from an ancestral "curse." In an attempt to untangle bloodlines and unify the plot, Faulkner ends his novel with an interracial funeral procession carrying the remains of Butch Beauchamp, a Black convicted murderer and the grandson of Mollie Beauchamp, who "doesn't care how he died [by execution]. She just wanted him home, but she wanted him to come home right."[2]

Getting things "right" motivates Jesmyn Ward to create intensely layered narratives about those she holds in a familiar embrace: Black folks in the rural South. Her own hometown of DeLisle on the Mississippi Gulf Coast is the inspiration for the fictional Bois Sauvage in most of her novels. Both are places "where family and community are sort of the same thing," and where generations survive despite the poverty, drug epidemics, and racism that are an ever-threatening presence in their lives.[3] They *endure*. Ward's own desire to escape Mississippi, where "the specter of all that we [Black southerners] have survived and died by" is "present in every flag, every street name, every monument, every vote," is offset by her attachment to the very place that she "loves more than she loathes."[4] After living all over the

Fig. 1: Juvenile Prisoners. Martha Alice Stewart, Time on Parchman Farm, 1930s Collection [mum01772_102_f15_9], Archives and Special Collections, J. D. Williams Library, University of Mississippi.

United States, Ward listened to a visceral call to *home*, a plot seemingly reimagined in Richie's return.

In *Sing, Unburied, Sing*, it is the lost histories of young boys like Richie who were exploited and tortured and killed while incarcerated that Jesmyn Ward recovers in her conjure tale. While traveling with his drug-addicted parents, Leonie (Black) and Michael (white), Jojo first encounters Richie, the ghost of his Black grandfather River's past. Richie was only twelve when he arrived at Parchman, and he immediately bonded with River, then *"a man of fifteen"* much wiser than his years imply (23). Experience belies age, as captured also in a rare archival photograph from the 1930s featuring juvenile delinquents whose nameless faces appear hardened by the unpredictable circumstances of growing up prematurely in the Jim Crow South and while enslaved at Parchman Farm (see fig. 1). They appear free of the external markings of enslavement (not wearing prison uniforms). They stand posed like little men, flanked by older prisoners and prison staff. Children left unprotected in "a brutal, predatory culture," where "first offenders were caged with incorrigibles, and adults with juveniles" and "'feeble-minded' convicts were everywhere," these are some of the boys whose fates went often unrecorded.⁵ Unspeakable terrors, as River recalls: when *"night guards at the doors to the shack go on a break, things can happen to a boy of twelve in the dark if he a crybaby"* (23). Ward performs an exorcism in her novel to alleviate the suffering of lost boys. Though Richie is not the protagonist, Ward allows him to tell his story alongside Jojo's in this coming-of-age novel. Their lives are intertwined by a history of oppression traceable to slavery and by racial strife and intimate violence in the present. Ward has this narrative mode in common with Faulkner. The art of storytelling is revealed in the way the authors blend the past and present lives of characters with the matter of race and place.

Enslaved African Americans and their descendants live in the webbed narrative of *Go Down, Moses*. However, the author's representation of the enslaved—and the "curse" of slavery that their descendants bear—is filtered mostly through the consciousness of another white southerner, Isaac McCaslin, and this "master narrative" of slavery does not allow Black characters to escape their tragic fates. Hence, Butch Beauchamp's demise is inevitable in the third-person omniscient narrative of the title story, with its sparse dialogue. To offer a counternarrative of the enslaved and generational curses, I read Ward's *Sing, Unburied, Sing* as a lyrical key to Faulkner's novel. Both works are haunted by a southern past though the landscape evolves into the contemporary world, from the plantation to the prison, where many African Americans appear enslaved on Parchman Farm, a narrative clue also found in *Go Down, Moses*. The aesthetics of the enslaved—spirituals and blues traditions, for certain—are liberating tropes in both novels and, yet, as I argue, Ward's use of such narrative tropes allows us to travel from Mississippi's Gulf Coast to the Delta (and perhaps other routes out of Yoknapatawpha), ultimately to emancipate not only enslaved African Americans and their descendants but also Faulkner from that slave past.

My reading of Faulkner and Ward concentrates on the figures of the enslaved reimagined as Black male convicts and the oral traditions that inscribe their bodies in the narratives. Slavery leaves a legacy of criminality for Black descendants in both novels. Academics and activists have long documented the transition from an enslaved labor force to the peonage system to mass incarcerations throughout the South, especially the practice of convict leasing, which became "worse than slavery" by many accounts.⁶ African American vernacular traditions offer varied responses to the conditions of Jim Crow society and prison culture as they developed around the turn of the twentieth century. Work songs and, later, blues music, when used as a survival mechanism, narrate the physical demands and psychological trauma of hard labor.⁷ Likewise,

**Fig. 2:** Prisoners lining up to go to work hoeing cotton. Martha Alice Stewart, Time on Parchman Farm, 1930s Collection [mum01772_102_f1_6_1], Archives and Special Collections, J. D. Williams Library, University of Mississippi.

archival images capture the shock, fear, and hopelessness of Black convicts working as chain gangs on public works projects, plowing fields with mule teams, and picking acres of cotton. In steady formation, withstanding the trusty guard's penetrating gaze and in range of the high-powered rifles, Black convicts toiled from "sun up to sun down" much like their enslaved ancestors[8] (see fig. 2). Photographed in motion under static conditions, subject to humiliation and destruction, Blackness is grafted onto the bodies of these convicts much as their uniforms identify them by the "ring-arounds" (horizontal strips for "gunmen") or "up-and-downs" (vertical stripes for trusty-shooters and on baggy dresses for female prisoners).[9] With the value of the enslaved exchanged for commodified convict laborers, by the early twentieth century, mass incarceration in the United States had become a profitable venture of plundering cheap flesh. Faulkner and Ward imagine a life thus enriched by what the imprisoned might have experienced. Black bodies tortured, contorted, and lifeless in these prison narratives, the visual imagery and the lyrical dimensions coalesce to achieve a necessary realism for emancipation. (See fig. 3.)

In *Go Down, Moses*, however, Faulkner's Black males cannot escape narrative entrapments; they remain enslaved by circumstance if not by moral convictions. Rider, in "Pantaloon in Black," while grieving the death of his wife, murders a white man in a dice game. Subsequently, Rider is lynched, as the story later is told from the perspective of a white

**Fig. 3:** Prisoners dumping cotton sacks. Martha Alice Stewart, Time on Parchman Farm, 1930s Collection [mum01772_102_f2_10_2], Archives and Special Collections, J. D. Williams Library, University of Mississippi.

deputy, which mirrors the narrative framing of the whole novel. The tragedy is in the double homicide and the indictment of white folks. Though the McCaslins do not appear in the story, their influence is a haunting presence nonetheless. Like the Black tenant farmers on the McCaslin plantation, Rider rents his cabin from Carothers ("Roth") Edmonds, descendant and the sole proprietor of the McCaslin estate (sharecropping acreage similar to the land upon which Parchman Farm was built in 1904). The home Rider makes with Mannie in six short months spent living there yields more freedom for the couple than the reader might imagine; he renovates the space and pays the rent in advance (avoiding debt slavery). With Mannie's death, however, the warmth from the fire on the hearth is extinguished, signifying also the extinction of Rider's will to live. The story transitions from the cabin to a boiler shed at the sawmill, where Rider kills Birdsong for cheating in the dice game, and, eventually, to a cell in the county jail. For Rider, these are not spaces of reform but of rebellion. And yet, at each turn in the narrative, Rider's imminent demise is predictable.

Faulkner uses a blues aesthetic—images and sound—to sharpen the contours of the character. We can understand Rider's grief, for instance, as an expression of the "down-hearted blues," signified in the narrative as follows:

And, once free of the bottom's unbreathing blackness, there was the moon again, his long shadow and that of the lifted jug slanting away as he drank and then held the jug poised, gulping the silver air into his throat until he could breathe again, speaking to the jug: "Come on now. You always claim you's a better man den me. Come on now. Prove it." He drank again, swallowing the chill liquid tamed of taste or heat either while the swallowing lasted, feeling it flow solid and cold with fire, past then enveloping the strong steady panting of his lungs until they too ran suddenly free as his moving body ran in the silver solid wall of air he breasted. And he was all right.... (141)

But Rider does not achieve the psychic release in this blues performance that Bessie Smith does as she sings, "World in a jug, the stopper's in my hand / Got the world in a jug, the stopper's in my hand."[10] He drinks to make sense of a world ordered by chaos (Mannie's untimely death) and racial destiny (his mortality). His desire to bottle his grief makes Rider a tragic figure, the persona of a bluesman, ultimately, as he struggles to live free in a world that destroys Black bodies.

His lynching prefigured in the narrative by what Ta-Nehisi Coates calls the "sheer terror of disembodiment,"[11] Rider lives on a former plantation and works at a sawmill, both controlled by white authorities. Such power relations are maintained in the narrative structure of "Pantaloon in Black," since we may experience Rider's grief in the first half with its omniscient narrator and understand it better in the second half as narrated by the white deputy. This *is* a story of the disembodied. Rider's fate is sealed by fear of the truth; he controls nothing, even his body is not his own. This fear is most evident in Rider's aunt's love; as his surrogate mother, she would sacrifice her own body to protect Rider's from the lynch mob. The deputy tries "to explain to her what would maybe happen to her too if them Birdsong kin catches us before we can get [Rider] locked up" (150). Later, she pleads, "'He was a good boy. He aint never been in no trouble till now. He will suffer for what he done. But dont let the white folks get him'" (151). That she does not fear also the white deputies who are "endowed with the authority to destroy" Black bodies suggests the exchange value of the enslaved compared to the convict.[12] "The life of the slave was valuable to his master, but there was no financial loss . . . if a convict died."[13] Considering how historical markings of slavery objectify the Black body in the novel, the back story humanizes Rider, though he remains an enigma to the deputy. The pain of losing his wife is accentuated by the generational Black pain of subjugation. The relative autonomy he achieves is a futile attempt to be free from this immediate and historical past: he defies a white foreman, assaults a white bootlegger, and kills a white cheat. His power to control his destiny, however, is limited by the narrative framing of Black bodies in *Go Down, Moses*.

Though he is a gambler, thief, and murderer, Butch Beauchamp's jail time is abbreviated in the narrative. We learn only that he inherits his vices from a "father who begot and deserted him and who was now in the State Penitentiary for manslaughter—some seed not only violent but dangerous and bad" (354). (Ward revises this father-son genealogy with River and Richie's relationship.) We meet Butch in the novel's final, title chapter, "Go Down, Moses," as he awaits his execution for killing a (white) policeman in Chicago. In a brief interview with a census taker, Butch reveals his birth name—"Samuel Worsham Beauchamp"—and scant details about his birthplace and family in Jefferson, Mississippi. Frustrated, the census taker pushes for more information: "'If they dont know who you are here, how will they know—how do you expect to get home?'" (352). Butch, however, is apathetic about returning "home."

That Mollie nevertheless insists on bringing her grandson home—albeit for burial—is a fulfillment of slave prophecy. She appeals to attorney Gavin Stevens to find her grandson: "Roth Edmonds sold my Benjamin. Sold him in Egypt. Pharaoh got him" (353), paraphrasing the lyrics of the spiritual "Go Down, Moses." She blames her former landlord for, in effect, enslaving and, thus, killing Butch/Benjamin after he is caught stealing and forced to leave the tenant farm. Mollie's plea for salvation appears only as the ramblings of an "old Negress," when her performance is much more. Like other "sorrow songs" cataloged by W. E. B. Du Bois, "Go Down, Moses" presents "the articulate message of the slave to the world":[14]

> Go down, Moses
> Way down in Egyptland
> Tell old Pharaoh
> To let my people go.[15]

The opening stanza issues a proclamation of freedom that echoes throughout the song:

> No more shall they in bondage toil,
> Let my people go
> Let them come out with Egypt's spoil.
> Let my people go
> The Lord told Moses what to do
> Let my people go
> To lead the children of Israel through.
> Let my people go.[16]

As an epic narrative drawn from the Old Testament, "Go Down, Moses" confirms Black humanity, the suffering and survival of enslaved African Americans and their descendants. It demonstrates Black creativity and genius, as James Weldon Johnson recognized in his praise for those enslaved "black and unknown bards" who were inspired to sing "songs of sorrow, love, and faith, and hope" to comfort and to liberate.[17] That self-emancipation for untold millions of enslaved African Americans carried over to their descendants, like Mollie Beauchamp, who wills freedom for her grandson too.

Faulkner weaves the lyrics of the slave spiritual "Go Down, Moses" throughout the story as if to offer a salve for deep racial wounds to conclude his epic narrative of southern redemption. However, with the song compressed in the narrative, Faulkner presents Black agency within the strict limitations of white southern paternalism. Interceding on Mollie's behalf, after all, Miss Worsham is the granddaughter of the slaveholder who once owned Mollie's parents. The decayed aristocrat underestimates the cost of bringing Butch's body home and insists that Stevens and other white townspeople defray the costs for the casket, flowers, and hearse. Ironically enough, a dead Black convict is worthless to the state's penal system though his funeral is quite expensive.

Though Miss Worsham's valuation of Butch's body astounds Stevens, he still collects funds "to bring a dead nigger home. . . . Never mind about a paper to sign: just give me a dollar. Or a half a dollar then. Or a quarter then," he bargains (360). Stevens thus figures as "Moses" in the narrative, a role befitting the scholar "whose serious vocation was a twenty-two-year-old unfinished translation of the Old Testament back into classic Greek" (353). But Stevens is ill-prepared for the task, as is evident when he tries to escape the chorus of accusations for Butch's death:

"Sold him in Egypt and now he dead."
"Oh yes, Lord. Sold him in Egypt." . . .
"Sold him to Pharaoh."
"And now he dead." (363)

Molly, her brother Hamp, and his wife are in deep mourning, for the past and present circumstances, but Stevens and perhaps Miss Worsham do not comprehend their chants. She concludes, "'It's our grief.'" Du Bois explains the layers of meaning and purpose in African American spirituals:

Through all the sorrow of the Sorrow Songs there breathes a hope— a faith in the ultimate justice of things. The minor cadences of despair change often to triumph and calm confidence. Sometimes it is faith in life, sometimes a faith in death, sometimes assurance of boundless justice in some fair world beyond. But whichever it is, the meaning is always clear: that sometime, somewhere, men will judge men by their souls and not by their skins.[18]

What justice the enslaved desired is obstructed in *Go Down, Moses*, and the "curse" remains for Faulkner's characters. The funeral procession does not untangle the plot nor the bloodlines, and Faulkner ends his novel with this cryptic scene. The hearse parades through the town, at once "circling the Confederate monument and the courthouse," carrying "the slain wolf" (364), as crowds gather along the streets to bear witness. The spectacle is reminiscent of ceremonial lynchings rather than a ritual "homegoing" in African American culture. Considering the monuments of white supremacy and the justice system in balance with a sacrificial Black body on display, reading *Go Down, Moses* today begs the question of how much the South has changed (if not the nation) since the days of slavery, the Civil War, or the post-Reconstruction eras.[19] In "Go Down, Moses," white authority silences the enslaved. Quite literally, we do not get the convict's story because Mr. Wilmoth, the editor of the county newspaper, refuses to print "'all of hit,'" as Mollie insists (365).

Reading *Sing, Unburied, Sing* as a lyrical key to *Go Down, Moses* gives the story of the enslaved a fuller expression. Ward acknowledges Faulkner's craft of storytelling as inspiring:

> I think about him [Faulkner] often, when I am writing my novels, because, first of all, I want my rendition of the South to have as much texture . . . and to be as alive . . . and also I think about him, too, because he champions characters who have really rich interior lives, but who may not, maybe, express it as clearly as they could, like in their dialogue, you know, when they're interacting with the other characters.[20]

In *Sing, Unburied, Sing*, we meet such characters living among the dead. Ward, however, uses the past to free the enslaved in the present. Hers is a prison narrative that inevitably has a blues soundtrack.

Parchman Farm is central to the racial drama we experience in *Sing, Unburied, Sing*. The past and present overlap in the stories that River tells Jojo about his time spent at Parchman during the 1940s, how he and his brother Stag were sentenced to hard labor there for minor offenses, like hundreds of other African American men and boys. *"Parchman the kind of place that fool you into thinking it ain't no prison, ain't going to be so bad when you first see it, because ain't no walls"* (21). Deceptively simple by design then, Mississippi State Penitentiary could "induce in the inmate a state of conscious and permanent visibility that assures the automatic functioning of power," according to Michel Foucault's model of panoptical prison design.[21] "*Parchman was a working farm right off,*" as River remembers, "*You see them open fields we worked in, the way you could look right through that barbed wire, the way you could grab it and get a toehold here, a bloody handhold there, the way they cut them trees flat so that land is empty and open to the ends of the earth, and you think,* I can get out of here if I set my mind to it. I can follow the right stars south and all the way on home" (22). Parchman operated as a large-scale, modern plantation and was notorious for labor exploitation and punishment.[22] River remains traumatized by his imprisonment, and Ward reconstructs his experience in a stream-of-consciousness narrative, with River both reporting action from the past (in italics) and experiencing it again in the present. Verb tenses shift—past, present, and conditional—in River's imprisoned mind, revealing how any time spent at Parchman carries a life sentence.

Enslaving Black bodies gave rise to the blues as a musical tradition of suffering and release. River tells Jojo about Black convicts working in the fields under constant surveillance by white "*sergeant[s]*" who "*come from a long line of overseers*" (22), and by inmate guards or trusty shooters who were most often callous murderers (see fig. 4). This is the blues experience reimagined in the lyrics of Booker "Bukka" White's classic "Parchman Farm Blues" (1940):

We go to work in the mo'nin
Just a-dawn of day
Just at the settin' of the sun
That's when da work is done, yeah[23]

In addition to blues songs like White's, prison work songs like "It Makes a Long Time Man Feel Bad" (1947) testify to the exploitative labor practices at Parchman by revealing the mental trauma that ensued:

Oh, Captain George, he was a hard a-drivin' man
Oh, Captain George, he was a hard a-drivin' man
Oh, Captain George, he was a hard a-drivin' man
Oh my Lawd
Oh, Captain George, would sho' drive us so hard
Oh, Captain George, would sho' drive us so hard
Oh, Captain George, would sho' drive us so hard
Oh my Lawd[24]

**Fig. 4:** African American trusty guards. Martha Alice Stewart, Time on Parchman Farm, 1930s Collection [mum01772_102_f16_4], Archives and Special Collections, J. D. Williams Library, University of Mississippi.

In ranking order—the "master"/superintendent, the sergeants, the drivers/captains, and the trusty shooters—the power structure recreated that of the most efficient planation. Black trusties and guards were a unique asset at Parchman. Like their white counterparts, Black trusties and guards were promised their freedom if they shot and killed a runaway convict.[25] In River's memories, he fears the trusty-shooters' thirst for blood as equaled only by the bloodhounds trained to tear apart Black flesh. Surviving Parchman, as River learned, meant to untether the spirit from the body. Work songs and blues music made such emancipation possible.[26]

In *Sing, Unburied, Sing*, Ward captures the blues aesthetic in themes and lyricism, images and ethos. She takes a cue at times from the "long line" form in blues music—repetitious in sound and reason much like Langston Hughes's performances in verse—and adapts it realistically to transport readers to experience the experience of Parchman.[27] River remembers working prior to his arrival at Parchman, *"but never like that. Never sunup to sundown in no cotton field. Never in that kind of heat. It's different up there. The heat.... Soon enough my hands thickened up and my feet crusted and bled and I understood that when I was on that line in them fields I had to not think about it"* (22). And of Richie, we learn also:

> They put him on the long line. From sunup to sundown we was out there in them fields, hoeing and picking and planting and pulling. A man get to

> *a point like that, he can't think. Just feel. Feel like he want to stop moving. Feel his stomach burn and know he want to eat. Feel his head packed full of cotton and know he want to sleep. Feel his throat close and fire run up his arms and legs, his heart beat out his chest, and know he want to run.* (68–69)

Living on Parchman also makes River "wanna holla," as the saying goes: "We was gunmen, under the gun of them damn trusty shooters. That was our whole world: the long line. Men strung out across the fields, the trusty shooters stalking the edge, the driver on his mule, the caller yelling to the sun, throwing his working song out. Like a fishing net. Us caught and struggling" (69). River's memories are "lined out" like the lyrics of a blues song, with repetitive imagery—"sunup to sundown," the "heat," and the "long line"—creating an antiphonal pattern of verse and commentary about the Parchman experience.[28] His rhythmic speech and raw emotions reincarnate the personae of great bluesmen like "Bukka" White, Eddie James "Son" House, and R. L. Burnside, all former Parchman convicts.[29] Like the songs they sang, Ward's blues narrative also offers temporary relief for the enslaved.

It is in River's stories about his time at Parchman that Jojo learns about generational curses that haunt the living. As Jojo pleads with his "Pops" to tell him the whole story about Richie, it unfolds instead throughout the novel as a series of monologues with gaps of memory and time. This narrative styling (often as stream-of-consciousness) Ward shares in common with Faulkner. Shifting from character to character, past to present, the spectral to the real, Jojo learns difficult lessons about survival. River tells him about Richie breaking a hoe and being whipped with *"Black Annie"* (120), a leather strap that was "the true symbol of authority and discipline at Parchman . . . three feet long and six inches wide."[30] Former convicts like River remembered "the sounds of Black Annie: the 'whistlin' air, the crack on bare flesh, the convict's painful grunt."[31] Such corporeal punishment was common practice on slave plantations and later it was used to discipline offenses committed by Black convicts, especially in the South.[32] Richie's abuse is one of the last memories River shares with Jojo, one of the last Jojo remembers before he arrives at Parchman with Leonie to pick up Michael, which is when he first encounters Richie. In transitioning from the past to the present, Ward collapses time, allowing Richie to escape Parchman, finally.

Understanding the convict's release—Michael's, Richie's, and River's—allows us to return to Faulkner's open-ended conclusion in *Go Down, Moses*. When Richie emerges in the narrative to tell his own story, he proclaims, "I'm going home" (126), echoing the desire of perhaps every inmate at Parchman. But their fates hung on the "luck—not justice" of receiving a pardon from Mississippi's governor, especially during the Jim Crow era.[33] The pardon system was used to release trusty shooters and other convicts who had earned the privilege, usually by killing anyone who attempted to escape Parchman.[34] Ultimately, according to historian David Oshinsky, white paternalism was the only guarantee for securing a pardon:

> In a prison system where most inmates were black and outside authorities were white, racial etiquette played a crucial role. There was a distinct ritual to the pardon process that everyone understood. In practical terms, it meant getting a number of prominent whites to vouch for the inmate's good character.[35]

In *Go Down, Moses*, Faulkner in effect offers an ironic "pardon" for slavery by sending Butch "home." Readers must contend with the incongruity of the actions of white folks (Faulkner and his characters) and with that of a convicted Black criminal whose lines of descent are traceable to slaveholders and their slave property.[36] "A bad son of a bad father," Butch was a self-confessed murderer, but that is who Stevens has to find and save. Once Butch is executed, Stevens's mission is not aborted: "'*We're bringing him home*,' he said. 'Miss Worsham and [the editor] and me and some others. It will cost—'" (359; emphasis added).

Understanding the meaning of "home" in Faulkner's novel leads back to reading *Sing, Unburied, Sing* as its lyrical key. Ward explores the meaning of home through song. Richie explains, "'Home ain't always about a place. . . . Home is about the earth. Whether the earth open up to you. Whether it pull you so close the space between you and it melt and y'all one and it beats like your heart. Same time. . . . The place is [a] song and I'm going to be part of the song'" (182–83). As he tells Jojo, Richie only began to understand home through River's stories about the Gulf Coast, the beauty of the ocean, and its changing colors as God's handiwork. River essentially never left his home because he carries it to Parchman in his freedom stories. Richie, however, wonders "if the reason I couldn't leave Parchman before Jojo came was because it was a sort of home to me: terrible and formative as the iron leash that chains dogs" (190–91). Butch's departure from and return to the Delta can be understood also in this way; marred by history and circumstance, it is a place that claims him nonetheless. Ward, however, riffs on the southern trope of the spectral to emancipate the enslaved in a way Faulkner does not. Black experience is metaphor in *Go Down, Moses*. Black experience is realized in Ward's narrative. Both novels conclude with rituals of the southern imaginary and African American culture, but Richie's *homegoing* is a ritual of release and Butch's *homecoming* is one of return. In *Sing, Unburied Sing*, Ward breaks the frame of Black male enslavement, spectrally and figuratively. Emancipating Richie is an act of justice, mercy, and love—largely missing elements in Faulkner's *Go Down, Moses*.

Writing a love story about Mississippi's history of slavery and Jim Crow is no small feat for any author. Ward manages to accomplish it in her lyrical narrative about a family burdened by this past of racial injustices. She takes her cue, though, from Faulkner, understanding that southerners inherit traditions that are often misunderstood. The lessons that Jojo are taught are those we all must learn about life, death, home, love, and, of course, time—universal truths that resonate in aesthetics of the enslaved. With the spirituals, work songs, and the blues used to resolve conflicts in the novels, the intertextuality of both works heightens reader appeal. While Faulkner, like his characters in *Go Down, Moses*, can remain trapped in the present by past sins of slavery, I recommend reading *Sing, Unburied, Sing* to understand and appreciate Faulkner's conundrum, and to consider how Ward emancipates with a song in continuum, a mystical phenomenon that is "something like relief, something like remembrance, something like ease" (284).

### NOTES

Thanks to research assistant Jonathan Puckett for his help finding archival images of African American inmates at Parchman in the 1930s as used in the essay.

1. Jesmyn Ward, *Sing, Unburied, Sing* (New York: Scribner, 2017), 281. Hereafter cited parenthetically.

2. William Faulkner, *Go Down, Moses*, rev. ed. (1942; repr., New York: Vintage International, 1990), 365; emphasis removed. Hereafter cited parenthetically. The Black Beauchamps are descendants of Lucius Quintus Carothers McCaslin, the white patriarch who had a child by his slave daughter, Tomasina/"Tomey." Butch's Black grandfather is "Lucas"/Lucius Quintus Carothers McCaslin Beauchamp, whose father was "Tomey's Turl"/Terrel. Lucas is the oldest surviving Black McCaslin, whose racial and financial inheritance complicates the narrative.

3. Jesmyn Ward, interview by Sam Briger, "For Jesmyn Ward, Writing Means Telling the 'Truth about the Place That I Live In,'" *Fresh Air*, November 28, 2017, www.npr.org/2017/11/28/566933935/for-jesmyn-ward-writing-means-telling-the-truth-about-the-place-that-i-live-in (accessed December 5, 2019).

4. Jesmyn Ward, "My True South: Returning Home to a Place I Love More Than I Loathe," *Time* (August 6–13, 2018): 49.

5. David Oshinsky, *Worse than Slavery: Parchman Farm and the Ordeal of Jim Crow Justice* (New York: Free Press, 1996), 138.

6. See Douglas A. Blackmon, *Slavery by Another Name: The Re-Enslavement of Black Americans from the Civil War to World War II* (New York: Doubleday, 2008), Richard Wormser, *The Rise and Fall of Jim Crow* (New York: St. Martin's Press, 2003), and Michelle Alexander, *The New Jim Crow: Mass Incarceration in the Age of Colorblindness* (New York: New Press, 2010). Most recently, Ava DuVernay's 2016 documentary *13th* charts the trajectory of African American enslavement to mass incarceration.

7. John and Alan Lomax's recordings of prison songs from Parchman are the most noted examples, well preserved in archives. See "Mississippi Prison Recordings 1947 and 1948," Association for Cultural Equity. research.culturalequity.org/get-audio-ix.do?ix=session&id=PR47&idType=abbrev&sortBy=abc (accessed December 5, 2019); "It Makes a Long Time Man Feel Bad," Library of Congress, www.loc.gov/item/lomaxbib000370/ (accessed December 5, 2019).

8. Part of the University of Mississippi's Archives and Special Collections includes the Martha Alice Stewart: Time on Parchman Farm Collection, featuring documentary photographs of Black convicts maintaining the operations of a large-scale plantation prison.

9. Oshinsky, *Worse than Slavery*, 137–38, 140.

10. "Down-Hearted Blues" was written by Alberta Hunter and Louie Austin in 1922. It became a hit song for Bessie Smith in 1923. The ability to control and create empowers the songstress, as she sings about dominating men despite the heartbreak she experiences.

11. Ta-Nehisi Coates, *Between the World and Me* (New York: Spiegel & Grau, 2015), 12.

12. Coates, *Between the World and Me*, 9.

13. L. G. Shivers, "A History of the Mississippi Penitentiary" (1930), qtd. in Oshinsky, *Worse than Slavery*, epigraph (n.p.).

14. W. E. B. Du Bois, *The Souls of Black Folk*, rev. ed. (1903; repr., Boston: Bedford/St. Martin's, 1997), 187.

15. "Go Down, Moses," in *The Norton Anthology of African American Literature*, vol. 1, ed. Henry Louis Gates Jr. and Valerie A. Smith (New York: W. W. Norton, 2014), 14.

16. Faulkner, "Go Down, Moses," 15.

17. James Weldon Johnson, "O Black and Unknown Bards," in *The Norton Anthology of African American Literature*, vol. 1, ed. Henry Louis Gates Jr. and Valerie A. Smith (New York: W.W. Norton, 2014), 784, 785.

18. Du Bois, *The Souls of Black Folk*, 192.

19. The spectacle of Butch's body brings to mind countless cases of Black victims abused/shot/killed by police that have gone "viral" on social media and featured in broadcast journalism and other media outlets. The names of victims—Breonna Taylor, Eric Garner, Sandra Bland, Michael Brown Jr., Tamir Rice, Philando Castile, Alton Sterling, and Laquan McDonald, among many others—have become hashtags for social media–sparked protests. Since 2013 activists with the #BlackLivesMatter (BLM) movement have spurred public protests against police brutality of African Americans, with events coming to a head with the death of George Floyd in 2020. See also Coates, *Between the World and Me*, 9.

20. Jesmyn Ward, "Off the Shelf," interview by publishers Simon & Schuster, Youtube, www.youtube.com/watch?v=52HqqzTYEsU (accessed December 5, 2019).

21. Michel Foucault, *Discipline and Punish: The Birth of the Prison* (1975), trans. Alan Sheridan (New York: Vintage Books, 1995), 201.

22. In addition to Oshinsky, see William Banks Taylor, *Down on Parchman Farm: The Great Prison in the Mississippi Delta* (Columbus: Ohio State University Press, 1999).

23. Booker T. Washington White, "Parchman Farm Blues" (1940), www.lyricsfreak.com/b/bukka+white/parchman+farm+blues_10053518.htm (accessed December 5, 2019).

24. Benny Will Richardson (hoe, vocals) and unidentified prisoners (hoe, vocals), "It Makes a Long Time Man Feel Bad," Association for Cultural Equity, research.culturalequity.org/get-audio-detailed-recording.do?recordingId=10702 (accessed December 5, 2019).

25. Oshinsky, *Worse than Slavery*, 147–48.

26. Several archives make prison songs by African Americans available for listeners. I consulted the Internet Archive and the Library of Congress to listen to rare recordings of songs like "It Makes a Long Time Man Feel Bad" and "Early in the Mornin'."

27. See Lorenzo Thomas, "Blues Aesthetic," in *The Oxford Companion to African American Literature*, ed. William L. Andrews, Frances Smith Foster, and Trudier Harris (New York: Oxford University Press, 1997), 87–89.

28. Langston Hughes's "The Weary Blues" (1926) is an example of this form in verse.

29. House's "Death Letter Blues" and Burnside's "See My Jumper on the Line" are classic blues about life at Parchman.

30. Oshinsky, *Worse than Slavery*, 149.

31. Oshinsky, *Worse than Slavery*, 151–52. In the 1940s, when folklorist John and Alan Lomax visited the prison to record blues songs, field hollers and work songs about Black Annie were cataloged too.

32. Oshinsky, *Worse than Slavery*, 149–52.

33. Oshinsky, *Worse than Slavery*, 180.

34. Oshinsky, *Worse than Slavery*, 179–86. Most pardons were granted in cases wherein a "humble negro" was involved in a Black-on-Black crime, where the argument for clemency emphasized Black inferiority as an innate criminal defect.

35. Oshinsky, *Worse than Slavery*, 181–82.

36. Parchman inmates convicted of a Black-on-white crime were much less likely to receive a pardon. See Oshinsky, *Worse than Slavery*, 187–90.

# Contributors

**Tim Armstrong** is professor of modern English and American literature at Royal Holloway, University of London. His books include *Modernism, Technology, and the Body*; *Haunted Hardy*; *Modernism: A Cultural History*; and most recently *The Logic of Slavery: Debt, Technology, and Pain in American Literature*. He is currently working on a study of modernist localism from 1926 to 1945.

**Edward A. Chappell** directed architectural research and historic preservation at the Colonial Williamsburg Foundation from 1980 to 2016. He and Carl Lounsbury studied and recorded buildings associated with slavery at the University of Mississippi for the UM Slavery Research Group. Chappell had degrees in history from William and Mary and architectural history from the University of Virginia.

**W. Ralph Eubanks** is the author of *Ever Is a Long Time: A Journey into Mississippi's Dark Past* and *The House at the End of the Road: The Story of Three Generations of an Interracial Family in the American South*. His essays on race, literature, and the South have appeared in the *Hedgehog Review*, *American Scholar*, *WIRED*, and the *New Yorker* and on National Public Radio. A 2007 Guggenheim Fellow, he is a visiting professor of English and Southern Studies at the University of Mississippi.

**Amy A. Foley** teaches in the English and cultural studies department at Bryant University in Rhode Island. Her work can be found in the *Journal of Popular Culture*, *Virginia Woolf Miscellany*, *Modern Language Studies*, and *Chiasmi International*. Foley's essay is an extension of her manuscript under review, *On the Threshold: Transitional Architectures in the Modern Novel*. She continues to write about fiction, modernism, architecture, and phenomenology in a global context.

**Michael Gorra** is Mary Augusta Jordan Professor of English at Smith College. His most recent book, *Portrait of a Novel: Henry James and the Making of an American Masterpiece* (2012), was a finalist for several prizes, including the Pulitzer Prize in Biography. His book-length study of Faulkner and the Civil War, *The Saddest Words: William Faulkner's Civil War*, is forthcoming from Liveright.

**Sherita L. Johnson** is an associate professor of English at the University of Southern Mississippi and a specialist in nineteenth-century African American literature, southern literature, and cultural studies. Author of *Black Women in New South Literature and Culture* (2010), Johnson also has served as a guest editor for two special issues of the *Southern Quarterly*: "My Southern Home": The Lives and Literature of 19th-Century Southern Black Writers (Spring 2008) and Freedom Summer 50th Anniversary (Fall 2014).

**Andrew B. Leiter** is professor of English at Lycoming College in Williamsport, Pennsylvania. He is author of *In the Shadow of the Black Beast: African American Masculinity in the Harlem and Southern Renaissances* (2010); editor of *Southerners on Film: Essays on Hollywood Portrayals since the 1970s* (2011); and coeditor (with Christopher Rieger) of *Faulkner and Hurston* (2017) and *Faulkner and Hemingway* (2018).

**John T. Matthews** is professor of English at Boston University. His previous books include *The Play of Faulkner's Language*, *The Sound and the Fury: Faulkner and the Lost Cause*, and *William Faulkner: Seeing through the South*. He is the editor of *A Companion to the Modern American Novel, 1900–1950*, *William Faulkner in Context*, and *The New Cambridge Companion to William Faulkner*. His articles on Faulkner and southern literature have appeared in *ELH*, *boundary 2*, *NOVEL*, *American Literary History*, *Philological Quarterly*, and elsewhere.

**Julie Beth Napolin** is assistant professor of digital humanities in literature at the New School. Her first book, *The Fact of Resonance: Modernist Acoustics and Narrative Form*, proposes a theory of aural phenomena in the works of Conrad, Du Bois, and Faulkner. In 2018–20 she was a Mellon Postdoctoral Fellow in the Price Lab for Digital Humanities at the University of Pennsylvania, working on a project titled "The Sound of Yoknapatawpha: An Acoustic Ecology."

**Erin Penner** is an associate professor of English at Asbury University. Her first book, *Character and Mourning: Woolf, Faulkner, and the Novel Elegy of the First World War*, was recently published by the University of Virginia Press. She has written on Faulkner for *Studies in the Novel*,

*African-American Review*, and *Mississippi Quarterly*, and has been an editor for *Digital Yoknapatawpha* since 2012.

**Stephanie Rountree** is assistant professor of English at the University of North Georgia, where she specializes in US literature and media, feminist and gender theory, and southern studies. Her scholarship has appeared in such publications as *Mississippi Quarterly*, *south: a literary journal*, *Ethos*, and *Carson McCullers in the Twenty-First Century* (2016). Together with Lisa Hinrichsen and Gina Caison, she is coeditor of *Small-Screen Souths: Region, Identity, and the Cultural Politics of Television* (2017) and *New Media and the US South* (in progress). Her current monograph project, tentatively titled "American Antiliberalism: Literatures of Enslavement and Public Health," investigates Black enslavement's formative role in the development of US public health as evidenced in post-Emancipation literature.

**Julia Stern** is Herman and Beulah Pearce Miller Research Professor of Literature, Charles Deering McCormick Professor of Teaching Excellence, and professor of English at Northwestern University. She is the author of *The Plight of Feeling: Sympathy and Dissent in the Early American Novel* (1997) and *Mary Chesnut's Civil War Epic* (2010). She is completing a manuscript entitled "Bette Davis Black and White." She has taught a course called "Race and Politics in the Major Novels of Faulkner" for more than twenty-five years.

**Jay Watson** is Howry Professor of Faulkner Studies and Professor of English at the University of Mississippi, where he has directed the Faulkner and Yoknapatawpha conference since 2012. He is author of three books, most recently *William Faulkner and the Faces of Modernity* (2019), and editor or coeditor of ten published or forthcoming volumes on Faulkner's work.

**Randall Wilhelm** is associate professor of English at Anderson University. He is the editor of *The Ron Rash Reader*, *Summoning the Dead: Essays on Ron Rash*, and the forthcoming *Conversations with Robert Morgan*. Wilhelm holds degrees in both visual art and literature, and has published on American, southern, and Appalachian writers, as well as interdisciplinary and transatlantic studies on the relationship between literature and visual art.

# Index

Page numbers in *italics* refer to illustrations.

Abdur-Rahman, Aliyyah I., 47
abolition, ix
*Absalom, Absalom!* (Faulkner), ix, xii, xiv, xviii, xix, xxi, xxv, 4, 11, 32–33, 38–41, 44, 76, 82, 84–85, 89, 117–18, 120, 126–27, 131, 134–42, 146–48, 187–88, 190; map, 100, *137*
Adams, John Quincy, 174
*Aeneas Africanus* (Edwards), 120
African Diaspora, 51
African Methodist Episcopal Church (Oxford), xi
Agamben, Giorgio, 126, 142
Agricultural Adjustment Act of 1933 (AAA), 111, 115
Agricultural Adjustment Act of 1938 (AAA), 115
Alabama, 28
Alabama Forestry Commission, 156
Althusser, Louis, 6
American antiliberalism, 156, 162, 168
American Association of University Presses, xxxi
Amis, Martin, 122
architecture: African, 49, 51; African American, 52; Anglo, 52; Colonial Revival, xviii, 71, 78; Euro-American, 54; German, 51; Greek Revival, 71, 75; I-house, 81n59; Irish, 51; Scottish, 51. *See also* Freud, Sigmund; Rowan Oak; slavery
Armstrong, Tim, xx, xxx, 4
*As I Lay Dying* (Faulkner), ix, 120
Atkinson, Ted, 107
Auld, Sophia, 37

Bailey, Ellen, 66
Bailey, Lucy, 80n32
Bailey Woods. *See* Rowan Oak
Ball, Charles, xvi, 37
Baptist, Edward E., xiii, xiv, xxix, 4, 5, 17n3, 19n13; *The Half Has Never Been Told*, 9, 17n3
Barbados, 13
"Barn Burning" (Faulkner), 35, 76, 117
Barnett, Ned, 69, 76
Barr, Caroline, 66, 69–70, 76, 80n42
Barthes, Roland, 13–31
Baucom, Ian, 4
Baylor College of Medicine, 159
Beckert, Sven, xiii, 3, 4, 5, 6, 17n3; *Empire of Cotton*, 17n3, 155, 169
Bederman, Gail, 47
Behind the Big House project, xi
*Beloved* (Morrison), 41, 110–11
Benjamin, Walter, 117
Berner, Seth, xxx
Berry, Daina, 5
Berte, Leigh Anne Litwiller, xxx
Bertholf, Garry J., xxx

215

Best, Stephen, xxx, 4, 132–33, 140
*Beulah* (McDaniels), 146
Bibler, Michael P., 176
bills of lading, slave, 9
*Black Thunder* (Bontemps), viii
BlackLivesMatter movement, 208n19
Bland, Sandra, 208n19
Blotner, Joseph, x, 180; *Portable Faulkner*, 93, 97
Boston, Massachusetts, 12–13
Boston University, 12
Boudreaux, Tony, xxix
Breaden, Dale, 113
Brer Fox an' Brer Rabbit, 114
British Empire, 95
Brooks, Cleanth, 84, 96
Brown, Michael, Jr., 208n19
Brown University, 13
Bruce, Eliza, 50
Bruinsburg, 79n16
Bryant, Sallie Bailey, 80n44
Bryant, W. C., 81n55
Bryant family (Coffeeville, Mississippi), vii
Burns Belfry, xi
Burnside, R. L., 205
Bush, Chet, xxx

Cambridge, Massachusetts, 86
*Capital in the Twenty-First Century* (Piketty), 3
capitalism, xiii, 3–4, 157; American, xiv–xv, 160; slave, 3–16; "Slavery's Capitalism," 155
Caribbean Sea, 21n28
Carothers, James B., xxx
Carver, George Washington, 111
Casanova, Pascale, 19n7
Castile, Philando, 208n19
Catlin, Roger, 174
Cellini, Richard, xxx
Cerf, Bennett, 81n54

Chappell, Edward A., xii, xvii, xxix
Chavers, Linda, xxx
Chesnutt, Charles, xx, 109; "Lonesome Ben," xxii–xxiii, 155–69; "Mars Jeem's Nightmare," 109
Christianity, 27
Civil War, viii, 32, 34, 58, 66, 67, 71, 93, 121, 126, 202; Civil War Amendments to the US Constitution, 29; Confederacy, 25, 87, 147; Confederate army, x, 28; Confederate Conscription Act (1862), 25; Grant's army, 28; United States Post Office, 111; siege of Vicksburg, 23; Union army, 25, 27–29, 32, 58, 148, 187; United States Colored Troops, 28–29
civilization, African and European ideologies of, 49
Claremont plantation, 61
Clark, Keith, 111
Clegg, John, 17n3–18n3
Coates, Ta-Nehisi, 199
Cobb, O. B., 79n22
Columbus, Mississippi, 62f, 63, 65
Commins, Saxe, 73, 81n61
Common Law, 108
*Common Law, The* (Holmes), 109–10
Concord, 63, 64
Confederate battle flag, removal, 3
Consolidated Association of the Planters of Louisiana, 19n13–20n13
copyright law, 144n32
Corinth, Mississippi, 28
cotton, cultivation of, xiii
Cowley, Malcolm, 106

daguerreotype, 173
Darrow, Charles, 114
Davidson, Suzanne, xxix

Davis, Thadious M., 96–97, 120; *Games of Property*, 119
de Bracton, Henry, 109
de Gaulle, Charles, 71
de la Serna, Ramon Gomez, 53
Derrida, Jacque: *Speech and Phenomena*, 127; *Of Grammatology*, 127
Descartes, René, 143n17
Digital Yoknapatawpha project, xxx, 92–93, 95, 101–3
Dimock, Wai Chee, 176
*Discourse on Inequality* (Rousseau), 113
Dixiecrats, 115
Douglass, Frederick, xvi, 30, 35, 37–38, 41, 93; "The Meaning of July Fourth for the Negro," (Douglass), 7; *Narrative of the Life of Frederick Douglass*, 35, 130; "What to the Slave Is the Fourth of July?," 94
Doyle, Don, 20n15
*Dred Scott v. Samford*, 123
Du Bois, W. E. B., 18n3, 24, 30, 48–49, 51, 200–201; "Africa, Colonialism, and Zionism," 49; *Black Reconstruction in America*, 161; "The Conservation of Races," 55n11; *The Negro American Family*, 48, 50; *Souls of Black Folk*, 29, 201; "What Is Civilization?," 49
Dussere, Erik, 112, 117
Duvall, John N., 175, 183
Duvert, Elizabeth, 100

E-Ah-Nah-Yea, 69
Eaton, John, 27
*Ebony & Ivy* (Wilder), x, 85
economy: credit, xiii, 149; cotton economy in Alabama and Mississippi, 8; riverboat, 8–9. *See also* slavery
Edison, Thomas, 132, 144n31
Ellis, Clifton, 50
Emancipation, ix, x, xxii, 49, 98, 126, 148, 155, 162, 166, 168
*Emancipator*, 15
Emanuel A. M. E. Church massacre, 3
*Essays on Liberty and Slavery* (Bledsoe), 88
Estrada, Kenneth, xxix
Eubanks, Ralph, xii, xviii–xix, xxix, xxx
Eudora Welty Awards in Creative Writing, xxix
"Evangeline" (Faulkner), ix, xxi, 138–40

*Fable, A* (Faulkner), ix, xviii, 77, 117, 120
Falkner, William Clark, viii, 25
Faulkner, Estelle Oldham, 67, 70–73, 74, 76–78, 80n48, 81n60
Faulkner, William: cartography by, 91, 98, 100; drawings, 174–90; gradualism, 115; illustrated and calligraphic booklets, 174; as Hollywood screenwriter, 84, 174; Nobel Prize, 69, 72, 76; silhouettes, 176
*Faulkner Journal*, xxix
Faulkner Society, xxix
*Faulkner's Imperialism* (Hagood), 45
Featherston, 62f
feudalism, 161–62
*Finnegan's Wake* (Joyce), 120
*Flags in the Dust* (Faulkner), vii
Flint, Wayne, 158
Flora (slave), 173–74
Floyd, George, 208n19
Foley, Amy, xvi, xvii, xxix–xxx
Forret, Jeff, xvi, 35, 36; *Race Relations at the Margins*, 36

Foucault, Michel, 119, 157, 203; *The Birth of Biopolitics*, 157
*Frankenstein* (Shelley), 149
Franklin, Malcolm, 80n42
Freedmen's Town, xi
Freud, Sigmund: on architecture as sign of civilization, 46, 48, 55n9; *Civilization and Its Discontents*, 46
Fugitive Slave Act, 133

Galle, Julian, xxix
gambling, 117–23
Gardner, Sarah E., xxx
Garner, Eric, 208n19
Garner, Margaret, 41
Genovese, Eugene, 18n5
geophagy (clay-eating), 163–69, 170n16
George, Henry, xx, 113–14
George, Lloyd, 114
Georgetown University, 13
Georgia, 28
Gilman, Sander L., 176
Ginsburg, Rebecca, 50
Gleason, Michael, xxx
Gleeson-White, Sarah, xxx
Glissant, Édouard, 130
*Go Down, Moses* (Faulkner), ix, xx, xxiv, xxv, 11, 32, 44, 48, 53, 60, 91–103, 107, 111–13, 115, 117, 119–20, 187, 194–207; "The Bear," 98–99, 108; "Delta Autumn," 99; "The Fire and the Hearth," 112, 117; "Go Down, Moses," xxiv; "The Old People," 99; "Pantaloon in Black," xii, xix–xx, xxiv, 97, 117; "Was," xix–xx, 53, 92–94, 96, 119, 121
"Go Down, Moses" (spiritual), 200–201
Godden, Richard, 19n13, 20n14, 39, 97, 111, 115

Gold, Lael, xxx
*Gone with the Wind* (Mitchell), viii, 34, 146; Mammy, 146
Gorra, Michael, xv, xxx
Graham, T. Austin, 188, 190
Grandin, Greg, 4
Grant, Ulysses S., 23, 27. *See also* Civil War
Great Depression, viii
Great Migration, 97
Great Mississippi Flood of 1927, ix
Greenfield Farm, 69, 72, 81n59

*Habeas Viscus* (Weheliye), 129–31, 134–35
Haiti, 39, 85, 146; Haitian Revolution, 7, 40
*Hamlet, The* (Faulkner), ix, 57
Hannon, Charles, 106, 188
Harker, Jaime, 187
Hart, Albert Bushnell, 11; *Slavery and Abolition*, 11
Hartman, Saidiya, xxi, 126
Harvard University, 11–13, 85, 21n21, 85; School of Law, 13
Hegel, Georg Wilhelm Friedrich, 20n14, 151; *The Phenomenology of Spirit*, 149; *The Philosophy of Right*, 133; master-slave relationship, 148–49
Holly Springs, Mississippi, xi, 62f, 63, 64f, 65
Hollywood, 67, 73, 80n48
Homeplace plantation, 87
hookworm, 156–69, 170n16, 170n18
House, Eddie James "Son," 205
House of Barring Brothers, 20n13
Howe, Irving, 32
Hudson, Peter James, 18n3
Hugh Craft House, 63
Hughes, Langston, 204
Hyppolite, Jean, 52

# INDEX

*If I Forget Thee, Jerusalem* (Faulkner). See also *Wild Palms, The* (Faulkner)
Indian Removal. *See* Indians, Southeastern
Indians, Southeastern, vii, xxv, 97; Chickasaw, 58, 106; Removal, xiii, xiv
*Intruder in the Dust* (Faulkner), ix, xx, 35, 60, 110–13, 115, 119–20, 122
Israelites, 27
"It Makes a Long Time Man Feel Bad" (traditional), 203

Jackson, Jeffrey T., xxix
Jackson, Mississippi, 61
Jackson, Robert, xxx
Jackson, T. J., 72
Jacobs, Harriet, xvi, 41; *Incidents in the Life of a Slave Girl*, 35
Jamaica, 79n24
James, C. L. R., 18n3
Jaurès, Jean, 18n3
Jim Crow, 29, 35, 77, 131, 139, 151, 166–68, 195–96, 206–7
John W. Hunt Scholarships, xxix
Johnson, James Weldon, 201
Johnson, Sherita L., xxiv–xxv, xxx
Johnson, Walter, xiii, 4, 8–9, 17n3, 20n16
Joiner, Jennie, xxx
Jones, Lydia, 80n42
Jordan River, 27
Joshua, 27
*Journal of Negro History*, 84
"Justice, A" (Faulkner), ix

Kentucky, 20n13
King, Richard, 111
"Knight's Gambit" (Faulkner), 44, 67
Kuyk, Dirk, Jr., 33
Kuzmanovich, Zoran, xxx

Lafayette (Marquis de Lafayette Gilbert du Motier), 71
Lafayette County, Mississippi, x, xxx
Landlord's Game, 114
Latham, Sean, 85, 97, 100–101
Lavater, Johann Kasper, 191n10
Lehigh University, xxix
Leiter, Andrew B., xvi, xxii, xxx
liberal democracy, United States, 157–60
liberalism, xxii
*Light in August* (Faulkner), ix, xi, xii, xxi, xxii, xxv, 52, 58, 73, 127, 130, 139, 150, 155–69, 187; "Dark House," 167
Lightweis-Goff, Jennie, xxx
Lincoln, Abraham, 28
Locke, John, 161
Lomax, John and Alan, 208n7, 209n31
Lorde, Audre, 156
Lost Cause, 187
Lott, Eric, 152
Lounsbury, Carl, xxix
Lowndes County, Alabama, 159
Lummis, Charles, 72
Lurie, Peter, xxx

Mabry, Jesse, 20n17
MacMaster, Anne, xxx
Magie, Elizabeth, 114
Mahurin, Sarah, 187, 190
malaria, 160
Manganelli, Kim, xxx
manliness/manhood, white, 47
Manning, Chandra, 28
*Mansion, The* (Faulkner), xii, 120
Marion, Andrew, xxx
*Marionettes, The* (Faulkner), xxiii, 176–90; "The Kiss," 177, *179*; "Marietta by the Fountain," 178–79, *179*; "Pierrot Standing," 177

Martin, Bonnie, 4
Martin, Gretchen, 33
Marxism, 49–50
Maryland, 20n13, 62; Baltimore, 35, 38
mass incarceration, African American, xxvn8. *See also* Parchman Farm
Massachusetts Bay Colony, 12
Matthews, J. E., 61
Matthews, John T., xiii, xiv–xv, xxx
McCarroll House, 62f, 79n24
McComs, Anna S., 61
McDaniel, George, xxix
McDonald, Brian, xxx
McDonald, Laquan, 208n19
McEwen, Narcissus, 69, 76
McKee, Katie, xxix
Medford, Massachusetts, 12
Memphis, Tennessee, 28, 149
mercantilism, 157–58, 160
Meredith, James, x
Meridian, Mississippi, 61
Merritt, Keri Leigh, xvi, 35, 36
Meyers, Maureen, xxix
MGM, 67
Middle Passage, vii, 130
miscegenation, 88, 97
Mississippi Constitution of 1832, 19n12
Mississippi Delta, xxx, 196, 206
Mississippi Gulf Coast, 194, 196, 206
*Mississippi Quarterly*, 85
Mississippi River Valley, xiii
Mississippi River, 21n28, 23
Mississippi State Penitentiary. *See* Parchman Farm
Monopoly, xx, 105–23, 116f
Montrose, 62f
Morris, Thomas D., 107
Moten, Fred, 130
"Mountain Victory" (Faulkner), ix, xvi, 34, 38, 42

music: blues, 196, 202–5, 207; blues aesthetic, 198; blues performance, 199; spirituals, 196, 207; work songs, 196, 204, 207
"My Grandmother Millard" (Faulkner), ix

Nadel, Alan, 111
Naeem, Asma, 173–74
Napoleonic Law, 109
Napolin, Julie Beth, xx–xxi, xxx
Nat Turner revolt, 35
Natchez, Mississippi, 65
National Portrait Gallery, 173
Neary, Janet, 180
Neiman, Fraser, 65
New Albany, Mississippi, xxx
New Deal, 118
"New History of Capitalism (NHC)," 17n3–18n3; Stephanie McCurry's critique of, 18n3
New Orleans, Louisiana, 30
Nietzschean superman, 111
North Carolina, 20n13, 162
"Notes on a Horse Thief" (Faulkner), 120
*Notes on the State of Virginia* (Jefferson), 161
Nunn, Erich, xxx

Oliver, Jack, 69
Olmsted, Alan L., 17n3
"On Privacy" (Faulkner), 55n9
one-drop rule, 82
Oshinsky, David, 206
Ovid, 143n17
Oxford, Mississippi, xxx, xxxi, 65, 72, 95
Oxford, United Kingdom, 95
Oxford Convention and Visitors Bureau, xxxi
*Oxford English Dictionary*, 120, 131
Oxford Falcon, 65–66

Parchman Farm, ix, xxiv–xxv, 194–207, *195*, *196*, *198*; chain gangs, 196; convict leasing, 196–97; juvenile prisoners, *195*; mass incarceration, 197; prison culture, 196; trusty guards, *204*
*Paris Review*, 86
paternalism, 164, 166, 189, 201
Peek, Charles, xxx
Pegues, Ben, 70, 80n42
Pegues, Evelyn, 70, 80n42
pellagra, 160
Penner, Erin, xix, xxx
Petty, Miriam, 146
Phillips, Ulrich B., 24, 30; *American Negro Slavery*, 24
Picketty, Thomas, 17n1
Plantation Monopoly, 114
Pocock, J. G. A., 118
*Poetics of Space, The* (Bachelard), 52
Polk, Noel, 69
Pomeranz, Kenneth, 15
poor whites, 32–42, 58, 159, 162, 172n46; relationship with slaves, 35–37
post-Emancipation reparations, 11
prediality, 108–9, 112, 114
*Price of Emancipation, The* (Draper), 18n3
Price, Andrew, 77
Primrose Place, 61
Promised Land, 27
*Pylon* (Faulkner), ix

Quashie, Colin, 114

*Radical Indigestion* (Tompkins), 164
Railton, Stephen, 93
Raymond, Yasmil, 180
Reconstruction, ix, xv, 11, 30, 40, 71, 107, 113, 126

"Red Leaves" (Faulkner), vii, xvii, 44, 58
*Reivers, The* (Faulkner), xx, 105, 118, 120–23
*Requiem for a Nun* (Faulkner), ix, xii, 132
Rhode, Paul W., 17n3
Rice, Tamir, 208n19
Rieger, Christopher, 93
Ring, Natalie, 11
Ripley, Mississippi, xxx, 25
Riverview, 62f
Rockman, Seth, 3, 155, 169
Rodden, John, 33
Romine, Scott, 33, 107
Roosevelt, Franklin D., 111
"Rose for Emily, A" (Faulkner), 52, 58
Ross, Charles K., xxix
Rothman, Joshua, xiii, 8
Roundtree, Stephanie, xxii–xxiii, xxx
Rowan Oak, vii, viii, ix, x, xi, xii, xviii, xxix, xxx, 63, 83; architecture at, 57–78; archeological survey of, xi; Bailey Woods, ix; slave dwelling at, xvii; slaves at (Simon, George, Dave, Lila, Frances, Phillis), 83
Royall, Isaac, 12–13
Ryan, Tim A., xxx

Sajet, Kim, 173
Saldívar, Ramón, 33
Salvant, Shawn, xxix
*Sanctuary* (Faulkner), ix, 187
Sartre, Jean-Paul, 105
*Saturday Evening Post*, vii, 188
Sciuto, Jenna Grace, xxix, xxx
Scoval, George, 61
Sedgwick, Eve Kosofky, 176
Sharpe, Christina, 138
Shaw, Gwendolyn Dubois, 180, 186
Sheegog, Robert, viii, x, xvii, xviii–xix, 63–72, *66*, *68*, 81n59, 83

Shreve, Henry, 21n28
silhouettes, xxiii, 173–90
Skipper, Jodi, xi, xxix, xxx
Slave Trade Act of 1807 (England), 95
slavery: abolition of international trade, 96; architecture(s), 45, 53; commodification of, xiii; defense of, 61; 1860 slave census, fictive kinship, 148; Great Britain, 17n3–18n3; human parasitism, 148; ideological reversal, 148; internal slave trade, 6; natal alienation, 148–49; neo-slave narratives, 32; New Orleans slave market, 7; slave housing, 53; slave economy, 33; slave narratives, viii, 32–42; slaves as contraband of war, 28; as social death, 148; University of Mississippi and slave labor, xi, 82–89
Slavery Abolition Act of 1833 (England), 95
*Slavery and Social Death* (Patterson), xxi–xxii, 148, 161
*Slavery in Black and White* (Fox-Genovese and Genovese), 35; "Slavery in the Abstract," 35–36
*Slavery in Mississippi* (Syndor), xviii, 83–84
social contract, white, 48
Somerset Case of 1772, 95
*Sound and the Fury, The* (Faulkner), viii, xii, xxi, 58, 75, 117, 120, 126–27, 129–30, 132, 135–42, 146–53; Sartre on, 105; "Twilight," 135
sound technology, 129, 134–35; phonography, 132–34, 144n33
Spillers, Hortense J., 129, 134, 139
Spratling, William, 55n11
Square Books, xxxi
St. Louis, Missouri, 30

State Colored Normal School in North Carolina, 165
Steeby, Elizabeth, 187
Stein, Jean, 86
Sterling, Alton, 208n19
Stern, Julia, xxi, xxix
Stockholm, Sweden, 72
Stoever, Jennifer, 128
Summers, Jill (née Faulkner), x, 69, 71, 76–77, 80n48
Sundquist, Eric J., 115
Sweeney, Erin, 33

Tannehill, Robyn, xxix
Taylor, Breonna, 208n19
Tebbetts, Terrell L., xxix
Ten Hills Farm, 12
Texas, 62
"That Evening Sun" (Faulkner), xxi, 58, 132, 134, 137
"There Was a Queen" (Faulkner), ix, 190
Thirteenth Amendment, ix
Thompson, Jacob, xix, 87
Till, Emmett, 76
*Town, The* (Faulkner), xii
Towner, Theresa, xxx
*Tuning of the World, The* (Shaffer), 129
Turner, Darwin T., 32
Twitty, Anne, xxx

*Uncle Tom's Cabin* (Stowe), 180
*Undoing the Demos* (Brown), 158
United States Post Office, Famous Americans stamp series, 111
University of Mississippi, ix, xxix, 83; antebellum and slave histories, xii; Arch Dalrymple III Department of History, xi; archives, xviii; Chapel, x; College of Liberal Arts, xxxi; Center for

the Study of Southern Culture, xxxi; Department of English, xxxi; Division of Outreach and Continuing Studies, xxxi; integration of, x; Lyceum, x; Museums, xviii, xxix; Observatory, x; Office of the Provost, xxxi; slavery at, xi; Southern Studies program, xi; University Greys, 82, 87; University of Mississippi Slavery Research Group, x–xi. *See also* slavery

University of Virginia, 84, 87, 132, 164

University Press of Mississippi, xxxi

*Unvanquished, The* (Faulkner), viii, ix, xv, xvi, xxiv, 23–30, 34, 42, 48, 53, 58, 107, 109, 113, 119, 187–90; "Ambuscade," 187–88; "An Odor of Verbena," xv

Upton, Dell, 51–52

Urgo, Joseph, 91

Usher, John, 12

Virginia, 20n13, 41, 94

Vonnegut, Kurt, 122

Waid, Candace, 175

Wakefield, 62f, 63

Walden Pond, 112

Walker, Anders, xxx

Walker, Kara, xxiii–xxiv, 173–90; *Black Out: Silhouettes Then and Now*, 173; critics of, 192n23; *The End of Uncle Tom and the Grand Allegorical Tableau of Eva in Heaven*, xxiii–xxiv, 180–90, *180*, *181*, *182*, *184*, *185*; *Kara Walker: My Complement, My Enemy, My Oppressor, My Love*, *181*

Walker, William Aiken, 59

Ward, Jesmyn, 194; *Sing, Unburied, Sing*, xxiv–xxv, 194–207

Warwick Castle, 95

"Wash" (Faulkner), ix, 34

Washington, Booker T., xxiii, 38, 48–49, 111, 164–65, 167; *Up from Slavery*, 49, 164, 167

Washington County, Mississippi, 59

Watson, Jay, 134

Weinstein, Philip, 33, 175

Wesson, Ben, 81n54

West Indies, 12, 21n18, 39–41

White, "Bukka," 205; "Parchman Farm Blues," 203

White Arches, 62, 63, 79n24

*Wild Palms, The* (Faulkner), ix, 120

Wilder, Craig Steven, xix, 4, 13

Wilhelm, Randall, xxiii–xxiv, xxx

Wilkinson County, Mississippi, 61

*William Faulkner and the Tangible Past* (Ruzieka), 45

William Faulkner Society, xxix

William the Conqueror, 95

Williams, Eric, 18n3

Williamson, Joel, 71–72

Wilson, Laura, xxx

Winthrop, John, 12

Wood, Ellen Meiksins, 161; *Empire of Capital*, 160; *Democracy against Capitalism*, 160

Woodson, Carter G., 83

Woodville, Mississippi, 61

Yoknapatawpha County, vii–viii, ix, 93

Žižek, Slavoj, 9

Zong massacre, xiii

www.ingramcontent.com/pod-product-compliance
Lightning Source LLC
Chambersburg PA
CBHW030618230426
43661CB00053B/2047